Issues of Regional Policies

A Report prepared by
A. EMANUEL
Former Chairman of the Industry Committee's
Working Party on Regional Development Policies

ORGANISATION FOR ECONOMIC
CO-OPERATION AND DEVELOPMENT

The Organisation for Economic Co-operation and Development (OECD) was set up under a Convention signed in Paris on 14th December, 1960, which provides that the OECD shall promote policies designed :

- *to achieve the highest sustainable economic growth and employment and a rising standard of living in Member countries, while maintaining financial stability, and thus to contribute to the development of the world economy;*
- *to contribute to sound economic expansion in Member as well as non-member countries in the process of economic development;*
- *to contribute to the expansion of world trade on a multilateral, non-discriminatory basis in accordance with international obligations.*

The Members of OECD are Australia, Austria, Belgium, Canada, Denmark, Finland, France, the Federal Republic of Germany, Greece, Iceland, Ireland, Italy, Japan, Luxembourg, the Netherlands, New Zealand, Norway, Portugal, Spain, Sweden, Switzerland, Turkey, the United Kingdom and the United States.

* *
*

FOREWORD

In 1970, the Organisation published a report of the Industry Committee's Working Party on Regional Policies entitled "The Regional Factor in Economic Development". This report was a factual and descriptive survey of the policies pursued by Member countries. Following this report, the Working Party decided to examine the problems raised by these policies with a view to presenting their conclusions in due course. In the meantime, and to assist the Working Party, the Organisation commissioned a special study of the issues of regional policies by Mr. A. Emanuel, formerly Chairman of the Working Party and now Consultant to the OECD.

The report prepared by Mr. Emanuel was submitted to the Working Party at its session of November 1972. The Working Party considered that the report made a valuable contribution to the subject and that it would be helpful to Member Governments in the continuing process of review of regional policies. In view of the growing importance of the subject and the policy implications, it recommended that it be published for general information.

The views expressed in the report are solely those of the author and do not necessarily commit the members of the Industry Committee or its Working Party on the facts they represent.

CONTENTS

Prefatory Note 9

  I. Introduction 13

 II. Strategies for Regional Development 17

III. The Regional Impact of National Factors 53

IV. The Problem of "Rectifying Imbalance" 79

 V. Unemployment Disparities 105

VI. Effectiveness of Financial Incentives to Firms ... 125

VII. Restraint Systems for Regional Policy 161

VIII. The Role of Infrastructure in Regional Economic
Planning 179

IX. Public Finance Aspects of Regional Policies 197

 X. The Problem of Organisation 213

XI. International Aspects of Regional Problems 229

XII. Conclusions 249

PREFATORY NOTE

This report was prepared in the Summer of 1972 and first presented to the OECD Working Party No. 6 on Regional Policies in November 1972. Its purpose is to assist the Working Party to give consideration to the major problems and issues which arise in the field of regional policies, on which the Working Party will in due course reach its own findings and conclusions and, it is understood, make its own recommendations. While the information on which the report is based is drawn mainly from the material supplied by members of the Working Party or from official sources, the views and opinions expressed in the report are those of the author as an independent consultant to the Organisation.

As indicated in different places in the report regional problems and policies, and the national contexts in which they arise, are subject to continuing change. Indeed there have been many important developments since the report was completed such as the declaration on regional policy included in the Communiqué of the Summit Conference of the EEC in October 1972 and the report issued on the authority of the Prime Minister of Japan on the remodelling of the Japanese Islands. There is therefore always an inherent danger of a report on regional policies being overtaken by events or becoming outdated almost by the time the ink is dry. The author has however sought to minimize this danger by concentrating on those issues which experience of countries over decades has shown to be of continuing importance and seem likely to remain important in the future. The report is an analytical rather than a descriptive document - descriptive accounts of regional policies are contained in other publications of the OECD. Statistical and other factual data in the report are given primarily to illustrate or justify the analysis. Events since the report was completed should not therefore have invalidated the basic approach adopted in the report even though the nature and significance of particular issues may have changed in individual countries.

9

It is desirable to stress also that the report has a practical rather than academic purpose. While, no doubt, the author's own theoretical approach will be discernible the report is directed towards the problems with which Governments tend to be faced. The approach is that of the layman (albeit, it is hoped an informed one) concerned with the way problems present themselves to administrations and to the lay public. It will have served its purpose if it contributes to a wider understanding of the nature of issues which are of growing importance to the lay public in many countries.

The report is arranged in twelve Chapters listed in the Table of Contents. The first five Chapters are concerned with the background to regional policies, the next five to problems of methodology, Chapter XI with international aspects and the final Chapter is not so much a summary as an attempt to highlight some of the more important conclusions which emerge from the report taken as a whole.

The Introduction gives some reasons for considering regional policies to be a matter of international as well as domestic concern. It points to the desirability of reaching some generally acceptable principles. Coupled with other chapters the thought is that regional policies can have harmful as well as beneficial effects.

The Chapter on Strategies is largely theoretical but points to the need to recognize the conflicts of objectives and the variety of alternative policies by which objectives may be achieved. An important point is that distinctions should be made between regional policies in their national contexts and policies for individual regions. The distinctions between "national" and "regional" policies is seen as a false dichotomy. National and regional policies are both parts of the comprehensive policy functions of Governments; they need to be pursued in parallel and in harmony and brought together in a manner which ensures consistency and appropriate attention to all the problems which are part of an interrelated whole.

The purpose of the Chapter on Regional Impact of National Factors is to show the importance of a correct understanding of the influence on regional development of the many factors which operate to determine the economic and social climate which is the background to all regional policies. Only if there is an awareness of the wide ranging influence of such factors on regional development can - in the Consultant's view - regional policies themselves be correctly attuned to the real needs of the situation.

The Chapter on Rectifying Regional Imbalance is partly theoretical but seeks to show, with practical illustrations, the inherent difficulty in giving this major objective of current regional policies any real meaning.

It brings out also the diverse way in which the concept is viewed in different countries and the basic conflict between remedying imbalance by the alternatives of transfer of resources and transfers of population. The thought that is emerging from the considerations in this chapter is that the degree of diversion of resources required to remedy imbalance is much greater than is likely to be made by any Government; that the concept of "imbalance" itself needs more precise definition in most cases; that insofar as migration and growth increases "imbalance" the necessary policies need to be adjusted to the problems of both growth and declining areas; and that regional policy needs to be seen as a policy for all regions which together constitute the whole country. Some doubt may also emerge from this chapter on the desirability, in economic terms, of seeking to divert a large proportion of such marginal national growth as can take place to regions which are unfavourably endowed with the conditions necessary for a healthy national economy. The doubts increase in proportion to the scale of the disadvantaged regions, in some cases of the order of 40-50 per cent of the area of a country. What this chapter may be suggesting is the need for a realistic view of what is desirable and feasible. This chapter may also throw some light on the relation between progress in the more backward regions and overall national growth, and why the "gaps" and "disparities" between more and less prosperous regions are not necessarily reduced despite vigorous regional policies.

The Chapter on Unemployment Disparities is essentially a continuation of the same themes as in the previous chapter, with special reference to regional manpower, employment and unemployment distribution. It contains a survey of trends in some countries for which statistics are available from OECD sources.

The Chapters on Incentives and Restraints discuss the workings of these two methods. They tend to bring out the importance of the general context in which they operate, which may nullify or diminish their usefulness. In these chapters, as in the preceding, the underlying thought is that policies which do not take account of the relevant considerations cannot only fail to achieve their objectives but can constitute a misuse of resources which few countries can afford. Some consideration is also given to the "distortion" effect of incentives and the need to reach some kind of international agreement on the extent to which they should be applied.

The Chapter on Infrastructure draws attention to the complementary role of investment in infrastructure, its various kinds, its impact on regional problems and the need to establish criteria to determine how far it is practicable to give favourable treatment to certain regions without misapplication of resources.

11

The Chapter on Public Finance examines the sources from which public finance can be applied to regional problems, the alternative methods for mobilizing them and the problem of determining the scale and criteria for their use. The chapter points to some of the disadvantages of a fragmented approach to public finance for regional purposes.

The Chapter on Organisation considers the tasks involved in developing regional policies and the problems of organisation to which this gives rise. It suggests that regional policies pose special problems in coordination for which a suitable organisational structure may be required.

The Chapter on International Aspects seeks to show the impact of regional policies on international economic relations, the need and scope for a degree of understanding and collaboration and agreement on limitations to rivalry in the fields of incentives and promotion efforts.

The concluding Chapter emphasizes the wide ranging nature of regional problems and their complexity. It seeks to define what would be involved in a more systematic approach to a long term and continuing effort to reconcile conflicts and to devise suitable policies within a framework of national policies and available resources.

Though each chapter must speak for itself, the general thought that underlies the report as a whole is that, because regional policies embrace almost every aspect of economic and social development, they cannot be put in a separate compartment from national policies as a whole. There would seem to be a need for a clearer definition of objectives; for a clearer indication of the resources that can be made available; for better tests of effectiveness of measures; and for a greater realisation that the growth or improvement of the economy as a whole may be hampered by the adoption of ineffective policies or policies which make a greater claim on national resources than can be justified by the results achieved. The impression left in the author's mind by this study is that there are many important issues still facing Governments, and that until greater clarity is achieved there is a real risk that the substantial resources devoted to regional policies will not bring about desired results and may constitute a hindrance to the processes of adjustment which are continually necessary in a changing world.

A. Emanuel
January, 1973

I

INTRODUCTION

Most, if not all, OECD Member countries participate in the work of the Working Party on Regional Development Policies. They do so because their Governments pursue, in one form or another, policies which are called "regional". What are these policies, how are they pursued, what are their effects and results, how do they relate to the general objectives to which Member countries of the OECD are pledged by their basic agreement setting up the Organisation, and what contribution can the OECD make, through a pooling of experience, to the better attainment of these objectives and others which Governments seek in the interests of the progress of their peoples? These, broadly, are the questions with which this report will seek to deal.

That these questions are important is demonstrated by the increasing attention paid to them, within Member countries and within groupings of countries such as OECD, EEC and EFTA.* They are important also because they call for the application of resources which, in the economists' sense, are always scarce or for which there are many competing claims. If successful, regional policies can influence national growth and development. If unsuccessful, they can impose a burden on national growth and represent a misuse of resources which countries cannot, given the universal desire for economic advance, afford. If they can be shown to be effective and useful, the question would arise of whether more resources should be devoted to them, and in what ways. If they are seen to be ineffective, burdensome or wrongly directed, the question arises of how they should be modified to make them more effective and more usefully applied. No Member country envisages their abandonment but equally no Member country could justify their continuance regardless of the benefits they bring or the costs involved.

* Developments since this report was completed, such as the declaration on regional policy by the EEC Summit Conference of October 1972, illustrate and reinforce this view.

Even though policies pursued for domestic purposes are regarded
as a matter of domestic political concern of the individual countries,
regional policies, like most other important policies affecting the national economy and its development, are of international concern. The
OECD, like other international organisations, is committed to the pursuit of growth policies in the common interest of its members. The
well-being of each country affects, and is affected by, the well-being
of others. Policies pursued in the name of regional balance of removing
regional disparities can have beneficial or deleterious effects well beyond
the borders of the country concerned. They can affect the pattern of
international trade, investment and capital movements. They may cause
unemployment to be exported. The use of special methods such as subsidies to regional growth arouse the interest of other countries whose
competing industries may be affected by them.*

Regional policies also provide an opportunity or forum for co-
operation. Countries with common borders, interlinked transport systems, common markets, with free or regulated flows of manpower and
capital and with trading arrangements can pursue policies for mutual
advantage in which account may be taken of the regional problems of
their partners. Co-operation can also take the form of devising accepted rules for the pursuit of regional policies so that they, in fact, work
to the mutual benefit of co-operating countries rather than the reverse.

All this could be sufficient reason for an organisation such as the
OECD to study the regional policies of its Members county. The
propose ways and means by which the policies could be improved. But
it is not the only reason. One thing has been made apparent in the work
done by the OECD so far, and that is that few, if any, Member countries
are satisfied with the results of their regional policies so far. Nor do
many countries regard the policies pursued so far as more than tentative and experimental. There is, however, no consensus of views
among them either on how far they should be pursued or on the methods
which are both effective and acceptable in terms of the desire of Member countries to co-operate fruitfully with each other. There is perhaps
consensus on one point, and that is that most countries have tended to
lack clarity in their regional policy objectives and few have as yet found
a consistent set of policies which will ensure the achievement of objectives
over a given period of time. The frequent changes and revisions which
have been made over recent years in almost all the Member countries
is evidence of this.

*
    Vide Report of OECD High Level Group "Policy Perspectives for International
Trade and Economic Relations", published August 1972, paragraph 105, which quotes
regional aids to production as an example of Government action "creating significant
distortions to trade".

The desirability of clarifying and pursuing effective regional policies is not a matter which interests Governments alone. By their very nature regional policies are intended to change the regional distribution of economic activity. Insofar as they do this they change the economic climate or environment in which those outside Government must work and make their own judgements of their future operations. Unless the private citizen, in particular the industrial or commercial entrepreneur has a clear view of what Government is seeking to do, his own plans for investment, production and location of his activities can be severely jeopardized. In all mixed economies, which characterize the majority of, if not all, the Member countries, the role of the private citizen in the economic life of the country is as important, or even more important, than that of Government. Certainly his activities complement those of Government. It follows that regional policies need to be so designed to permit this complementary role to be performed in harmony with or with due regard to them. If they are not, then the private sector will be less able to make its contribution to the regional objectives and indeed to the more general objectives of Government.

The origins, nature, purposes and methods of regional policies differ greatly among all countries, for their own conditions greatly vary. One can ask how countries as different as the United States from Luxembourg, or Japan from Denmark can face similar problems in matters of a "domestic" character, or how experience in one country can have any useful lesson for countries of totally different size and structure. A "region" of the United States can be several times larger in all senses than some Member countries, while a region in a small country may be no larger, or not as large, as an English county. The diversity of economic, social and political conditions in European countries cannot be disregarded. Yet it is not an illusory task to consider regional policies in general terms which may apply to such diverse countries. The nature of the economic problem of choice between alternative actions is not necessarily different because of the number of noughts in the equation. However that may be, Member countries find in practice that there are common underlying features in their aims and methods. If this report assists countries to increase their understanding of the common ground it would amply repay the effort put into its preparation.

This report is not a descriptive survey*, though some descriptive material relating to individual countries is included, or used as an illustration of the themes discussed. It is intended as an objective and critical examination or appraisal of the regional policies of Member countries as a whole. At the same time it seeks to offer constructive

* A descriptive survey, though out of date in some details but still valid in broad principle, is provided by the OECD report published in 1970 "The Regional Factor in Economic Development".

comment which may be of use to any Government considering its regional policies.

The problems, perplexities and dilemmas which are inherent in regional policies have been well set out in "The Growth of Output 1960-1980" published by the OECD in December 1970, pp. 133-138. The present report is an attempt to examine some of these problems and issues in a way which it is hoped may prove helpful in the continuing process of reviews of regional policies and in the context of the wider general economic background which form their setting. The task is a formidable one for any single individual and the writer is conscious of his own limitations. The last paragraph of the text referred to offers both justification for the attempt and some excuse for its failings. It is quoted here as a fitting conclusion to this introductory chapter:

"It is because regional policies are important, and of increasing relevance, that it is essential to be aware of the problems and difficulties which surround them. In view of the complexity of the field, these difficulties are not surprising; and given their relation to ultimate political options, it would be idle to think that they are capable of definitive solutions. But it should be hoped that further work and accumulating experience will help to clarify some of the elements on which decisions have to be based."

II

STRATEGIES FOR REGIONAL DEVELOPMENT

All attempts to change the course of events in whole regions of countries imply that those responsible, viz. Governments, regional and local authorities or other special bodies on which the task may be laid, have some broad concept both of the regional situation with which they have to deal and of the methods which they deem to be appropriate to achieve the objective. Regional policies are pursued by the carrying out of plans, projects and programmes in a wide variety of fields, economic, social and environmental, or in physical infrastructure, and by measures to foster or restrain those developments which are, respectively, in accord or incompatible with the policy objectives.

Separate authorities with their own responsibilities and powers and their own ideas of what is necessary, may of course pursue incompatible and mutually conflicting policies and varying success may attend efforts to co-ordinate their activities or reconcile their objectives. Differences of political philosophies between authorities, as well as differences of view on particular schemes, may prevent agreement or the adoption of common concepts. In Federal States clashes of view can occur between Federal and State authorities. In unitary States powerful local authorities may be able to pursue independent policies according to their own statutory powers, from those of the central Government. Agencies entrusted with the provision and development of services such as power supplies, road and rail communications, etc., and with powers to implement their own policies may be able to take an independent line from that of other authorities.

It may be the case that the lack of common policies or common concepts behind the actions of separate and conflicting authorities can give rise to a serious economic problem in that it can bring about a wasteful use of resources by the mutual frustration of their separate endeavours. Such frustration can occur for example, if separate authorities adopt different assumptions about needs and prospects: if

17

authorities responsible for housing adopt different population growth
assumptions from those responsible for schools and hospitals; if
authorities responsible for industrial development and those responsible
for water, power and communications adopt conflicting forecasts.
Waste of resources can occur when roads are constructed to carry
traffic that does not materialize; when land is reserved for industrial
or housing use where industry or people are not available to make use
of it; or when local authorities devote resources to the preparation
of industrial estates in areas for incoming new industry in which central
Government restraints may operate to prevent it.

The conflict of policies, objectives and plans may also lead to
economic loss when authorities are unable or unwilling to take the
complementary action to support projects of another authority, or of
the private sector. Industrial growth in the private sector can be
frustrated by failure to provide complementary facilities in power and
water supplies, communications, health, education and manpower
training facilities. Expenditure on the improvement of the environment or on the creation of new centres and urban centres and development of the infrastructure may be nullified by the failure of complementary action on the part of the authorities responsible for location
of industry policies.

The point does not need to be laboured. Comprehensive regional
development, to be successful, requires a measure of administrative
co-ordination between the many separate authorities and other bodies.
This is a subject which will be considered in a separate chapter. It
also requires the elaboration of a series of self-consistent regional
policy guidelines which will help the separate authorities, if not to
harmonize their activities, at least to appreciate what is likely to happen
to the regional context in which they are operating as a result of other
authorities' activities.

It is perhaps an encouraging feature of regional policies in recent
years that many countries have come increasingly to recognize the
need for what, for want of a better word, can be termed "regional
strategies". A perusal of the country studies made by the Working
Party in their "Salient Features" reports shows that the term is not
universally adopted. Nonetheless many countries have found it necessary to formulate comprehensive regional development plans, and to
conceive them not as static lists of proposed development projects but
as dynamic assessments of a continuingly changing regional situation
and a vehicle for a definition of the kind of policies which are called
for. Such plans are seen as a means of conveying to the separate
authorities concerned the "strategic framework" within which their own
projects and schemes are most likely to achieve the desired result of
regional improvement, growth or development.

18

In the United Kingdom the use of the term "regional strategy" has become an accepted part of the vocabulary of regional economic planning. The regional Economic Planning Councils set up in 1965 have had assigned to them as a main task the preparation of "strategies" for the medium and long term, for the consideration of Government and the local planning authorities. Several such strategies have been produced. The local planning authorities are required, in preparing development plans for their areas, to take account of the proposed regional strategies and Government decisions on them. In Italy and France regional authorities have been encouraged or obliged to make comprehensive surveys and appraisals of the economic features of their regions and to indicate the main lines on which they are to be tackled, a process which can be described as formulating a strategy. In the United States regional inter-State commissions and inter-county organisations and local bodies have been required, as a condition for the granting of aid by the Economic Development Administration, to formulate overall economic development plans (OEDP's) which indicate their concept of the problems facing the area and the way in which particular types of schemes will fit into that concept.

In some countries other terms have been used to denote the same thing, such as "integrated programme co-ordination", "comprehensive regional planning" and similar terms. "Regional planning" is also used to denote a concerted attempt to bring separate and unco-ordinated plans or programmes into one coherent and self-consistent whole. While drawing attention to the diverse vocabulary, often, and regrettably, lacking precise definition, we use the term "strategy" to embrace all these concepts to convey the notion of a general approach to the problem of providing a common framework or setting for regional development activities of separate and disparate authorities.

The term "regional strategy" does, of course, carry within it the seeds of some confusion. It is used to denote the strategy proposed for particular regions. It is also used to denote the principles on which national policy is based to bring about shifts in the distribution of economic activity between regions. Regional policies can be pursued both by national authorities and by authorities within regions. Both may have their separate strategies to achieve their objectives which may or may not be reconcilable with each other. The need to distinguish between the two types, i.e. between "national" regional strategies and "regional" regional strategies, is not only a semantic one. Coherent and effective policies for particular regions can only be achieved if there is some degree of consistency between the two. It is unfortunate that much of the official literature in many countries fails to distinguish between them. It may be added that the problem of harmonizing strategies is not confined to regional strategies. The picture is only complete when account is taken of national or "global" economic strategies all of which (for reasons which are gone into more fully in the chapter on national factors affecting regional problems) can have their impact on regional strategies in both senses in which the term is used.

A further source of confusion can also arise if care is not taken to distinguish between regional strategies designed for different purposes, for example between economic strategies and, say, land-use strategies. The aims of the former may be to bring about a different economic struc- ture of a region: the aim of the latter a different spatial distribution of that structure. A comprehensive regional strategy may seek to harmo- nize both, but they can also take their separate directions if the authori- ties responsible for each operate in isolation from each other and in so doing bring about an uneconomic or ineffective use of resources.

Having taken the precaution of drawing attention to the different uses to which the term "regional strategy" can be put, we shall continue to use it, with such qualifying adjectives as may be required in the con- text.

In the remainder of this chapter we shall be concerned with the problems and difficulties which arise in attempts to formulate strategies for regional development conforming with both national and regional policy aims. The Working Party has itself identified this as one of the more serious and difficult questions facing Governments pursuing active regional policies. It is important also in the context of overall econom- ic policies seeking to foster soundly based economic growth, an aim common to OECD countries and to others. It is for this latter reason that the Working Party has given particular attention to the principles involved in drawing up regional economic strategies in relation to na- tional economic strategies. A number of specific questions were listed in their consideration of the subject and, for convenience, are appended at the end of this chapter. Our discussion will in large part be directed towards them.

It may be useful to begin by attempting to distinguish those matters which relate to "national" regional strategies and those which relate to "internal" regional strategies.

As we see it "national" regional strategies comprise those policies and measures which are specifically designed to bring about a particular pattern of regional development. It need not be automatically assumed that the desired pattern is different from the one that would be brought about by the free play of economic forces and the normal working of ec- onomic and social institutions and policies. A country may have the choice and may prefer the regional pattern which emerges naturally from that which would be brought about by intervention. Not all coun- tries have considered it necessary or feasible to modify, to any serious

20

degree, the "imbalance" between regions. There can be, as indicated in "The Growth of Output" a conflict of aims, between the desirability of encouraging growth and between some concept of regional equality. As the same report says, "neither aim can be regarded as absolute". "If regional policies were to be viewed exclusively as a means to maximize growth of output, the resulting conclusions might be inacceptable to most countries. Nor can absolute regional equality be regarded as an overriding aim. It is, moreover, not immediately evident why all regions should have the same level of average income, or the same rate of growth ...".

The first and primary question for "national" regional strategy is therefore how far is it, or will it be, necessary to modify the inter-regional pattern that results from known trends in the economy? If the answer is that it is necessary to modify it to a given degree the second question to be faced is that of the methods which are appropriate and what may be expected to result from their application.

Our study of the information made available to the OECD through the Working Party has not thrown up any instance of a country approaching this question in any systematic way. In most countries national regional policies have grown up "like Topsy" in response to political pressures and the frequent changes which are made in weight and direction of regional policies indicate some uncertainty about how far it is right to seek equality rather than uneven growth.

Even in countries such as Italy and the United Kingdom where the degree of regional imbalance of employment, incomes and social conditions provides the main motive for regional policies the degree to which modification rather than elimination of the imbalances is desired can only be inferred from broad statements of aim and from the actual measures.

The generalisation, in "The Growth of Output" (p. 137), that in most countries the problem of regional imbalances of these and other kinds has been increasing can, as the report says, indicate that regional policies have not been applied with sufficient energy and that regional policies take a long time to produce the desired effect. It is also a fair inference from the same fact that few Governments desire the effect so much that they would be prepared to adopt the policies which would be needed to achieve it. In other words "national regional strategies" involve no more, in the first place, than an attempt to strike some sort of balance between possibly conflicting objectives of national policy, such as overall economic growth and a more satisfactory regional balance than would be obtained from the working of ordinary economic forces and policies.

It would be unrealistic to suggest that Governments should define their national strategies in terms of unattainable targets, or in terms of attainable targets for which too high a price in restricted growth might have to be paid. In both cases Governments would suffer embarassment, either as the passage of time demonstrates that stated targets are not being achieved or as the measures of policy are seen to be clearly inadequate to their attainment. Equally, to limit targets to what is attainable, or to what does not involve paying too high a price, can lay Governments open to the charge of underestimating the gravity of the regional problem and give rise to constant pressures to do more than the Government judges to be desirable. In other words targets are hostages to fortune as far as Governments are concerned and in democratic countries free gifts of ammunition to their critics and oppositions. In these circumstances it is not surprising that national objectives of regional policy, such as overcoming regional imbalances, congestion and the like, tend to be stated in broad general terms with no quantitative definitions of the residual degree of imbalance or congestion which is ultimately to be accepted or of the time scale over which "unacceptable" imbalances are to be eliminated.

The dilemmas facing Governments in choosing between conflicting objectives are real. Vague and question begging formulations of aims, such as "striking a suitable balance" between economic and other social objectives, or a "suitable interregional imbalance" leave open what is meant by "suitable". In the democratic world of competing and other political philosophies it can only be regarded as inevitable that the "suitable" balance is not a matter for economic formulae alone but is one of judgement expressed in terms of the political will of a nation through its political institutions.

Nonetheless it remains true that "strategies" which are not geared to defined objectives can hardly be meaningful. There is no standard by which their appositeness or effectiveness can be judged; no way of telling whether more or less resources should be applied to implement them; no way of reconciling or making them consistent with other strategies; and no way of telling if it is the objectives themselves, rather than the strategies which need to be modified to achieve the "right balance" between conflicting objectives. The case for some degree of precision in defining objectives is also reinforced if the co-operation, understanding or sympathy of other authorities is needed, a point which is of course particularly relevant in the international field. Finally, vaguely stated objectives can lend themselves to alternative and even opposing strategies, and until more precision is given to the objectives the bases for a rational choice between strategies hardly exists.

These generalizations can be illustrated by a few examples expressed in more concrete terms.

The general objective of "rectifying" or improving regional imbalances in employment opportunities, incomes, social conditions, etc. offers no guide to the appropriate strategy since it can be achieved by alternatives of "taking work to the workers" or "workers to the work". If the objective is qualified to posit a preference, for or against interregional migration, the appropriate national strategy for the regions will depend on the degree to which migration is posited. Similarly if it is qualified by adherence to another objective of national economic policy, such as the maintenance of an adequate national growth rate, the appropriate regional strategy will vary according to the capacity of the regions to contribute to national growth. The objective of "reducing congestion", in large urban conglomerations by itself offers no guide to the appropriate national strategy for dealing with congested urban centres in different regions. The choice may be between improving employment opportunities in less congested regions to discourage migration, or recognizing migration as an unavoidable consequence of economic conditions and tackling the resulting problems in the congested regions.

More generally, if the resources devoted to overcoming regional imbalances are insufficient, the choice for national regional strategy lies between increasing them or recognizing the need to alter the strategy to deal with the resultant problems in whatever way they are distributed interregionally. It cannot be assumed dogmatically that the former choice is always to be preferred, since resources available to overcome imbalances are not unlimited, and no Government is able to ignore the actual problems that result from the changes which take place, despite regional policies, in the interregional distribution of economic activity.

In practice no Government pursues one objective of policy to the exclusion of all others. The resultant "mix" of objectives and policies is a compromise based, in the last resort, on what is judged to be politically acceptable. Of none of the OECD countries whose regional policies have been studied can it be said that they are pursued without regard to their influence on overall growth, or that growth policies are pursued without regard to their effect on the regions. Nor can any Government be accused of confining their attention, in the pursuit of regional policies, to the problem of the disadvantaged regions to the exclusion of those of the other regions.

The OECD report "The Regional Factor in Economic Development" (p. 24) points out that the principal aims of regional economic policy are complex and interrelated and that regional policy is geared to the central objective of economic growth as well as the correction of imbalances in regional employment and incomes. The descriptions of the objectives of the countries studied show how varied they can be, yet still fit this general formula.

If this were all that could be said there would however still be no answer to the question of how the objectives of national regional strategy can be more closely defined, despite the acknowledged difficulties of quantifying targets. The Working Party has given considerable attention to this problem and, in doing so, exposed some of the semantic confusions to which the subject seems particularly liable.

To avoid these confusions it is necessary to distinguish between those ultimate objectives of society which infuse the whole of its activities and those objectives in more limited spheres the achievement of which is conducive to the ultimate objectives. These latter have been referred to by the Working Party as intermediate objectives, though they could equally well be described as derivative from, or secondary, objectives to the ultimate objectives.

Ultimate objectives can be listed in great, sometimes contradictory, detail - higher standards of life for all, full employment, maximum leisure, social justice, equality, adequate reward for effort, freedom from want, security, abolition of poverty, quality of life, etc. They are summed up in such phrases as "the health, wealth and happiness of all citizens". Most countries would subscribe to this as the ultimate objective but give different weight, according to their social and political philosophies, to particular aspects.

If "Reality" - sometimes harsh - has the unfortunate and, no doubt, regrettable habit of breaking through Utopian clouds, it does not destroy the vision. It also serves the purpose of concentrating the mind wonderfully on the practical choices which are open, in reality. It is not necessary to discuss the problem and difficulties in defining or selecting ultimate objectives. They exist however and are the background against which the choice of intermediate objectives is made. They serve to explain the difference in emphasis given to secondary objectives in different countries.

A further "semantic" distinction that the Working Party have made is between intermediate aims and the specific objectives for the achievement of the aims. Thus an intermediate objective (of regional policy) is to secure a better balance between regions. Specifically this will mean a relative rise in the standard of living in certain regions compared with others. The intermediate objective does not define the specific objectives. A change in regional imbalances can be brought about in alternative and opposite ways; viz. by outward migration from the disadvantaged region or by diversion of resources to it (we discuss this question as a major issue in the chapter on regional imbalances).

The intermediate objective of decongestion of urban conglomerations can be achieved by a whole variety of alternative means, each of

24

which gives rise to a different specific objective, such as the creation of new towns in determined areas, or the removal of factors causing congestion in the urban conglomerations themselves.

The intermediate objective of coping with the depopulation of rural areas or raising living standards may require the adoption of specific objectives varying with the causes of depopulation, viz. lack of remunerative employment for labour rendered surplus by advances in agricultural techniques, unattractive conditions compared with urban centres owing to lack of scale or concentration in units sufficient to provide necessary services.

The intermediate objective of enabling disadvantaged regions to compete more effectively with others may give rise to alternative specific objectives of improving their communications, infrastructure and labour skills or injecting new types of industry to replace those unable to compete.

Examples of the difference between intermediate and specific objectives can be multiplied ad infinitum. The important reason for making the distinction is, as already noted, that each intermediate objective does not define the specific objectives but gives rise to a range of choices which can only be made on the basis of a judgement of which is the better designed, in the particular circumstances, to achieve the intermediate objective.

A further distinction needs to be made, between specific objectives and the method by which these are to be achieved. The specific objective of, say, creating twenty new towns, can call for a variety of methods. They may range from institutional changes (viz. the creation of new systems of town administration such as the Development Corporations in the United Kingdom), methods affecting the allocation of public expenditure for infrastructure and public services, and methods for encouraging the movement of people or industry to the new towns. It may itself be an intermediate objective of regional policy to create conditions which enable these methods to work.

There is thus an interaction between methods by which specific objectives are to be achieved and the intermediate objectives themselves. The method of encouraging the movement of industry to disadvantaged regions can vary from the grant of financial incentives to firms (a subject discussed in another chapter) the imposition of restraints on industry in other regions or developing the infrastructure and services to make conditions in the disadvantaged regions more attractive. Here again, there is an interaction between methods and intermediate objectives - and some methods may not be consistent with some intermediate objectives. Thus if it is an intermediate objective to encourage the

spread of efficient competitive industry to disadvantaged regions the
adoption of incentives to firms which put a premium on inefficiency or
uncompetitiveness generally will be inconsistent with that objective.

It has been noted that intermediate objectives are an aspect of a
wider ultimate objective. Within the ultimate objective, however defined,
there are numerous intermediate objectives all of which stand in some
relation to each other. An intermediate objective of securing an improvement in the general economic prospects of a country will be related to several other intermediate objectives, such as avoiding inflation,
securing a satisfactory balance of payments, enhanced industrial productivity. It can also be related to complementary objectives in the
social field, such as improving health and education and the "quality
of life" generally. Some of these objectives may clash, for example
industrial growth, or the exploitation of natural resources may clash
with environmental considerations. Similarly, specific objectives (and
the methods used) designed to achieve one intermediate objective, may
clash with other intermediate objectives and the specific objectives and
methods that they entail. The specific objective of developing service
employment by, for example, the encouragement of tourism may clash
with the intermediate objective of conservation of the countryside, the
sea coasts and their traditional values. Regional differences in, say,
health and education may have a different pattern from employment and
income levels and the objectives in the former may have different regional aspects from the latter. It may, and almost certainly will be in most
countries an intermediate objective in itself to avoid or reduce the clash
between different intermediate objectives and the specific objectives and
methods to which they give rise, including their regional emphasis.

All this somewhat theoretical analysis is designed to bring us closer
to the answer to the question of how the objectives of national regional
strategy can be more closely defined. It also brings us nearer to identifying the essential elements in a "national regional strategy" as opposed
to an internal regional strategy. The conclusions reached so far can be
summed up in the following way:

1. A "strategy" is a unifying concept which brings together ultimate, intermediate and specific objectives, and their related methods into a coherent whole. It therefore defines the objectives
themselves and the way in which they are to be achieved.

2. Presupposing the ultimate objective for a good life for all can
best be taken for granted, a "national regional strategy" is concerned with one among many of the intermediate objectives of national
policy. Since these may clash and be mutually frustrating the
strategy will need, inter alia, to indicate the relationship of its
objectives with other intermediate objectives.

26

3.   The intermediate objectives of a national regional strategy do not by themselves define the specific objectives which are appropriate. The same intermediate objectives can be achieved by the adoption of a variety of specific objectives. The choice of specific objectives can only be made by a comparative assessment of the merits of the alternatives. Similarly, a variety of methods can be used to achieve the same specific objective and the choice can only be determined after examination of comparative merits in given circumstances.

4.   Specific objectives and methods, and their regional patterns, can, like the intermediate objectives themselves, clash with other intermediate objectives. The national regional strategy would therefore need to indicate the relation between the specific objectives and methods and other intermediate objectives and their related methods.

This formulation helps to bring out some of the component elements in a national strategy and their interrelations. It constitutes only a skeleton or the "bare bones". The effectiveness of a strategy cannot be determined by its skeletal structure but by its relevance to the facts, the appositeness and feasibility of the objectives and methods adopted.

On this basis the pre-requisite for a strategy is a knowledge and understanding of the "facts" or the factual situation with which the strategy is to deal. A strategy which is geared to non existent "facts" or to abstract notions of what ought to exist in some ideal world can have an academic interest but will not serve the purpose of dealing with real situations; and it is real situations with which Governments are faced. The question has to be asked therefore: what are the facts with which national strategy for regions should be concerned.

The first observation to be made is that the only facts relevant to a strategy are those which relate to the future. The past has gone; and though it may be a guide to what can happen in the future nothing can be done to alter the past. Unfortunately for those who have to deal with the future, it cannot be precisely predicted and the past may be a bad guide to what will happen in the future. At any specific point in time those past trends may have worked themselves out and new trends may be in operation which can only be faintly discerned. For example the rundown of agricultural employment, or the staple industries in particular regions, can have reached their limits, while the accumulation of new economic circumstances or the accumulative effect of regional policies and measures previously adopted may have laid the foundations for new future trends which will produce a totally different regional situation from that of preceding years.

27

The important developments of recent times, the considerable migration of population, the changing birth rates, the development of advanced technological industries, the relative growth of "service industries", the "rundown" of employment in coal and textiles, the revaluations of currencies, the discovery of new resources, the improvement of national communication networks, new transportation systems (such as the "container revolution") and the progress towards a wider membership of the EEC, - all mean that the national contexts in which regional strategies have to be worked out now is a very different one from that of the early sixties.

Secondly, the future is not a single period: it stretches out, through the immediate future to the short, medium and longer terms which can only be seen as through a glass darkly. Even the immediate future cannot be seen very clearly. The "strategist" has, at all times, to allow for change that cannot be foreseen and the errors that are inevitable in all attempts to penetrate the mists of the future. If the past is a guide to anything, it is to the ever present possibility of error in judging the future. This does not mean that attempts at strategies are foredoomed to failure at the start. It emphasizes the importance, however, of systems of constant monitoring of change, so that aims and objectives can be altered as new situations and new predictive techniques require. It calls also for setting the parameters of strategies in terms of ranges of possibilities rather than a set of single predictions for each aspect of a situation with which the strategy is to deal.

This being said it can now be asked what are the basic facts which need to be assembled, relating to the future, before a suitable strategy can be divised? This is not a matter on which anyone be dogmatic. Nor are there, to the writer's knowledge, any national regional strategies extant which offer a model which all Governments could be advised to follow.* The Working Party might perhaps usefully attempt to frame such a model. In the meantime the following should only be regarded as tentative suggestions.

---

* A number of OECD countries have published national strategies for regional development as part of, or separately from national plans. They vary in structure and the degree of which they provide the factual and predictive data on which the strategic objectives are based. The United Kingdom study "Long Term Population Distribution in Great Britain" published by HMSO for the Department of Economic Affairs in 1971 is an interesting attempt to provide the long term parameters for a strategy. The fact that it took 5-6 years to prepare is some indication of the difficulties involved. It is difficult to judge how far it constitutes the basis for current United Kingdom long term regional strategies.

FACTUAL REQUIREMENTS
FOR A NATIONAL REGIONAL STRATEGY

1. The demographic facts. Ranges of forecasts showing:

   a) Total population, its age and sex distribution and household composition for given periods ahead;

   b) The population of working age derived from (a) for given periods ahead;

   c) The regional distributions of (a) and (b) on the basis of previous trends corrected (i) by known new trends and (ii) by the predicted effects of regional policies and measures.

2. The economic facts influencing the regional structure, viz:

   a) Predictable change in national resources, output and consumption, income and investment;

   b) External economic factors: world market forces affecting import and export capability or trends; foreign trade orientation of the national economy; trends in competing or associated countries;

   c) Structural changes: rising, declining and stable industries and occupations (broadly categorized - primary, manufacturing, technological, service industries, etc.);

   d) Economic control policies for stimulation or restraint; the ratio of public to private sector consumption;

   e) Overall demand for and supply of manpower (labour and skills) of various main classes resulting from (a) - (d); employment and unemployment.

3. The physical infrastructure:

   a) Energy supplies;

   b) Communications (surface, air and telecommunications), ports and harbours, transport systems;

   c) Land availability and land use.

4. The social framework

   a) Progress in education and the effects on skills;

   b) Progress in housing, health and welfare;

c) Changing social objectives and their influence: progress towards equality, leisure versus work; environmental improvement.

5. Regional patterns emerging from (1) to (4).

Ideally this would show, for each particular subject, the positive
or negative effect on each region, quantified to the extent the data allow.
The same region could of course be positively or negatively affected by
different factors, for they do not necessarily work in the same direction.
It would no doubt be possible, after analysis of the regional effects of
each set of "facts", to sum the regional situation up for each scheduled
period, and by giving "weights" to each element, reach a conclusion on
whether the resultant situation is one to be accepted or corrected, and in
which respects. It would be a complicated but not impossible task. It
would certainly be a necessary one in any systematic approach to the
problem of defining what the objectives of a national regional strategy
are to be. Assuming it could be done, a tabular presentation could help
to identify the areas with which the strategy would be concerned. The
following schematic form (on page 31) is only partial but serves to show
a possible way of indicating the regional patterns.

Leaving aside the problem of giving proper meaning to the plus
and minus signs a construct of this character enables certain features
of the hypothetical country to be simply described.

It has a rising population and, taken overall, the trends are satisfactory. The main problems which give rise to concern are employment demand, adverse external economic factors and the environment.

The region in the apparently worst situation is Region V. It has
a declining share of the national population, its economic indices are
all negative and the only positive feature is that its infrastructure is
relatively improving. Region II also has an overall unfavourable situation. While its population is rising in proportion to the national total
its share of national output is declining and it is beset both by structural
and external economic problems causing decline in employment demand.
Nonetheless its share of the national income is rising (despite the relative fall in output) perhaps because its favourable and improving environment attracts large numbers of well-to-do residents in retirement
and social security benefits are generous. Regions I, III and IV are all
satisfactory "overall" but in I the rise in output reflects heavy external
investment the benefits of which accrue largely outside the region so
that while employment demand is rising the region's share of national
income is in fact declining. In Region III the pluses are largely due to

30

	REGIONS					COUNTRY
	I	II	III	IV	V	
Influence of changes in: Gross population (regionally as proportion of national) + = increase - = decrease	+	+	-	+	-	+
Output (regionally as proportion of national) + = increase - = decrease	+	-	+	+	-	+
Income (regionally as proportion of national) + = increase - = decrease	-	+	+	+	-	+
World economic factors + = favourable - = unfavourable	+	-	+	+	-	-
Structural changes + = favourable - = unfavourable	+	-	+	+	-	+
Employment demand + = increase - = decrease	+	-	-	-	-	-
Infrastructure + = (relative) improvement - = (relative) worsening	-	+	-	-	+	+
Social Framework: Education + = adapted to change - = not adapted	+	+	+	+	-	+
Environment + = improving - = worsening	-	+	+	-	-	-
Overall + = satisfactory trends - = unsatisfactory trends	+	-	+	+	-	+

the relative fall in population, its favourable position in regard to world economic factors and to its industrial structure. In IV the main weaknesses are in the infrastructure, and environment but they do not offset the favourable economic and social (educational) factors.

It is not difficult to see what kind of national and "national regional" strategies are likely to be suggested in this sort of situation. The global problems for the economy are international competition and a decline in employment demand. These problems, together with structural change, are common to both regions with overall unsatisfactory trends, namely II and V. The better placed regions are not uniformly satisfactory however. Regions I and III and IV all suffer from a relative worsening of their infrastructure and the environment is worsening in I and IV as well as in V. Economic strategy would be concerned especially with regions II and V and the strategy for the infrastructure with I, III and IV.

It would of course be possible to invent an entirely different pattern, as would show, for example, that world economic factors are unfavourable to all regions and that favourable employment demand is confined to regions less susceptible by their structure to the influence of world factors.

Nor do the regions with overall satisfactory trends necessarily correspond to the regions which have been "more prosperous" in the past. The test is, as has been said, what is likely to happen in the future and it cannot be automatically assumed - anywhere - that the conditions which have led to prosperity of a region in the past are guaranteed to continue for ever in the future. If that were so, many of the regions which are now suffering from decline of the industries which were formerly the source of their prosperity would not now be "problem" regions. It can hardly be too strongly stressed that, unless a realistic appraisal is made of the future prospects of regions in the total national context, any objectives of national regional policy based on concepts of past and current states of prosperity will be misconceived or directed towards the wrong targets.

The schematic presentation adopted above shows only the sort of matters about which national judgements need to be formed. It helps also to provide answers to the first three questions listed in the Appendix to this chapter. The general views of the Working Party on these questions were that, in the context of a national framework for regional policies, strategies are required for each region, "prosperous" and "less prosperous" alike, for the reason that national economic strategies are concerned with the economy as a whole and must be attuned to the prospective situation of the country as a whole, i.e. its several regions. The national assumptions to be fed into each regional strategy must be defined and add up to a mutually consistent whole. Separate strategies which produce a total population greater than that predicted for the whole country would be meaningless. So would strategies which provide for more than the total output, or total employment than can be predicted from global calculations.

These views are endorsed by all that has been said so far in this chapter.

The first stage in any systematic approach to a national regional strategy is to survey the regional bearing of separate national intermediate objectives. Thus, using the above construct as a model the national intermediate objectives are:

1. Making the economy less vulnerable to adverse world economic factors;

2. Ensuring a higher level of employment demand;

3. Dealing with the worsening environment.

A less simplified or limited construct would extend the list. Other intermediate objectives which find a place in many countries would include:

4. Fostering necessary structural change to lessen reliance on declining or unviable industries and increase the role of viable, modern, high growth and profitable industries;

5. Modifying the ratio of private or public consumption (or vice versa according to political philosophy);

6. Modernizing the infrastructure to cope adequately with new developments or technologies;

7. Adjusting the technical, professional and vocational aptitudes of the population to changing technological and occupational demands;

8. Ensuring adequate standards of social provision for housing, health, welfare and social security;

9. Dealing with the problem of leisure and recreation arising either from greater affluence or diminishing demand for labour time;

10. Lessening social hardship from economic change while ensuring adaptability to it.

This is not an exhaustive list but is sufficient to show that each intermediate objective is likely to have its own particular regional pattern which may differ from that of the others. Thus (1), (5), (7), (8), (9) and (10) may be a country wide objective; (2) may have a different regional pattern from (3) and (6) and (4) may be required everywhere, but in different degrees.

The second stage in a systematic approach to a national regional strategy is to define the policies appropriate to each objective and the degree to which the policies should be regionally differentiated. Common to both tasks will of course be an assessment of the priorities to be attached to coping with each of the intermediate objectives. The priorities are important. If, for example, a higher priority is given to (8) than (6) the resources available to deal with (6) might be insufficient to deal with more than the minimum necessary in each region, leaving no room for a specially high level of infrastructure development in the particular regions where it is relatively worse. Alternatively, if the highest priority has to be given to (1) and (2) the possibilities of dealing with imbalances in regional patterns in the other fields will be correspondingly limited. Similarly, if (7) were regarded as among the highest national priority objectives the regional pattern of deficiencies in education would be a pressing element in the national regional strategy. If it were to outweigh (3) the policy would be to give more importance to regional imbalances in education than those in the environment.

Once the problem of assigning priorities to the various intermediate objectives has been resolved the next question facing the systematic strategist is that of the policy or policies appropriate to dealing with the objectives. Each objective can give rise to controversy over which is the right policy, and it is only according to which way the main argument is resolved that it becomes possible to decide how far regional differentiation is a necessary part of the policy.

Thus the policy for (1), (2) and (4) might be a combination of monetary and fiscal measures to control the total demand; of placing reliance on competitive forces to oblige industry and commerce to adjust to change, allowing the weak or inefficient to go to the wall in the hope that the strong and efficient will best secure the long term viability of the economy; giving special support, through financial assistance or other measures, to selected industries offering the best hope for a continuingly viable national economy; or confining support measures to the "propping up" of weak or declining industries for which no employment-giving replacement is in sight.

It would not be hard to find examples of all these policies operating, sometimes, simultaneously and in conflict with each other, in most countries.

Each of the policies will have a different regional impact and therefore in themselves reflect a different approach to national regional strategy. Monetary and fiscal measures increasing global demand will give
a "boost" to those industries able to take advantage of it irrespective of
the regions in which they may be situated. Financial support measures
to selected industries, e. g. in advanced technology, aviation, electronics,
ect. , will bear on some regions more than others; the "propping up" of
weak or inefficient industries for which there is no replacement in sight
might bear particularly on those regions where the overall employment
position is weak but can of course also apply to areas within regions
– the special pockets of unemployment.

A national regional strategy which combines all these policies clearly
cannot be defined in terms of a single intermediate objective, such as
"securing a proper balance between regions". It would be more correct
to say that the regional strategy is designed to achieve that regional
balance which will result from the pursuit of the necessary national policies. It is worth putting some emphasis on this, since it is the combination of policies which flow from numerous intermediate objectives
which really constitutes the regional policy that is truly being followed.

The national regional strategy which emerges from the combination
of policies referred to above can now be stated, in a different way from
the more traditional formulation of "rectifying imbalances", as follows:

1. The national regional strategy follows consequentially on the
adoption of main national policies or goals – in this case international viability, employment growth and structural change for modernisation. It is not designed to bring about a preconceived regional distribution of economic activity incompatible with these
main objectives.

2. Growth is welcomed of industries which are (a) responsive to
demand, (b) capable of adjusting efficiently to competitive conditions, (c) able to contribute to future growth of and viability of the
economy as a whole.

3. Weak and inefficient industries will be allowed to fade out,
except in areas where there are inadequate alternative employment
possibilities (and migration on an adequate scale is not feasible or
desirable).

4. Special support measures will be given so far as necessary to
ensure an adequate proportion in the economy of modern, viable
growth industries able to face competition: they will also be given,
as necessary, to cope with the problem in (3).

35

If other main objectives of national policy are incorporated the national regional strategy would be modified accordingly. The appropriate policies would depend on what gave rise to the need for the policy.

Thus the "worsening of the environment" could be due to the pollution effect of the new viable industries, or to the modernization of the infrastructure, e.g. the improvement of roads to permit an unlimited number of new cars to pollute the atmosphere. The "modernization" of the infrastructure itself may be required to facilitate industrial development in those regions in which it can be expected to take place. The "raising of standards of social provisions" in, say, housing, may require rapid building of houses for people who can afford to pay the cost, and for subsidization of housing for all those who cannot afford the cost - even irrespective of the regions in which they live and work. Coping with the problem of leisure and recreation can involve the provision of facilities where local resources are insufficient. The alleviation of social hardship arising from changing economic circumstances may present a choice between palliatives measures in the shape of adequate social security benefits or changing main economic objectives to give more support to industries in decline. Each of these objectives involves a choice for the policy makers. The choice that is made is then a determinant of the regional patterns.

The "national regional strategy" emerges from the choice made between the alternative approaches to these objectives. We can add some further components to our hypothetical strategy, presupposing certain policy choices.

5. Environmental problems will be tackled in harmony with the main economic objectives of national growth. Priority in the allocation of public resources will be given to overcoming the effects of necessary new technological developments. Clearing of dereclict land due to past industrial development will be given special support (a) where it is conducive to economic growth and (b) where it will provide facilities for amenity and recreation in under provided areas;

6. Priority for infrastructure in the shape of roads, power and water supplies will be governed by the needs of the industrial and commercial growth of the country. It will take place in accordance with criteria for determining where the best rate of return on investment can be secured. Thus low priority will be accorded to road construction in areas where existing and prospective traffic can be coped with, and high priority where overloading and congestion are bad and likely to worsen as a result of further industrial development and the growing car ownership;*

* This particular policy of course involves a rejection of the alternative of spending money on roads to give employment or to use the improvement of roads, irrespective of potential traffic needs, to increase the attractiveness of an area to incoming industry. It also

7.   Housing policy will aim to ensure a rapid provision of houses in areas of population and employment growth, and where the existing housing stock is insufficient, or where demolition and slum clearance necessitates replacement. Land use planning for housing will be geared to a satisfactory matching of residential and industrial areas, with due regard to communications, minimization of commuting and protection of environment. These principles will be followed in all regions and applied according to local circumstances.

In this systematic and theoretical approach the national regional strategy emerges as the expression, in regional terms, of a series of national policies. Under this concept it is no longer appropriate, or necessary, to think in terms of "conflict" between regional and other national policies. National regional strategy becomes the way in which national policies, with their different objectives, are applied territorially. The advantage of this approach is that it eliminates the totally artificial distinction between a country and its regions. A country is its regions and the artificial distinction leads in some countries to the misuse of the term "regions", confusing it with backward, "declining" or otherwise "disadvantaged" regions. It also leads to the use of the term "regional policy" or "regional planning" confined to selected regions. One of the disadvantages of this terminology is that it tends to give rise to a need for an apologia or defensive posture in regard to policies which permit development to take place outside the so-called "development" regions. This is unreal since no country is able to develop its full potential unless it makes use of the capacities of all its regions. The adoption of a defensive posture, when policy implies the development of those regions more favourably placed to meet a country's requirements, is not only misplaced. It carries with it the danger of creating a psychological climate for diverting resources to selected regions irrespective of the effect on the progress of the national economy as a whole. It is not, of course, wrong so to divert resources. It is wrong however by a country's own criteria, if the diversion is such as to frustrate the country's various national objectives seen as a whole - and hardly appropriate to make a special defence of those policies which conform with them.*

involves a rejection of a policy of allowing road congestion to become so bad in overloaded zones that it acts as an incentive to firms to establish themselves elsewhere. These are choices which have to be made. We shall deal with infrastructure policy as a separate issue and our hypothetical strategy does not imply that one choice is necessarily better than another.

    *   As the question of terminology is raised a plea (no doubt a purist one) might be made for the abandonment of such terms as the "development regions". Under most national policies development is sought, promoted, supported, encouraged or permitted in all regions. Economic development policies themselves require complementary policies for the development of the infrastructure, the environment, education, health and so on. In some countries, with vigorous "regional" policies the most rapid development may take place in "non development" regions. The term "industrial preference regions" would have the advantage of avoiding this sort of semantic obfuscation.

37

SPECIFIC OBJECTIVES OF REGIONAL POLICY

Once the intermediate objectives of national policy and their regional components have been established it is possible to specify the particular objectives by which the strategy is to be realized.

The fourth stage involves stating the intermediate objectives of national policy in regional terms, the choice being based on policy decisions as to priorities and methods for dealing with given problems. A few illustrations in concrete terms will help to indicate what is meant.

The intermediate objective of enhancing the competitive strength of the economy as a whole may require different degrees of attention in different regions. If the industries in Regions A to C are judged to be modern, efficient, well managed and with adequate access to sources of manpower, markets and supplies whereas in Regions D and E industries are judged to be deficient in some or all of these respects, the specific objectives of national policy may be to improve the "performance of Regions D and E". This presupposes a judgement that the "measures" necessary are feasible, and compatible with other intermediate objectives (for example a proper return for public expenditure that may be required).

The same situation could however lead to a different specific objective. It might be judged that the problems of Regions D and E could not be solved except at prohibitive cost and that a better return, in terms of national competitive capacity, would be obtained by enhancing still further the performance of Regions A to C. The specific regional objectives of national policy might be to secure a rundown of Regions D and E and to "cushion" the social effects while improving still further the performance of Regions A to C and enabling them to cope with such consequential problems as an inflow of migrants from Regions D and E.

The choice made will be a political one and similar situations in different countries will be resolved differently. The decision to adopt one specific objective rather than another is however a decision of national regional strategy.

To take another illustration. The intermediate national objective of enabling the road system to cope with the traffic load arising from expanding industrial activity can give rise to general specific objectives, viz. (a) the creation of a network of efficient main roads (say motorways) linking each major industrial centre to each other and to selected external links, (b) the improvement of the road system in major urban centres, (c) improvement of secondary road systems where this is most urgently needed and the benefits justify the expenditure.

The adoption of the "programme" over a given time scale, in accordance with priorities, the resources available and technical factors involved means that the intermediate objective can be stated in regional terms. The specific objectives are then defined as the completion of parts of the programme, in the several regions, by given dates.

The decision may reflect the political priorities and preferences of development in different regions but they, also, are decisions of national regional strategy.

A further illustration can be given by reference to an intermediate national objective of lessening excessive growth of major cities or excessive concentration of industrial development in "congested" areas or regions. The policy or method by which this objective is to be achieved may be the development of new free standing cities, satellites, "growth" points or zones and "métropoles d'équilibre". The policy can only be implemented through a definition of the number, size and rate of development of the new cities, growth points, etc. in each of the regions in which they are to be created.

The specific objectives of the national regional policy can then be described as "two cities" (etc.) in Region A, five in Region B, four in Region C and so on, each with the proposed size on given time scales. The alternate political choice may turn on an appraisal of resource cost, urgency of need in the several regions, feasibility from various angles, relationship with other objectives, such as the employment growth and national productivity and so on. Once the choice has been made however, each project becomes a specific regional objective linked to the national objective and an integral feature of the national regional strategy.

It is not necessary to multiply the illustrations to establish that each set of specific regional objectives follows from the way in which particular intermediate objectives are to be obtained, and that the distribution of these specific objectives between regions is an indication of the national regional strategy that is being pursued. The methods by which the intermediate objectives are to be achieved, will, as has already been discussed, throw up policy choices as well as technical problems. While the technical problems must be resolved by the technicians, i.e. the project planners, engineers, surveyors, economists and sociologists, the policy problems or the way they are resolved constitute part of the strategy. Thus the decision to build up new towns or "métropoles d'équilibre" may be accompanied by a strategic decision to provide more favourable financial terms to the constructing authority in some regions rather than in others, expressing thus a regional preference. A strategic decision may also be made to limit the rate of growth of new towns in particular regions to what can be achieved through its inherent attractiveness to industry. Alternatively the rate of growth can be speeded up by granting financial incentives to industry in those towns located in problem regions.

The use of wage subsidies may be a method by which employers are encouraged to increase their labour force. A decision to limit such subsidies to regions of high unemployment would be one for national regional strategy, relating to methods.

To recapitulate, we may sum up the preceding analysis by saying that a national regional strategy for regional development involves five stages, viz:

1. The assembling of the national intermediate objectives which have a bearing on regional development;

2. Determining the way in which the intermediate objectives are regionally differentiated;

3. Considering the policies which should govern the choice of specific objectives;

4. Selecting the specific objectives, in conformity with policies, necessary in the regions, to secure the intermediate objectives;

5. Adopting the methods best designed to fulfil the specific objectives.

There is, of course, nothing in this abstract formula to suggest what the "right" national strategy would be in given circumstances. Nor does it indicate how far it is right, in the pursuance of national intermediate objectives, to differentiate in favour, or discriminate against particular regions on applying general policies. This is the very stuff of the debate that has to go on in each country before the policy decisions are made and the objectives and methods adopted. What the formula does show is that the debate on what constitutes the "right" national regional strategy is not about a single issue but about many inter-linked issues each of which has its distinct regional implications. The "right" strategy is the one that emerges from proper consideration of them all.

Nor does it indicate the administrative methods appropriate to dividing up a national strategy or suggest that this is a task for national, central Government authorities acting alone. The administration procedure will vary between countries, its constitutional structure and the degree in which different authorities will need to co-operate in preparing a strategy in which they will have a part to play. However the problem

of co-operation and co-ordination is resolved does not of itself affect
the necessary content of a strategy. A reading of the country studies
of the Working Party suggests that few countries, if any, have as yet
sought to adopt the systematic approach that is implied in the above
formula. The difficulties in doing so are formidable. Knowledge of
the relevant facts is usually fragmentary, forecasting techniques are,
at best, experimental, conflicting policy aims are hard to reconcile.
The fact that many elements in strategy formulation are the responsibility of separate, often rival, agencies inhibits the kind of co-ordination
of approach required for a comprehensive national regional strategy.
Political pressures are such that Governments may sometimes prefer
any decision at all to the indecision that results from seeking too perfect
an answer.

It can, however, perhaps be claimed for the systematic approach
which has been elaborated, at possibly over great length, in the foregoing, that it has certain advantages over a less systematic approach.
It points the way to improvement of methods of formulating a national
strategy, where this may be desired. It would help to diminish vague-
ness of objectives, apparent conflicts between them and focus attention
on the real choices that confront Governments. It lessens the over-
emphasis on vaguely stated single objectives. From an economic
standpoint it could lead to the more effective use of scarce resources by weighing all the competing claims on them against a coherent
and meaningful strategy. The inference has been drawn that Governments do not necessarily desire to achieve alleged objectives of regional policy at the expense of all others. The drawing up of a comprehensive
national regional strategy which gives a proper place to other objectives
with regional implications has the advantage of giving a truer and more
intelligible picture of what Governments are seeking to achieve. In so
doing the policies pursued can be realistically geared and resources
allocated accordingly to the real rather than the supposed objectives of
regional policy.

Finally, a valid national framework can be provided for strategies
for development of individual regions, the subject of the following section.

STRATEGY FOR INDIVIDUAL REGIONS

Though some reasons have been given, in the earlier parts of this
chapter, for the production of strategies for individual regions it is not
self-evident that they are necessary in all circumstances. Economic
development has, after all, taken place in regions over the centuries
without anything that can be called a regional strategy. Even in those
countries in which regional planning is most advanced the role of formal

regional strategies still plays only a very limited part in shaping the course of development. The mainsprings of regional development are usually not to be found in the concerted plans of central and regional authorities but in the response of the national and international community to the opportunities which a region offers. The response does not come only within the region. It often, and sometimes mainly comes from outside. Since enterprise and capital are directed towards the most profitable ends open to them investment and productive effort flow towards and away from regions according to the relative scope they offer for development.

Many of the decisions as to what shall be developed and how, or as to what industries and economic activities are feasible are made from outside a region. Central Governments can decide how to locate public resources between regions: the bigger the role of central finance in public expenditure the more the development of the infrastructure and public services will depend on the decisions of central Government. Institutions and organisations in the public and private sector located in capital cities or elsewhere, may have the deciding voice in the use of capital. It is their decisions which may determine the provision of power and water supplies, airports and air services, mineral development, the location of manufacturing establishments and commercial services, wholesale and retail distribution, advertising and marketing, etc. Local individuals, organisations, institutions and companies will play their part, but it will only be one part in a complex of interrelations in which purely regional influence will vary from region to region and from sector to sector.

Here lies the first important difference between national and regional strategies. A central authority - the Government - has the ultimate power to decide the strategy - including the regional parts of it - for the country as a whole in its national and international setting. There will of course be constitutional and political and practical limitations on the exercise of its power. Allowing for these limitations it still remains true that the way in which the power of central Government is exercised, especially in the key sectors of national legislation, currency, fiscal policy, the regulation of trade and commerce and the setting of standards and criteria is a major determinant of the progress of a nation as a whole and of its constituent regions and parts. By contrast a strategy for an individual region - irrespective of the authority that prepares it - can be designed only to influence the development of a region within the national setting and can only be effective if it makes proper allowance for that setting.

Ideally this would mean that a precondition for an effective strategy for a region or number of regions is the existence of a defined national regional strategy. In practice however this is more often an aspiration rather than a reality. Few Governments have sought, and still fewer succeeded, in developing a comprehensive national strategic framework for the regions taken together. National strategies have tended to be confined to the "problem regions", on the assumption that the others can be adequately cared for through the working of the economic system and the related, regionally undifferentiated, policies. Even then they have to be largely inferred from the specific objectives and methods adopted, themselves liable to frequent change. This is not the only difficulty. As experience has taught, national regional strategies do not necessarily succeed in achieving their objectives. A realistic strategy for an individual region requires a judgement as to the likely effects both of the national strategy and of other factors which will influence the region's development.

A further significant influence on the development of a region is that of the other regions. Regional economies are not closed systems but interrelated through the inter-regional movements of people, goods and services, the existence of inter-regional enterprise and infrastructure and through the progress of development in other regions.

The background to the development of any region is therefore (a) the trend of the national economy, (b) the national strategies and policies at work, (c) the trends, developments and strategies in the other regions. It is worth stressing from the start that knowledge of all these things is likely to be limited among national and regional authorities alike: acknowledgement of this basic limitation is the beginning of realism in the preparation of any regional strategy.

To recognize the limitations on what is possible is not to declare that the task of preparing regional strategies is an impossible one and should be abandoned. For the reason given earlier the need for regional strategies exists. The problem is to define the objectives and select the methods and measures with adequate regard to the limitations imposed by the realities of the national and inter-regional situations. The task is one that calls for co-ordination between national and regional authorities. However this co-ordination is effected - a subject for separate consideration - the only effective regional strategy is the one that takes proper account of these limitations.

As with national strategies, regional strategies can only be meaningful if they are geared to defined objectives. The selection of objectives, general and specific, and of the appropriate methods equally presupposes a survey of the region's problems, an appraisal of its future prospects and a choice between alternative policies and measures.

Since each region will have its own characteristics and range of problems of differing degrees of importance, regional strategies will

differ significantly, certainly in content and often in form. Their mutual
validity will however still depend on the degree to which common assumption for those aspects which they have in common with other regions are
adopted. Thus a series of regional strategies which are based on population forecasts which in total exceeds that of the national population, or
growth will lack mutual validity. Regional strategies which pre-empt the
growth in labour supply, or the development of particular industries will
conflict rather than complement each other. No strategy can be realistically, and finally, adopted or made to work unless it belongs to a self-
consistent national pattern of regional strategies.

One method that is frequently used for fixing objectives of regional
strategy is that of comparative need: measuring for example the discrep-
ancies between income and employment levels in the region and that of
the country as a whole. The objective is then defined as the elimination
or reduction of this discrepancy or gap to a more "satisfactory level".
Using the reasoning in the earlier part of this chapter this kind of objective belongs more to the category of "ultimate" objectives or aspirations.
It suffers from the same disadvantages and from having little to do with
what can actually be achieved within a given time-scale and with the resources available. Its achievement will depend not only on what can be
done within the region itself but on what will happen to the other regions
tending to increase or lessen the gap. Its adoption as a real or "intermediate" objective can only be justified if certain preconditions can be
satisfied, such as the capacity of the region to develop more rapidly than
elsewhere and/or the allocation of sufficient resources to enable it do so.

It may be considered to be a weakness of many of the strategies which
have been formulated by regional bodies - for example in some of the
earlier productions of the regional Economic Planning Councils in the
United Kingdom - that their objectives have tended to be presented as
catalogues of "needs" on the basis of desirable standards. The real
problem that has to be solved by the strategist is to select those objectives which are feasible in the prevailing or expected circumstances,
taking account of the region's potential and the national needs and policies which will bear on the region. The first step towards an effective
regional strategy is therefore the selection of the "intermediate regional objectives" which can be regarded as practicable.

Since there is aloways an element of choice in the selection of
objectives it is not possible to generalize about the appropriate objectives for a given regional situation. A region which is suffering from
decline of its staple industries and migration of workers to other regions can present a choice between accepting its run-down as inevitable
and cushioning the effects by social security measures, or counteracting
the run-down by special support measures for existing industry and/or
generating new industries to replace it. Conversely a region which is

expanding rapidly owing to its inherent capacity for growth may warrant encouragement in the interest of national growth and of the declining regions or throw up problems calling either for restraint of the growth or for measures to control its harmful effects. In both cases the decision can only turn on what is feasible, the costs and benefits of the alternative courses and the availability of the resources required.

The strategy which follows from the basic choice can then call for a number of related objectives, each of which will present a choice of methods or measures. Among the objectives which usually find a place in regional strategies are the following:

In regions of declining or slow growth:

a)   Removing or overcoming the causes of decline in particular industries;

b)   Accepting that some industries will fade out and creating conditions favourable to the development of new industries;

c)   Facilitating the resettlement or retraining of labour;

d)   Adjusting investment on infrastructure to the level of economic activity expected;

e)   Making up deficiencies in local resources required to maintain or develop necessary social services.

In regions of potential expansion:

 i) Removing hindrances to the full exploitation of the potential capacity;

 ii) Imposing restraints to counteract harmful consequences;

iii) Facilitating settlement of incoming or migrant labour;

iv) Ensuring adequate development of infrastructure required for economic growth;

 v) Adjusting social services to meet the needs of a growing economy.

These are not exhaustive lists of possible "intermediate" objectives and they provide no automatic guide to the appropriate strategy for regions facing decline or expansion. The feasible strategy will always depend on the actual circumstances, viz. the reasons for decline, the causes and consequences of expansion and the availability of resources to be applied to the chosen strategy.

In some countries, such as Italy and the United Kingdom, the emphasis for the declining regions is clearly on strategies designed to counteract decline. In others, such as the United States and Spain, the emphasis for the growth regions is on coping with the problems presented by the growth. Since most countries have both declining and expanding regions the strategies in each type place a different degree of emphasis on counteracting and corrective objectives according to the underlying philosophy of regional policies as a whole.

It is noteworthy that in the United Kingdom the most advanced regional strategy is that for the South East, hitherto traditionally and economically the most prosperous growth region. An examination of that strategy suggests that most of the objectives (i) to (v) play a part in it. The strategies for the regions of the Mezzogiorno in Italy include most of the objectives in (a) to (e). The examples of which there are others in Japan, Sweden, France, Belgium, Spain and the United States show that a positive strategy may be required in growth regions as well as those of decline.

This leads on to a second feature of a regional strategy, namely that it is required not only to deal with the economic aspects of growth or decline but also with the problem of the spatial organisation of the region. This is essentially a land-use problem but the important conclusion that appears to be emerging from the way regional policies have developed in the past decades is that regional land-use strategies cannot be dealt with in isolation from the economic context of the region concerned. A further objective of a regional strategy can be seen therefore as ensuring a correlation or co-ordination between land-use strategies and the economic development which is envisaged.

The need of this arises in a variety of ways. Economic development itself requires land for agriculture, manufacture, and commerce, for factories and offices and for the accomodation of the work people of all kinds. It needs also an infrastructure of communication, power and water supplies, drainage and sewage disposal. People's needs for housing land, for amenity and recreation compete with the needs of the economy and with those for the social infrastructure, schools, hospitals and institutions of all kinds. However large a country may be, the way in which these multifarious needs for land is met is a determinant both of the efficiency and costs of economic activity and of the quality of life of the citizens. It determines the extent of travel to work or for leisure purposes and the degree of congestion of road systems as well as atmospheric and other forms of pollution of the environment.

Where land, and the resources available for communications are abundant a policy or strategy of dispersal may be more feasible than where they are scarce. The problem of competing uses for land are of

46

course most acute in countries with high population densities such as Belgium, the Netherlands, the United Kingdom and Japan. They are not however confined to such countries, since the most favourable conditions for economic growth are not evenly distributed throughout a whole country but may be concentrated in certain areas or regions. Quite apart from competing uses for the same land, the complementary nature of economic and social activity, of town and country, will require economic and other development to take place in some degree of proximity. Alternatively dispersal may, as in the United States, throw up the problem of unbalanced communities, the impoverished city centres surrounded by affluent dispersed residential zones. The objectives of a strategy for any particular region may therefore include finding a satisfactory relation between the spatial patterns of different activities.

The selection of the objectives of a strategy for the development of an individual region produces many difficult problems for which there is bo self-evident solution. Economic questions include:

1. In a primarily agricultural region in which improved productivity creates a surplus of labour should the objective be to open up more land for agricultural use (by land reform, irrigation, etc.) or provide stimuli to the growth of manufacturing industries for which infrastructure or manpower skills must be provided at high cost?

2. In a primarily agricultural region of low output per man, due to inferior soils, poor organisation or land ownership systems, should the emphasis of the regional strategy be on improved methods and systems for agriculture or be directed towards the provision of alternative sources of employment?

3. In a region in which the original primary industries, e.g. coal, mineral extraction, forestry, fisheries, are running down either from exhaustion of the natural wealth or through lack of demand for the products, what cost/efficiency limits should be placed on the development of alternative industries? Should the emphasis be placed on encouraging migration, training, the creation of self-supporting industries or the development of an infrastructure as a basis for the attraction of new industry?

4. In a region in which there is a mixed economy but a low rate of adaptation to change in market conditions, technological progress, management techniques and organisational requirements, should the objective be to remedy these deficiencies or create new and more efficient industries to displace the old? If the latter, how far should it be a complementary objective to improve the infrastructure to suit the requirements of new industry?

5.   In a region in which economic conditions are more favourable to expansion but in which deficiencies in infrastructure social services or environment hamper the realization of its potential should the objective be to deal with the deficiencies or restrain or discourage the growth?

6.   In a region in which unemployment in manufacturing tends to increase as a result of changing production techniques - etc. - should the objective be to foster the growth of more manufacturing industry or that of "service" industry calling for greater use of man-power?

7.   In a region in which average income levels are "unsatisfactory" should the objective be to encourage the high income/low cost, producing industries at the possible risk of creating an inflationary demand for labour and of contraction in the low income/high cost industries?

In the land-use sphere equally difficult questions may present themselves, viz:

a)   If industry is more efficient in urban centres should town growth be accentuated as a means of providing employment for labour released by the run-down of agriculture in rural areas?

b)   Should economic growth be concentrated in and around the main "nodal" points of the communications system?

c)   Should the objective be to limit major cities to a defined size to avoid congestion, pollution and environmental disutility at the expense of economic growth necessary to achieve income or employment aims?

d)   If existing industrial areas are environmentally unsatisfactory but still economically efficient, or capable of becoming more efficient, should the objective be to reconstruct them to remove their environmental disabilities?

e)   Alternatively to (d) should the objective be to create new viable cities or centres adequately planned to avoid the disabilities of the older centres?

f)   Should the objective be to develop the region's infrastructure so as to cope more effectively with the existing distribution of population or so as to encourage growth on a new regional pattern?

All these, and similar questions, will find different answers in different countries and indeed in different regions of the same country. As with national strategy the knowledge and data necessary for a rational answer will often be lacking and current fashions in sociological and economic thought and the accompanying political pressures may have a more potent influence than a careful weighing of the merits of the alternatives. All that can be said is that such questions need to be posed, and as well founded answers as possible sought, if regional strategies are to be worthwhile and the appropriate specific objectives are to be identified and their feasibility judged in terms of costs and benefits and the best use of what resources are available, including those supplied from outside the region.

The methods by which the objectives can be achieved can also influence their selection. Where economy in the use of resources is important the preference may go to the specific objective which can achieve the general (intermediate) objective at lower cost. The development of new methods can also exercise a powerful influence in the regional strategy. Thus the improved methods of road construction which have made the creation of super-highways or motorways more economic have given a boost in many countries to regional strategies based upon rapid communication between major centres. At the same time it has in some cases increased the relative attraction to industry of the larger centres with radial communication in several directions and been a significant factor in the location of the newer centres. Towns or cities less well placed in relation to the motorway system become relatively less attractive. Similarly the adoption of new techniques for slum clearance, house building, clearance of derelict land offer greater possibilities of rectifying the disabilities of older but important industrial cities. In early post-war years the technical methods that were then available made it more difficult than today to envisage the total redevelopment of existing cities as a feasible way to cope with the problem of demographic and economic growth. Conversely, factors which operated against the dispersal of manufacturing or office establishments to smaller cities or country areas have been modified by such developments as the power grids, air travel and telecommunications.

SUMMARY AND CONCLUSION

This chapter has been largely a theoretical one. It has sought to clarify what is involved in preparing regional strategies in national and regional terms. It has indicated that strategies can only be meaningful if defined in terms of their several interrelated objectives rather than in terms of a single purpose. Leaving aside those ultimate objectives which can only be regarded as general aspirations we have classified the main objectives as intermediate objectives, each of which can imply a variety of specific objectives and methods. The difficulties in adopting a systematic approach have been recognized but it has been argued that there is a need for such an approach if effective regional strategies are to be pursued.

The principle that each national intermediate objective has its own regional component is of some importance since it enables the objectives of national regional strategy to be stated in realistic terms. It obviates the dichotomy between a policy of regional balance and a policy of national growth. Neither can be, nor is in practice, pursued to the exclusion of the other. The national regional strategy is in fact one which shows how the different objectives of national policy are to be pursued regionally.

Strategies for individual regions are dependent on the national strategic framework within which they are set, and are mutually interactive with strategies for other regions. They also pose difficult questions of choice between objectives and methods but it is only through an examination of the merits of alternative choices that a realistic strategy can be divised.

APPENDIX

Questions Posed for the Consideration of the Working Party*

1. Are regional economic strategies required for each region, "prosperous" and "less prosperous" alike, and why?

2. Can strategies for particular regions be pursued independently of a more or less complete "national" framework of regional strategies and in what circumstances?

3. What are the "national" assumptions that must be fed into each regional strategy to ensure maximum inter-regional consistency?

4. How can regional strategies allow for changes in the condition of the national economy as a whole and for changing forecasts of basic factors such as population growth, etc? (The question of the relation of regional policies to national anti-inflation policies is part of this).

5. How frequently should a regional strategy be revised to take account of changes in regional or national conditions?

6. If regional strategies are long-term frameworks for policy in different fields and are "flexible" enough to adjust to changing conditions, how can they be "firm" enough to be of practical value?

7. Can, and should, the effects of a strategy for a particular region or other regions be calculated and allowed for in the development of the national economic ctrategy? What tests should be

* These questions were set out in an unpublished paper "The Principles Involved in Drawing up Regional Economic Strategies in Relation to National Economic Strategies".

applied to monitor the effects or "success" of a regional strategy in relation to both its regional and national aims?

8.   Should the preparation of a regional economic strategy be regarded as an exercise for the joint effort of those concerned with national and regional policies, or a purely regional exercise? If the latter, in what ways and at what stages would consultations between the regional and central authorities be appropriate?

9.   Is there a built-on conflict between the aims of promoting growth of less prosperous regions by discriminatory methods and promoting the growth of the national economy as a whole? How should a balance be struck between the two aims?

10.   For those regions for which a particular strategy is regarded as unnecessary, to what extent is any regional economic planning required at all and for what purposes?

11.   To what extent should a regional economic strategy include strategies for physical and social development? Should the planning of the regional physical and social environment be geared to the needs of the regional and national economy or vice versa?

12.   Which is the chicken and which is the egg? The economic or the social, physical or environmental structure? Should a regional strategy in general be primarily an economic one designed to influence the industrial and commercial activities within the region or a physical/social one designed to achieve environmental aims within pre-determined limits set by economic conditions? How far is it feasible to restrain "natural" growth within a region for environmental purposes without excessive cost to the national economy?

III

THE REGIONAL IMPACT OF NATIONAL FACTORS

Regions are not separate countries but parts of countries and they are subject therefore not only to the influences which are internally generated within the region but also to those from outside. Many influences operate throughout a country - we use the term "national" influences or factors - but their impact can be very different on different regions. Nor are all influences affecting the economy as a whole, dependent only on factors domestic to the country concerned. Countries themselves are not isolated from the interplay of world economic forces and forces external to a country can have nationwide and therefore regional impacts. Regional policies which do not take account of the nature of the changes which permeate the economy as a whole, whether they originate from inside or outside a country's borders, are likely to be misconceived. Change in national factors can affect regions to their advantage or disadvantage. In the short term they can offset altogether the effects of measures designed to improve the economy of particular regions. In the longer term they can make the proposed remedies irrelevant, if not introduce rigidities which make adjustment to change more difficult.

It is not a paradox but a simple truth that change is about the only constant factor in all economies and an assessment of the direction of change in the future is a prerequisite of rational policies for the future. Policies do not affect the past. They can only influence the future. However much a present situation can be explained by reference to history and past trends the future will be determined by the way current trends operate and by the new factors which may arise as the future unfolds.

Regional policies are often presented as an attempt to correct a situation resulting from trends operating in the past. Unless it can be shown however that those trends will continue to operate in the future and will not be offset or accentuated by significant new factors they will be seeking to correct a situation which may no longer exist. In a dynamic world policies to be effective must be attuned to the real, ever-changing situation rather than to the static past. It is the object of this chapter to draw attention to some of the dynamic forces of change affecting the economy as a whole and to their implications for regional policies.

The following is a short list of factors affecting the economy as a whole, changes in which could have important implications for regional policy.

1. Population, its age and sex composition, proportion of working age and geographical distribution and densities.

2. The industrial and occupational distribution of the population of working age: gross and sectoral employment or unemployment levels.

3. The level of education, technical skills or competence of the working population.

4. The value, in real terms, of the GNP.

5. The nature and composition, volume and value of real resources, land, mineral, buildings, plant equipment and infrastructure – the capital assets of the nation.

6. The external balances of trade and payments and the composition of import and export trade.

7. Technological change and the rate of substitution of capital for labour intensive techniques.

8. The habits, tastes and consumer preferences of the population, including attitudes to mobility, urban life, leisure, amenity and recreation.

9. The degree of inflation of prices and incomes.

10. Public revenues and expenditures and their scale in relation to priority objectives.

Any analysis, statistical or otherwise factual, would show considerable contrasts in the way these factors operate in different countries. Each country has its own absolute levels and the rate of change would vary in each according to its special circumstances. Our purpose at this stage is not to carry out such an analysis but to indicate in general terms the bearing such factors can have on the regional situation and therefore on the policies designed to affect it, using

54

available statistical material mainly in illustration of the generalisations that can be made.

POPULATION

Population affects the regional problem essentially by posing a question of its distribution. The question can arise in situations not only of rising but also of falling or static populations but changing economic capacity. Since in all Member countries population has been and is continuing to rise this special case can however be disregarded.

The capacity of a country to absorb or provide for its own population growth is not only determined by its own economic growth rate but also by the opportunities afforded in other countries to emigration, and attitudes to such migration. Historically emigration from Europe to countries overseas has, of course, played a major part not only in facilitating or accelerating the overall growth of the recipient countries but also in relieving population pressures in the countries of emigration and in the regions where the pressures are greatest. There are no economic "laws" which indicate that a country can automatically adjust its economic growth to that of its population and emigration has provided one means by which adjustment has been effected. There can be little doubt that, without emigration, the situation in the pressure regions could have been much more difficult to cope with than it has been. This is not a phenomenon confined to less advanced countries with predominantly agricultural economies. It has occurred in "advanced" industrialized countries such as the United Kingdom where indeed it has been at a higher rate in the recent past than in some countries with a lower level of industrialization.

Nor has inward immigration been confined to overseas countries such as the United States and Australia. Advanced European countries such as Germany and France have had a marked high level of net immigration mainly from countries, including European countries, in which economic conditions were less rapidly progressing. However much the social consequences of such movements beyond frontiers may be considered undesirable, no country has as yet sought, or been obliged, to assume that it must achieve a rate of economic growth proportionate to its population growth. This point needs to be made simply to avoid the not uncommon misconception that the scale of the regional problem of the future can be related to projected national increase of populations. The fact that the rules of the EEC are intended to permit a much greater degree of freedom for migration between Member countries seems to emphasize the importance of making allowance for the potential effects of external migration in estimating the scale of regional problems following from population growth.

It may be noted that the 1970 net inward migration into Germany and France totalled about three quarters of a million representing a job total far in excess of those created by regional policy measures in most of the other European countries put together.

Nonetheless populations have grown in all the Member countries, ranging during 1960-1970 from an annual average increase of 4 per thousand in Ireland and Finland to 25 per thousand in Turkey. In other European countries it varied: 16 per thousand in Switzerland, 12.5 per thousand in the Netherlands, 10.5 per thousand in France, Germany and Spain, and 8 and 6 per thousand in Italy and the United Kingdom respectively. In overseas countries rates varied from 20 per thousand in Australia, through 18 per thousand in Canada, 12.5 in the United States and 10.5 in Japan. As a broad generalization the countries with the higher population growth tend to be those with the higher net immigration, while those with lower population increase, such as the United Kingdom and Italy, have had net emigration. *

If population growth figures alone were taken as index of the severity of regional problems the United Kingdom and Italy would appear to be countries with relatively less severe problems. The figures cannot of course be used in this way since they provide no indication of the economic problems of the countries or their regional disparities. The size of the population increase nevertheless plays some part in determining both the scale of economic growth that is needed simply to maintain the standard of living per head and the possible role of internal migration. If all regions of a country had the same potential for economic growth a rise in population could be spread throughout the country without substantial migration. It is because regions do not have the same potential for growth that the alternative arises - as we discuss elsewhere (Chapitre IV) - of transferring resources or accepting internal migration.

In countries with a large amount of relatively under-developed or under-utilized territory or resources a high rate of population growth may be accompanied by a high internal migration, from more to less developed regions, much as population moves internationally from countries of lower to countries of higher opportunities. In countries with an already dense settlement pattern and a more or less equal level of development the opportunities for or benefits from internal migration may be considerably less. Relatively densely populated countries such as Belgium and Holland, the United Kingdom, Germany and Japan provide

* OECD statistics.

56

comparatively less opportunity for internal migration orientated policies than do those of relatively sparse population such as the United States and Canada. Though the distribution of resources may be uneven in the former group, social resistance may mitigate more against migration than in countries in which the population distribution is still relatively fluid.

However our only conclusion is that the scale of growth of population is an important facet of the regional problem and that unless resource growth can be matched in the regions in which population growth occurs the choice may be between external and internal migration or lower conditions of life in them. It is important therefore that countries should constantly assess the predicted population growth after allowing for external migration and consider the feasibility of the alternatives of migration or resource growth before determining their regional policies. Because there is no natural economic law or process which ensures an automatic matching of resource growth to population, a policy which seeks to maintain an existing pattern of population distribution irrespective of its growth would seem to be somewhat unrealistic.

INDUSTRIAL AND OCCUPATIONAL DISTRIBUTION

It is a well known fact that the composition of the employed population varies considerably between countries in different stages of development and over time as they progress from one phase to another. In the early stages the predominant occupations tend to be in agriculture, fisheries, forestry, mineral extraction and handicrafts or small scale manufacture. As skills and techniques improve and subsistence needs are met manufacturing processes and greater specialization are developed, producing a wider variety of consumable goods and a more complex pattern of exchange and markets. As the economy as a whole expands a new web of basic services, of communications, transportation and urban centres develop, together with supporting commercial activities in finance, banking and trade on a national and international scale. As new skills are required in each industry old occupations disappear and new ones take their place. The process of change never ends but the occupational picture at any one point of time may be very different from that in preceding eras.

The process is not confined to primitive economies but pervades all economies other than those which stagnate in a situation of repetition of what has gone before. It is the "stationary state" rather than the "progressive state" which is more a figment of the economist"s imagination. The latter corresponds more to reality than the former.

57

Because society exists in a finite spatial world, changes in the industrial and occupational pattern involve changes in the spatial distribution of work. Areas previously flourishing may decline in terms of their employment opportunities as for example agricultural productivity changes - absolutely or in relation to the competitive growth elsewhere - as forestry or mineral areas are "worked out" and new sources take their place. As cities based on industries which become obsolescent fade unless new occupations are found for their populations the centres of gravity in a country may shift periodically as has been seen in earlier times. In the United Kingdom, the home of the 19th century industrial revolution, the changes brought about by the shift from agriculture to iron and steel, ship building and textiles, meant a shift in population distribution broadly from South to North. During this century the growth of new industries and the development of services occupations brought about a relative growth in the South and Midlands. Similar shifts, as the occupational structure changes, can be observed in most countries.

Structural changes are not brought about only by domestic factors. Development in outside countries can have an impact on particular industries inside a country, as for example the development of textile industries in the under developed world has had an effect in the areas of traditional textile production in the industrially advanced countries of Europe and North America or as "extensive" agriculture of the newer countries has competed successfully with the intensive agriculture of the older. Such changes and the development of new industrial and commercial opportunities give impetus to a different occupational pattern.

It is not necessary to describe in detail the variations in industrial structures between countries in order to make the point that considerable variations exist. Of the OECD countries the United Kingdom has the lowest proportion of civilian employees engaged in agriculture (2.9 per cent) and Turkey the highest (72.1 per cent). Between these extremes the variations in the highly industrialized countries range from 4.4 per cent in the United States and 4.8 per cent in Belgium on the one hand, 9.0 per cent in Germany, 14 per cent in France, 17.4 per cent in Japan and 19.6 per cent in Italy on the other. Similarly large variations occur in "industry" (including mining, manufacturing, construction, electricity, gas and water). Of the heavily industrialized countries Germany has a proportion of 50.3 per cent compared with 46.5 per cent in the United Kingdom, 43.7 per cent in Italy, 38.4 per cent in Sweden, 35.7 per cent in Japan and only 32.3 per cent in the United States. By contrast the United States has 63.3 per cent classified as "other", compared with 53.5 per cent in Sweden, 50.6 per cent in the United Kingdom, 48.8 per cent in Norway, 46.9 per cent in Japan and 36.7 per cent in Italy.* These global categories hide a multitude of variations in industrial occupational classes.

* 1970 data.

It would not be possible, without taking time series, to establish how far these proportions are rising or falling. They would no doubt show that there is no complete parallelism between countries and that whereas in some the proportion of people engaged in one group of occupations may fall, in others they may be rising. The further decline of the proportion engaged in agriculture may in some countries lead to an increase in the proportion engaged in industry while in others it may lead to a rise in the proportion in the "other" category. The value of output is of course not necessarily proportionate to the numbers of employed. Thus the proportion of GNP derived from agriculture tends to be less than the proportion of people engaged in agriculture.

Variations in industrial and occupational structures between countries and over time can be of importance in the determination of regional policies. This is so partly because they are a feature of the regional distribution of population. It also means that the success of efforts to improve the regional situation depends on the extent to which they take account of the potential for expansion of the occupations chosen to bring about the improvement.

Thus to take a hypothetical example, a country may have a given expansion potential in manufacturing industry. But unless the industries are those suited to the conditions of the regions it is desired, as a matter of policy, to bring forward, overall national industrial growth may not, unaided, promote industry in those regions. By the same token if a country is tending to expand in the so-called "services" industries the task of injecting new manufacturing industry into a backward region may be the more difficult insofar as it would require the relocation of existing industry, or the development of totally new and more sophisticated technical accomplishment in a backward population.

The use of broad classification such as "manufacturing industry" can obscure the fact that the occupational structure within an industry may be rapidly changing. In many countries the mechanisation of agriculture alters the balance between farm labourers, skilled mechanics and machine operators not to speak of supervisors and financial controllers. In manufacturing industry automation increases the emphasis on control system or computer operations, and lessens that on bench work skills. The increase in output of all kinds increases the proportion of people required for distribution, sales, marketing, advertizing, accounting and similar occupations; and though these may be functionally related to manufacturing they are not necessarily directly linked in geographical or spatial terms. Occupations connected with entertainment, leisure, recreation, amenities and tourism may play a more important part in the growth of GNP. All of these may have different location determining factors from those of industries with a different range of occupational skills.

We do not do more than seek to emphasize that changing trends in industrial and occupational structures can be a key factor in determining the policies suitable for regional growth. They can affect the aims and feasibility of a regional plan, the nature of the vocational training and guidance schemes required to adapt a regional population to change, the selection of industrial or commercial enterprises from which growth, is sought and the scale and nature of investment required to employ a given population fruitfully. The point deserves emphasis if only because in the past it has tended to be neglected and policies of regional development have been seen as basically policies for the introduction of manufacturing industry in regions in which they either did not previously exist or in which existing manufacturing industry no longer provided an adequate level of employment. Clearly the industrial pattern either has to suit the existing occupational "mix" or the "mix" must be changed to meet the requirements of the industrial pattern proposed. Since particular industries and occupational groups have their own location determining factors an examination of the changes occuring in them sould seem to be a prerequisite for the formulation of any realistic regional policy.

EDUCATION AND TECHNICAL COMPETENCE

No apology need be made in a work primarily directed towards economic questions for referring to the subject of education. Education, or the process of bringing out in individuals the full potential of their personalities, is a major force in the economic progress of society. Education affects not only the skills of individuals, but their tastes and aspirations including their choice of vocation. It also influences the demands they make on society for the satisfaction not only of material wants but all those which go to make up the "quality" of life. Perhaps, viewed historically, no single factor has done more in the past century to transform society. Not only has it immeasurably increased the scientific and technical skills of the populations, but in so doing, it has influenced the productive process, the nature of the goods produced and the methods by which they are produced.

In no country has the progress of education reached its peak. The length of time devoted to education of the young has been rising in most countries and there has been a continuous process of extension of all forms of higher education for the adolescent and adult population through post school colleges, technical institutions, polytechnics and universities.

Because education is increasingly universal and open to all, it falls within the category of "national" factors. Because it is a "national" factor it has an impact on regions, and on regional policies. It is of course both an end in itself; and a means of achieving other ends. It has, perhaps, two main regional implications: First it produces a need

60

and demand for levelling out the regional facilities for education. Secondly it affects the tastes and aspirations of people in terms of the work they are prepared to do, and their choice of location in which they seek to work.

The Working Party has not so far carried out any examination of the part that educational change plays in the regional problem. In the absence of detailed study only a few generalizations can be offered the validity of which may vary considerably from country to country.

In general people tend to seek work corresponding to their aptitudes and training. It has been a feature of relatively undeveloped societies, in which education has not extended to more than a few, that employment is sought or obtained in manual work of a low level of technical accomplishment, in agriculture, in manufacture or labouring work generally. In industrialized societies in which education for the mass has gone little beyond the acquisition of the three "R"s, a high proportion of the population tend to be engaged in simple, often repetitive, manual work calling for uncomplicated dexterity rather than mental exertion. In such societies the degree of employment and its location will depend on the available resources and industries which require only those corresponding levels of skills. In more advanced societies not only do the levels of skills in manufacturing rise but also a wider diversity of occupations reflects the greater range of the talents and aptitudes which the educational process extends, sharpens and refines. One result in such societies is that a high proportion of the population becomes adapted to and interested in pursuits outside the direct production field of the primary or manufacturing industries, such as the various "white collar" employments, commerce and the professions - and the arts. The same processes produce a shift in the "social" composition of society and "social mobility", i.e. movement of individuals between income and social classes becomes more marked.

In a society in which educational facilities and the opportunities for the individual benefitting from them to obtain employment congenial to him are reasonably matched in localities or regions, the enhanced occupational and social mobility which education confers do not necessarily imply a corresponding geographical mobility. In this respect countries differ a great deal. There are those in which both the better educational facilities and the employments matching them tend to be concentrated in certain areas. There are those in which both are more widely spread throughout the country. In the former the extension of educational facilities - wherever they may be located - unmatched by a corresponding development of employment opportunities or environment, may lead to a geographical displacement of the beneficiaries. In concrete terms, a person successfully completing a university course or obtaining a professional qualification is less limited to the locality of his birth and chilhood than before and has a greater freedom of choice in determining where he wishes to live and work. In the former case considerable geographical movement may take place, often to the metropolitan cities or other major centres. Growing urbanization, by no means necessarily evenly distributed, can be a reflection of the redistribution of population with the increased talents due to the education process. The characteristic divergence between life in capital or major central cities and provinces and the "magnetic" attraction of the former to the higher talents can, in this view, be considered as an illustration of the effects of the education process on the distribution of population.

Examples of social mobility combined with geographical displacement would probably not be hard to find in most countries. So far as interregional, as distinct from local movements, are concerned they may be less apparent in countries which have a high degree of decentralization in Government, business administration and the broad "cultural" field, and in which modern industry is also widely dispersed. Perhaps Germany would be the prototype of such countries. By contrast they might be more apparent in countries in which large regions are significantly different from others in their industrial and occupational structure, where there is a high degree of centralization in Government, professional, cultural, administration functions in capital cities, and where modern industry is more highly concentrated in certain regions. Italy, the United Kingdom and France might be examples of these. In large countries in which the growth of agricultural productivity proceeds pari passu with the development of education and training in the modern skills and techniques the movement of the educated population to the large cities or their environs may also be an example.

Considerable research would be needed to establish how significant this phenomenon is in the particular circumstances of individual countries. The point we are seeking to make here however is that the pattern of the regional distribution of population will depend to some extent on the degree to which there is regional response to the changing occupational requirements of the population brought about by the progress in education. One significant conclusion might be that it poses the problem of the need to look beyond manufacturing and primary industry in determining the occupational "mix" in regions in which it is desired to hold population at a given level. Another way of putting the same point is that, as education and other social processes increase the scope and significance of the administration, professional, technical and commercial "services" of a society, so the aim of securing a given regional population distribution can only be achieved if due weight is given to this factor.

While, undoubtedly, many countries pay a great deal of attention to the need to provide a better regional distribution of education facilities, schools colleges, technical institutions and universities, a failure to develop corresponding opportunities for employment of the "output" from these institutions in the regions may accentuate rather than alleviate the problems flowing from population migration.

GROSS NATIONAL PRODUCT

"Gross national product" is simply a measure of the global change in an economy. It is not a cause of the change but a summation of the many changes, positive and negative, occuring throughout an economy as a whole. By its nature it hides or obscures the changes which are taking place in its component elements.

Before discussing the implications of the concept for regional policies it may be useful to quote some figures showing the way in which it has changed in recent years in a few countries. For convenience annual average percentage population 1960-1970 increases are shown at the same time.*

In the United States GNP, at 1958 market prices rose from 475.9 billion (i.e. thousand million) dollars in 1959 to 727 billion in 1969, an increase of about 54 per cent or 5.4 per cent per annum on average (arithmetical). (Population increase 1.25 per cent per annum).

In Canada it rose, at 1961 market prices, from 33.4 billion dollars in 1959 to 61.1 billion dollars in 1969, an increase of about 85 per cent or an average of 8.6 per cent per annum over ten years. (Population increase 1.8 per cent per annum).

In Japan it rose, at 1965 market prices, from 17.3 thousand billion yen in 1959 to 50.7 thousand billion yen in 1969, an increase of 193 per cent or an average of 19.3 per cent per annum over ten years. (Population increase 1.05 per cent).

In Germany, at 1963 market prices, it rose from 1959 to 1968 from DM 288 billion to DM 467 billion, an increase of 62 per cent or of nearly 7 per cent per annum average over nine years. (Population increase 1.05 per cent).

In France, at 1963 market prices, it rose from 1959 to 1968 from 323 to 530 billion francs or 61 per cent, an average of nearly 7 per cent per annum over nine years. (Population increase 1.05 per cent).

---

* Source: Main Economic Indicators, 1959-1969 and OECD Observer, February 1972.

In Italy, at 1963 market prices, it rose from 24 thousand billion Lire in 1959 to 40 thousand billion in 1968, an increase of 66.6 per cent or an average of 7.4 per cent per annum, over nine years. (Population increase 0.8 per cent).

In the United Kingdom, at 1963 market prices, it rose from £ 27 thousand million in 1959 to £ 35.5 thousand million in 1968, an increase of 31 per cent or an average of 3.4 per cent per annum over nine years. (Population increase 0.6 per cent).

In Sweden, at 1963 market prices, it rose from 72.6 billion Kroner in 1959 to 106 billion in 1968, an increase of 47 per cent or an average of 5.2 per cent per annum over nine years. (Population increase 0.75 per cent).

In the Netherlands, at 1963 market prices, it rose from 43.8 billion guilders in 1959 to 70.1 billion in 1968, an increase of 60 per cent or an average of 6.6 per cent per annum over nine years. (Population increase 1.25 per cent).

In Belgium, at 1963 market prices, it rose from 570 billion Francs in 1959 to 852 billion in 1968, an increase of about 50 per cent or an average of 5 per cent per annum. (Population increase 0.55 per cent).

In all these cases there has been growth in GNP and in population. The country with the lowest rate of growth - the United Kingdom - also has one of the lowest population growth rates.

These figures may also be compared with the change in the labour force shown in the first column of figures below:

	PERCENTAGE INCREASE 1957-68	PER CENT AVERAGE (APPROX.) PER ANNUM - 11 YEARS -	
		TOTAL LABOUR FORCE	"CIVILIAN" LABOUR FORCE
United States	17.9	1.6	1.6
Canada	30.9	2.8	2.9
Japan	15.9	1.4	1.4
Germany	2.1	0.2	0.1
France	4.0	0.3	0.5
Italy	(-)8.8	(-)0.8	(-)0.8
United Kingdom ...	4.0	0.3	0.5
Sweden	11.0	1.0	1.0
Netherlands	11.4	1.0	1.0
Belgium	3.0	0.3	0.3

These figures have been extracted from the OECD publication "Labour Force Statistics 1957-1968" (published 1970).

While, with the exceptions of France and the United Kingdom, total and civilian labour forces appear to have changed at about the same rate the contrast between either column of labour force figures and those of GNP is marked. GNP has risen substantially more than the labour force and in Italy the latter has declined noticeably. The labour force has risen more than the population only in the*cases of Canada, Sweden and the United States and since population has grown, GNP per head (at constant market prices) has tended to rise in all cases by less than total GNP.

It would take a full analysis to determine the contribution to the growth of GNP of individual sectors of the economy. Since the "services" sectors have in many countries been a principle factor in overall growth it may be useful to add figures for the same countries showing the change in civilian employment in categories 6-9 of the ISIC (viz. commerce, transport, storage and communication, services and "others not specified).

The OECD "Labour Force Statistics, 1957-68" is our source of the following figures:

PERCENTAGE OF CIVILIAN EMPLOYMENT
IN SECTORS 6-9
(SERVICES)

	1958	1968	CHANGE % 10 YEARS
United States	57.5	61.2	6.4
Canada	50.4	59.1	17.3
Japan	39.6	45.7	14.4
Germany	36.7	41.6	13.3
France	37.3	43.8	17.4
Italy	29.7	35.7	20.2
United Kingdom ...	46.6	50.2	7.7
Sweden	43.4 (1961)	49.7	14.5 (7 years)
Netherlands	45.9	50.7	10.4
Belgium	44.6	49.6	11.2

These figures do not show the contribution made to GNP since earnings vary between sectors. (The sectors excluded (0-5), are the primary industries: (agriculture, forestry, mining, etc.) manufacturing, construction, electricity, gas, water and sanitary services).

The figures may be considered striking. In all cases the proportion of civilian employment in these sectors has risen substantially. In the United States and the United Kingdom respectively, where the growth has been least, the absolute proportion was approaching, and above, half in 1958 and exceeded half and three fifths in 1968. In Italy, where the proportion was lowest in 1958, the increase was higher than in all other countries with the marginal exception of Sweden.

The contrast with the "industry" sectors 1-5 is also marked as the following extract from the same source shows:

PERCENTAGE OF CIVILIAN EMPLOYMENT IN SECTORS 1-5 (INDUSTRY)

	1958	1968
United States	33.6	33.8
Canada	35.3	32.3
Japan	27.6	34.4
Germany	47.7	48.2
France	39.0	40.4
Italy	35.4	41.8
United Kingdom	48.9	46.7
Sweden	42.2 (1961)	41.0 (7 years)
Netherlands	41.5	41.3
Belgium	47.2	44.9

Only Italy and Japan show a significant increase reflecting a closely corresponding decline in the proportion engaged in agriculture, forestry and fishing. All the others have been virtually static or declining and this applies also to countries with a relative high proportion of between 40 per cent and 50 per cent. In France, where the proportion engaged in agriculture, etc. fell from 23.7 per cent to 15.8 per cent (or 8 points), the proportion in the sectors 6-9 accounted for most of this fall - rising by 6.5 points (37.3 per cent to 43.8 per cent).

Though only a limited number of countries have been quoted the general impression given is that expanding sectors in the national economies are those classified "others" and that industry, including manufacturing, accounts not only for substantially less than half but is static or declining.

GNP does not of course rise steadily from year to year, nor do past trends necessarily demonstrate the shape of things to come. Nor, as has been said, does GNP necessarily move in proportion to the change in sectors defined in employment terms.

However the figures suggest a high degree of probability for the view that in employment terms the growth sector of modern economies is to be found outside manufacturing and construction. Insofar as this is true the consequences for regional policies could be significant. Attempts to generate growth in regions affected by agricultural decline or the obsolescence of previously established industries primarily by the introduction of industrial enterprise are presented with an overall limiting factor of the lack of growth in this field. It does not follow automatically that such policies are not feasible. The overall growth of the "other" (6-9) sectors may lessen the demand or scope for industrial growth in regions in which conditions for their expansion may be particularly favourable and increase the relative suitability for industry of the other or backward regions. This too could however be an optimistic or wishful thinking assumption, since, in many cases, the declining regions are not necessarily those most suited for what industrial growth there may be.

The contribution that the various sectors make to GNP is not of course directly related to the numbers employed in the sectors. The volume and value of output in any sector is a function also of the use of capital equipment, the technical efficiency of its use and, generally speaking, the productivity of the industry. Capital investment in new plant and machinery and modern technology together permit an increasing value of output by a given labour force. Because modern manufacturing industry has tended to become more "capital intensive" it will still have contributed to the rise in overall GNP, despite the relative lack of growth in the labour force. The regional distribution of growth in the value of output cannot be easily ascertained since few if any countries have as yet produced adequate statistics of regional output. It may well be the case that output per head in manufacturing industry - as in mining and agriculture - has tended to increase in most regions where modernization and re-equipment have taken place under the pressure of market forces and competition. However, to the extent that modernization and investment take place more in the regions which are favourably placed for development and growth the overall growth in GNP can involve a relative regional shift in the distribution of output towards the better placed regions. It certainly cannot be assumed that the overall rise in GNP due to investment, improved techniques and higher productivity would distribute itself evenly throughout the regions, irrespective of their particular characteristics, and there would seem to be a strong presumption that overall growth of GNP is inevitably accompanied by shifts in the regional distribution of output.

To some extent "service" industries, e.g. retail distribution and local administration, commerce and finance, may tend to follow or group themselves in or around the foci of manufacturing industry but again there is no fundamental necessity for a close correlation of manufacturing and other employments in given regions.

67

Our main conclusion is that regional policies which are founded on the belief that regional aims can be better achieved in situations of over-all growth of the GNP are not necessarily well founded. Further reasons for this view are given in the discussion of the central problem of dealing with regional "imbalances" (Chapter IV). Certainly we consider that the full impact of the changing sources or composition of GNP needs to be examined in each country before any facile assumptions can be made of the bearing of GNP on regional problems.

CHANGE IN RESOURCES

Change in resources - natural and man-made - available to a country is a potent factor determining the regional distribution of output, employment and income levels. Regional problems arise in many cases because the original resources cease to be important or diminish in importance, either as they are run down and exhausted or as new resources elsewhere provide a better and more competitive source of the materials for industry. Man-made resources in the shape of capital equipment can cease to be of economic value as they become obsolete or obsolescent, or face competition as a result of development elsewhere, in other regions or countries.

Examples of the former are to be found in all countries at varying stages of their economic development. The working out of the richer mineral seams, the exhaustion of soil from intensive agricultural use, the over exploitation of forests and fisheries all represent decline in natural wealth bearing particularly on the regions in which they are located. Such run down of natural resources may not necessarily be due to policies of deliberate over exploitation but to the working of economic forces which encourage the use of resources up to the point where the marginal return on capital invested or labour employed is equal to that obtainable from other uses. For this reason natural resources may cease to be exploited well before they are physically exhausted.

The run down or going out of operation of man-made resources - the capital equipment of industry - may also reflect the same problems. Typical cases are the textile, shipbuilding and steel industries in countries in which they originated. As renewal and replacement becomes necessary the decision whether to do so turns on the competing claims of other industries for capital and labour and the rate of return is affected by the growth of competitive industry in the same fields in other countries. Since neither the national or international economies are static the "old" industrial pattern gives way to new, and what were formerly man-made economic resources become heaps of disused machinery, derelict factories and buildings. This process too has its implications for the economic life of the regions affected.

The reverse process also takes place in a dynamic economy. New natural resources are discovered and brought into production, or better techniques for the utilization and conservation of existing natural resources are applied. New man-made resources, in the shape of new industries producing new products, are developed taking the place of the old. In agriculture not only have new lands been opened up in the past century as countries such as the United States and Australia have developed but existing lands in the "developed" countries have been better farmed, irrigated or conserved. The process can affect whole regions, as in the area of the Tennessee Valley Authority in the United States, or the Mezzogiorno in Italy. Both extension of area or improvement of utilization of agricultural land can represent a net increase of agricultural land resources. More spectacular, perhaps, in recent times have been the harnessing of water power for energy and the discovery and development of natural gas and oil in the north European offshore areas.

In the man-made field new inventions and new products have given rise to whole new ranges of industry from motor vehicles to advanced engineering, radio, telecommunications and electronics, plastics, atomic energy and aviation.

Overall these changes represent a growth in resources and permit a rising standard of living measured in material consumptions, as well as leisure, recreation and amenities. They also have a significant impact on regional growth and change according to the way their effects are disseminated throughout the regions of a country.

Much of the increase in wealth brought about by this resource increase has been utilized for the development and improvement of the physical and social infrastructure. The development of motorways and land communications generally, housing, electricity, water supplies, etc., if never reaching the probably unattainable target of satisfying all needs has been both the product of modern resource development and a contributor to it. Regionally the distribution of investment in infrastructure may tend to follow the growth of economic resources but it is also susceptible to deliberate national policy decisions and, to some extent, can influence the areas in which development proceeds. The improvement of communications and the development of the social infrastructure can create not only new opportunities, for example, manufacturing and processing for wider markets but new leisure industries such as tourism and recreation.

Our conclusion is again only a general one. In no field more than that of resource development is the dynamic pattern of change in the national economy more apparent. Its effects on the regions of each country can obviously be far reaching and only if sufficient account is taken of these effects can suitable regional policies be devised.

INTERNATIONAL TRADE

There are few factors which play a greater part in the determination of national economic policies than the course of a country's external trade. A serious disequilibrium in the balance of trade and payments can lead to change in internal monetary and fiscal policies, corrective measures to encourage exports or discourage imports or to devaluations or revaluations of currencies. The effects of these policies can be nation-wide, putting a damper on growth and employment or stimulating it, as the case may be. They can increase, or decrease the role of imports and exports in the national economy and change relative price levels and the profitability or otherwise of whole ranges of industry according to their degree of dependence on international trade.

The size of the gap between imports and exports or in the balance of payments may of itself be no measure of the severity of problems involved in conditions of disequilibrium. Often more important is the size of the gap in relation to a country's reserves and international credit standing and the expectations of international monetary institutions based on prospective trends. The confidence factor can be a key determinant of the policies which must be pursued in given circumstances of disequilibrium.

Whatever the size of the gap the effort to close it varies with the structure of a country's economy and the adaptability of its sectors to the influences of the corrective measures.

It is the relation between imports and exports and between payments and receipts rather than the actual size which determines whether there is an external balance of trade or payments problem. Thus the United States has had severe external balance of payments problems although external trade plays a much smaller part in its total economy than in most other countries. The part played by international trade does in fact vary very considerably. In 1970 (calculated from OECD "Main Economic Indicators" 19th March, 1972, pp. 122-138) exports bore the following relation to GNP:

	%		%
Canada	22	Germany	18
United States	4	Italy	14
Japan	10	Netherlands	38
Belgium	47	Sweden	24
France	12	United Kingdom ...	14

Both overvaluation and undervaluation of currencies can cause a situation of disequilibrium and the corrective policies, including a change in exchange rates, are designed in essence to increase the export/import ratio in the one case and the import/export ratio in the other.

The effect - and effectiveness - of these policies on the regions depends on the make-up of their industries and their ability to respond to the changes of profitability in exporting or importing. There is certainly no reason to suppose that the effects of corrective policies would be evenly distributed throughout the regions. It would of course need an examination in depth of the actual situation in each country which has had balance of payments problems to ascertain how the policies bore in practice on the different regions. It may however be said that during the period in the United Kingdom, of vigorous measures to deal with the balance of payments problem, say from 1964 to 1971, the relatively depressed regions - broadly the "development" or assisted areas - continued to remain relatively depressed: indeed as the balance of payments problem finally seemed to disappear in 1971 the overall economic situation in these areas worsened materially. While unemployment increased throughout the country it increased at an even higher rate in some of the development areas, notably Scotland and the North of England.

Too much should not be made of an example of this character if only because other factors were operating, such as the degree of "cost push" inflation and the tendency towards reduced labour demand in all regions, including some that were previously high employment regions, such as the West Midlands. All that can perhaps be said is that national measures of wide general effect, such as those designed to deal with a particular external trade and payments problem can have very different effects in different regions. It would seem reasonable also to suppose that regions which are not well placed to expand exports or import substitutes will be the last to benefit from national measures designed to this end. In formulating policies to secure certain regional aims it is clearly important to assess the role that international trade is expected to play in the development of the national economy and the contribution that will be required and be possible from the various regions.

TECHNOLOGICAL CHANGE

As has been seen technological change is a potent factor in reshaping national economies and leading to new industrial, sectoral and geographical patterns. We use the term not so much to denote changes in the methods of production, though technological change can materially affect the whole system of production, but the development of new

71

products and activities arising from the advances in scientific knowledge. The use of new materials, such as plastics, new techniques, such as computers, data banks and microfilm records are only some examples. These changes can have radical effects on local industrial structure, the complex linkages between industries, the markets, national and international, for the new products and on the skills required from the "labour force". The rate at which industries can develop from the new technologies is also affected by the degree to which their needs can be met in areas or regions hitherto devoted to other types of industry.

The new technologies do not represent only an addition to the range of existing industry. They can result in the displacement or total disappearance of older industries based on older products or techniques – just as in byone days, the stage coach gave way to the railway train and the latter, to some extent, has given way to the motor vehicle (and as this may give way in the future to the electric car or gas turbine). The industries they displace may be located where historical circumstance have placed them not necessarily of course in the regions which have suffered decline for other reasons.

The degree to which these new industries are capital or labour intensive can be a determining factor on whether they would, in the absence of state intervention, locate themselves in areas in which labour is available or in areas in which more importance attaches to other factors, such as linkages or market accessability. It would not seem possible to generalize. Some of these industries, e. g. certain types of electronics, are in fact labour intensive and the example of Japan shows that many of the modern industries provide employment for, initially, unskilled labour (including females). On the other hand the use of computer techniques and automation is widely applicable both to old and new industries.

Perhaps the most significant feature for regional policy purposes of the new technologies is the rapidity and extent to which they have been transforming the industrial structure. Because of this they can have widespread regional effects not confined to specially disadvantaged regions. Again a proper assessment of these effects would seem to be a precondition of suitable regional policies.

INFLATION

Since inflation has been a feature of the economies of most of the OECD countries in recent years it can properly be regarded as one of the "national factors" whose impact on the regional situation should be considered. It is no part of our task to examine the cause and cures of inflation (for this see the OECD report "Inflation: the present problem",

December 1970). Inflation is however a dynamic influence on the economy as a whole and its regional components, and its effects can vary from region to region. There is also an interplay between measures seeking to restrain it and the pattern of regional change. In the OECD report referred to regional policy measures are themselves seen as relevant to the control of inflation. These include regional policies to ease structural adaptation (p.41), geographical mobility, incentives and regional development subsidies (p. 53), moving jobs to workers in the interest of regional balance (p. 54) and the development of a "rational and coherent set of sectoral and regional policies". It is pointed out (p. 106) that the "burdens of global anti-inflationary policies, falling unevenly on different regions" can be lessened by selective manpower measures. Also that geographical mobility may be dependent on effective regional planning (p. 106): and that the anti-inflationary aspect of balanced regional development is particularly stressed in countries dominated by large urban conurbations (p. 107). Subsidies for the use of labour are seen as geared to "stimulate fuller utilization of existing capital equipment in problem areas" (p. 107).

The report "The Regional Factor in Economic Development" itself suggests that "the introduction of a regional component to national policy can ... contribute to running the economy at a high level without creating inflationary pressures and weakening the balance of payments" (p. 10). It points out that "high levels of demand can still leave substantial areas of depression and unemployment", while, "unless counteracting measures are taken, the pressure on physical resources, especially in periods of inflationary pressure, in the large urban conurbations and the living conditions of their inhabitants could well become intolerable" (p. 96).

In its (unpublished) report on "The Incidence of Large Conurbations on Inflationary Pressure", the Working Party suggested that conurbations played a different part in the inflationary process according to the individual location and characteristics and to the nature in the inflationary process in particular countries. They were also concerned to point out that the measures to control inflation could have important effects on regional development and on the attainment of the aim of regional policies.

The Working Party expressed the classical relationship between inflation and the regional problem in the following terms:

" ... when excessive demand pressures had built up in the more prosperous areas and counter-inflationary measures had to be taken, these had much more marked effects on the less prosperous regions giving rise to excessively high rates of unemployment there. Conversely, when the overall pace of economic development is

73

particularly rapid, the economies of the less prosperous regions are also affected in the same direction but at a lower rate. Consequently one of the objectives of regional development policy was to reduce national inflationary pressure by redistributing demand in such a way as to diminish the pressures in the regions where theyre were the greatest, while still maintaining or even expanding the level of activity in those regions where they were least."

They went on to say however that "recent experience of some countries suggest that the problem (now) presents itself differently particularly in countries where demand-push inflation is giving way to cost-push inflation and where high levels of unemployment affect "prosperous" and "less prosperous" regions alike.

They also drew attention to the possibility that some conurbations can have an anti-inflationary impact, the reasons being, broadly, their advantages of external economies and economies of scale, for industrial, commercial and service undertakings, the size and fluidity of the labour market, the lower cost per head (in some cases) of urban infrastructure, the strong consumer market, with very competitive supply conditions, and the above average tax revenues.

The report also drew attention to the role of sectoral influences on the process of inflation and the fact that wage settlements determined in the region with the tighest labour situation are transmitted to all other parts of a country, despite the excess of labour supply over labour demand in other regions.

The work done so far therefore seems to establish fairly clearly that there is a relationship between inflation and the regional situation, though it is a complex one and simple generalizations may not fit all cases.

A few further points can however be made. The process of inflation can be generated in many ways, through internally generated money and credit expansion, through external financial movements, countries "exporting" inflation to others, "demand-push" and "cost-push". Its results (or accompanying symptoms) are rising prices - too much money chasing too few goods - rising incomes - attempting to keep pace with rising living costs; and shortages of labour in some sectors. However its own momentum generates changes in "propensities" to save, or consume, or invest, derived from changes in the "confidence" factor which may mitigate against pressure on labour supply. Thus the phenomenon of high unemployment and low investment can be observed in periods of inflationary price and income rises.

If we consider (as a simplified "model") the effects on "high pressure" and "low pressure" regions (corresponding to "prosperous" and "less prosperous" progressing or "declining", "developed" or "backward" regions) it might be said that the effects of inflation are more immediate on regions with relatively little slack and derivative on the others. In the former there are fewer surplus resources to be drawn upon so that demand pressures exert a more rapid influence on prices and incomes; in the latter the availability of unused capacity enables extra demand to be cushioned by extra supply.

The model obviously over-simplifies in certain respects. In countries with a national market for consumer goods price disparities between regions would tend to be minimal. Significantly higher prices in one region would drain off goods from the others until some sort of equilibrium was reached. However not all countries do have national markets for all goods and it is conceivable, for example, that inflationary processes in Northern Italy would not, on this count, spread equally to the whole of the country.

Because labour is less mobile or less responsive to short-term influences the pressure of demand on labour can more easily translate itself into higher wages, or labour "poaching" in pressure regions than in others. If there were disparity in wage levels demand would tend to rise where there was a surplus of labour, and inflation could thus, in a sense, mobilize that surplus. It could of course be argued that sometimes the existence of large areas of unemployment is due to a "deflationary" situation in the economy as a whole and that a corrective inflation could be a remedy for this. However the "remedy" would not work as advantage cannot be taken of wage disparities if these are eliminated as a result of common wage levels throughout the economy. In that case inflation simply increases the pressure in the "pressure" areas without permitting the "slack" to be taken up in the non-pressure areas. It could thus be argued (as in the OECD report on Inflation) that, in an inflationary situation, wage subsidization in the non-pressure areas could be a means of counteracting the effects of national common wage settlements. The alternative is of course a system of wage settlements which allow demand and supply to operate in the labour market.

The effects of moving "jobs to the workers" in an inflationary situation can be both beneficial and harmful. Demand for workers would be reduced in the areas of high pressure, presumably thereby lessening the pressures for higher wage settlements and distributing the available employment more "equitably". On the other hand, if cost factors in the non-pressure areas are not dissimilar from those in the pressure areas or if the disadvantages of the non-pressure areas entail higher costs of production the net effect on the economy as a whole may be to increase costs and hence be inflationary in influence.

75

The alternatives of "moving workers to the jobs" may also be harmful or beneficial. The extra supply of labour may reduce the inflationary pressures in the pressure areas, and costs of production. It may however generate inflationary pressures on rent, housing, land, transport and public services generally, at least in the short term. Whether it will in the longer term depends on the rate at which these services can be expanded to cope with the increase in the labour supply. In the non-pressure regions it may raise costs, if, for example, it accentuates a shortage in certain types of labour which might be short even in such areas; it can reduce the load on public services but increase the cost per head.

In our view correct policy cannot be determined by reference to generalizations. The answer must depend on the circumstances of individual countries which vary in most of the material respects - influence of national wage settlements, adaptability of regions or local areas to inward or outward flows, degree of mobility of industry and of the work force, etc.

A distinction needs to be drawn between inflation as a short-term phenomenon and as a continuing force in the long term; and also between degrees of inflation. If inflation is overcome in the short term major structural changes in the economy, such as may be entailed in moving "workers to the work" or "work to the workers", would have little relevance to the problem. In the longer term it could have more relevance insofar as inflationary pressures are continuously generated by a maldistribution of work in relation to the location of the work force. As has been pointed out the solution could be either way. A permanent disparity between demand and supply of labour in the major industrial centres can be a permanent predisposing factor to inflation. It can then only be overcome by dealing with the root cause - by either method.

We share the view of the Working Party that such evidence as there is does not necessarily lend support to the view that the costs of "congestion" in the large conurbations are necessarily inflationary. They can be. On the other hand it can also be surmised that in some cases it is failure to deal with the costs of congestion, or a belief that such costs cannot be reduced, that leads to a policy of favouring movement of work from the more congested to the less congested areas. It should not be overlooked that constraints placed upon development of the larger cities and conurbations, often of course for good social and environmental reasons, can be inflationary. Restrictions on land use have the effect of limiting its supply and putting up its price. Failure to overcome transport problems can result not only from their insuperability but from deliberate decisions in planning expenditure on "infrastructure", giving preference to places where problems are less urgent. Detailed study would be required in each case before a conclusion could be reached on how serious are the problems of expanding infrastructures in regions more suited to economic growth than others. It is only possible, without such study, to advance the hypothesis that regional policy could in some circumstances contribute to overcoming some at least of the root causes of inflation if sufficient resources were devoted to reducing the deficiencies in the areas in which it tends to be generated, and to making possible a greater degree of mobility from areas where work is not available to those where it is. On the same hypothesis the man-power training and resettlement schemes which are being adopted in many countries and which include schemes to encourage mobility of labour may be frustrated unless they are accompanied by measures designed to reduce inflationary pressures resulting from restraints in housing and other forms of social services.

The inferences from this brief and possibly superficial analysis are that regional maldistribution of industry and labour can be a potent contributor to the inflationary process; that the inflationary process itself and some measures to control it can increase the maldistribution; that some measures to diminish the maldistribution can be inflationary; and that the key problem in determining regional policy in relation to inflation as a continuing, longer-term phenomenon, is how it can best bring about the balance between supply and demand for labour in the regions. The answer is not necessarily one way but must depend on the individual circumstances of particular countries.

IV

THE PROBLEM OF "RECTIFYING" IMBALANCE

The problem of bringing about a given state of "balance" between regions can perhaps usefully be considered with the aid of a theoretical model. We can imagine a country in a pristine state of economic innocence or health in which no malformation exists; or, in other words, where there are no imbalances. This would mean a generalized condition of evenness: evenness of distribution of population as between regions, evenness of economic structure, evenness of employment, activity rates, income, social welfare. Climatic and other environmental factors are equally attractive (or unattractive) to the inhabitants. A state of this kind is of course a purely conceptual notion and exists nowhere in the real world, nor could it possibly exist. The concept serves however to permit the introduction of variables that upset the evenness of the country and to consider the problem entailed in restoring it.

To clothe the model with a little more flesh we assume that like the Romans in Britain the Government divides the country into five regions, I, II, III, IV, V. Each of them has by definition, one fifth of the population, one fifth of the total capital, one fifth of the employment and one fifth of the gross and nett national income. The inhabitants of each region can obtain no marginal advantage by moving from one region to another and, being pure and undiluted "economic men", are (at least in aggregate) content to stay put in their regions; i.e. there is no net inward or outward interregional migration. (Case A).

Into this happy and stable world we introduce an element of change. We ignore the time factor and compare only the changed situation with the original one.

The element of change can be likened to a sudden malady which affects only region V. For some reason which need not be elaborated and only imagined, the region ceases to be "equal" in all economic respects to the others and remains equal only in respect to its share of the population which remains at one fifth of the national population. In other respects it suffers a halving of the economic indices, i.e.

its capital is halved and its income per head is halved. A "gap" has appeared between its economic state and that of the other regions equal to 50 of the economic level of the other regions or 100 of the level of region V.* The Government discards leaving things as they are as being politically intolerable and considers the alternatives open to it. It bases its initial consideration of the problem on the assumption that it has no means open to inject new factors into the economy as a whole, which depends entirely on the resources and labours of the people. Its first approach is therefore based on the concept of regional redistribution. It finds immediately that there are several alternative courses of action which could result in a restored condition of evenness.

It can allow economic "laws" to take their course. Since the society is a free one and the inhabitants are all "economic men", and seek their advantage where they can find it, this course would entail a movement of part of the population from region V to the other regions until incomes per head are equalized throughout the country at a lower level. Since we have assumed that, for an unexplained reason, the GNP has fallen by one tenth, incomes per head in each region have also fallen to nine tenths of the previous level. However the population in region V is less than it was before and the difference - the migrating element - has redistributed itself evenly throughout the other four regions. Since we do not wish to complicate the model by calculating the rates at which marginal incomes change as population shifts we shall simply assume that region V finishes up with half its original population (or ten per cent of the total) and that the remaining four share 90 per cent equally. In other words, each has grown from 20 per cent to 22 $\frac{1}{2}$ per cent of the total population. Similar shifts must, for the sake of this model, be assumed to have occurred in the capital and economic structure. Under this course the equalization of incomes has been achieved at a lower income per head (inevitable under the conditions of the model) and a simple redistribution of the population. (Case B).

It can use the powers of the state to compel a shift of resources from the other four regions to region V, sufficient to maintain an equal distribution of population between the regions and an equality of income per head. (Case C). This involves retaining 20 per cent of the population in region V and in each of the other regions. As before, average income per head falls to 90 per cent of the previous income but this has been achieved by a redistribution of the country's income producing capacity. The other regions will each have sufficient capital to produce 90 per cent of their previous income and (since models work without

* The concept of random shock is of course not necessary. A gap can simply be assumed to exist, as a matter of fact. The concept is needed solely to dramatise the awareness of regional imbalance.

friction) this means their capital has fallen by 10 per cent. Region V will have been placed in the same position and instead of having only half of its original capital will also have 90 per cent. Each of the other regions, in this model, will have contributed 2/90 of the new (reduced) total national income.

The three cases, A, B and C can be summarized in the following table:

	CASE A "BEFORE THE FALL"		CASE B REDISTRIBUTED POPULATION	CASE C CAPITAL AND INCOME REDISTRIBUTED
	Regional income		Regional income	Regional income
I		20	10	18
II		20	20	18
III		20	20	18
IV		20	20	18
V		20	20	18
GNP		100	90	90
Population		100	100	100
Income per head	1		0.9	0.9

On reflection the Government finds neither case B and C tolerable. In both cases the populations of four regions have suffered a fall in income per head, for no apparent fault of their own. In the former case half the population of region V has had to move while the remaining population instead of being grateful for the transfer of resources to it remains equally conscious of the general fall in income per head. In the latter case too the population of region V while remaining in situ still suffers a decline in income per head and obstinately disregards the fact that, without the Government measures to transfer resources to the region it would have been even worse off.

The Government being conscious and responsive to political reality - and here the model approximates to the real world - decides that it must change the rules. The only way it can meet the aspirations of the population is to disregard the assumption that it cannot inject new factors into the economy as a whole. Contentment can only be secured by replacing the lost income producing power of region V. A reduced national income of 90 per cent of the original national income must be turned again into 100 per cent. The economy (as it stands after the Fall) must be expanded by 10/90 or 11 per cent (cumulative).

A Government, with a magic wand could do this overnight, and restore the lost wealth of region V by one wave. Not even the most unrealistic model should have a Government of this sort and the Government in our model considers two alternatives.

(Case D). Special measures to generate real growth in the whole country for transfer to region V in replacement of the lost wealth. Since we have ruled out a magic wand the Government has to allow the measures to take time. According to its judgement as to what would secure the acceptance or acquiescence of the population of the region, sufficient to avoid movement to other regions, it can seek to devise special measures which would have the desired effect by a given time. It realizes that the longer the time scale it allows the less need be the annual growth. At the rate of an (arithmetical) average of one per cent national growth rate per annum it would take 11 years to achieve the target. The transfer of the whole of the growth to region V would raise its income from 50 per cent of its original income by an average of about four and a half per cent (= 50/11) per annum. The other four regions would not get any benefit from the national growth and special measures and their presumed discontent would remain. It would still take 11 years for region V to reach equality with the other regions. On both counts the Government therefore refuses to contemplate such a slow solution to its problem.

A further alternative (Case E) is to concentrate the "special measures" on region V alone. No growth is required from other regions (the Government considers they have reached their peak) and no transfer from them to region V. Their income level remains at 100. To bring region V to parity with them and back to its former level of 100 would involve a doubling of its production potential or 100 per cent growth. At the (arithmetical) rate of one per cent this would take 100 years. An average growth of $4\frac{1}{2}$ per cent would take 22 years. This alternative - a policy of raising region V by its own "bootstraps" - is initially discarded.

It prefers measures that would work more rapidly, i.e. a national growth rate higher than the average one per cent per annum, i.e. a cumulative total of 11 per cent. It makes the assumption that the underlying reasons for the decline in the economy of region V and the static condition of the rest of the economy were not due to irremediable causes. The Government decides to solve the problem in half the time, or $5\frac{1}{2}$ years, which it judges to be acceptable to the people as a whole. In this case (F) it must adopt special measures which will double the rate of growth.

The model assumes that any growth brought about by "special measures" is real growth. It is of course possible for Governments to bring about an apparent growth by inflation, but as this would distort the picture, an inflationary solution is excluded from the model. In the real world inflation does occur and can mask the lack of progress in reducing regional imbalances.

The figures in the model can of course be infinitely varied and it would need an econometric formula to work out the results of any large number of variations. However, an example can be given to illustrate the results of changing the quantities in the model.

A basic simplification is obtained by assuming a country has only two regions North (N) and South (S) reflecting the characteristic "dual" system. *

N constitutes 60 per cent and S 40 per cent of the population and economic wealth. In the initial equal distribution system (Case A) income per head is equal throughout the country.

After the "random shock" introduced in region S its income potential is assumed to be reduced by half. Total national income falls from 100 to 80, income per head to 0.8. In Case B half the population of S is assumed to migrate, or have migrated to N. N now has 80 per cent of the population and S 20 per cent. The total income of N is 64 and that of S 16.

In the alternative Case C the population of S remains in situ and the necessary transfer of resources and income from N to S is effected by the Government. The income of N is reduced from 60 to 48 and the income of S is 32.

As before, neither situation commends itself to the Government and it seeks to replace the lost income. It now has the task of finding the lost 20 per cent equal to 25 per cent of the reduced gross national product. An average growth of 1 per cent of the reduced national product of 80 would produce only 0.8 per annum. It would therefore take 20/0.8 or 25 years, to restore the position in which the whole country enjoys the same gross income and there is complete regional equality. The time taken to restore regional equality alone by transferring the whole growth of income to region S would be 16/0.8 or 20 years.

* See the article by J. G. Williamson in Regional Analysis, edited by L. Needleman, Penguin Modern Economics, 1968.

Obviously neither of the two examples in the model itself bears any relation to reality. Regions do not lose half their sources of income, and regional populations cannot be transferred overnight. The gross income of a region receiving population does not remain static, so that the same "cake" is merely shared by a larger population. Nor does the gross income in the region suffering the "random shock" adjust itself proportionately to the shift of populations to other regions. Similarly transfers of resources cannot be made automatically to match the sudden decline in the region losing resources.

The same points can be expressed by saying that a loss of X in the product of one region does not, in the real world, simply reduce the national product by X. Repercussion effects may increase or decrease the income in the other regions so that the national product may be higher or lower than the original minus X.

In our model we have assumed for simplicity that a transfer in population leaves the total product in the declining regions unchanged. In classical economics a rise in population increases the national product but the "law of diminishing returns" produces a falling marginal product for each marginal addition to population. Conversely, a fall in population raises the marginal product. Equilibrium, in the sense of equality of income per head between regions would be reached in our first example (of five regions) by a smaller shift of population than one half X. But the classical concept of the law of diminishing returns is now recognized to be a special case. An increase of population may in fact increase the marginal product by producing a larger scale economy. A shift of population from region S to region N could enhance the performance of N's economy. Equilibrium might therefore be reached only by an even greater number of population. Alternatively the disparities between regions would widen rather than be diminished.

Our model also assumes that the national income would be static except for the change in the "random shock" region. This is also far from reality. The national income is constantly changing, upwards or downwards, as a consequence of numerous factors of the development of new resources and skills, the loss or obsolescence of capital equipment, technical change, changes in demographical conditions, etc. If national income is steadily rising the problem of making good a loss suffered in a particular region would appear easier to the Government but if the growth were spread proportionately between the regions the period of time to secure complete equality would still be prolonged. Since the model simply seeks to isolate the effect of "random shock" the possibility of changes in the national economy, which could be for better or worse, has been ignored. Similarly, it does not make provision for change in the region receiving the "random shock", whether for better or worse.

The model oversimplifies another important aspect. It assumes a proportionality between population, capital, resources and income per head. It uses total regional income and income per head as interchangeable measures of regional disparity. In the real world there are other measures of disparity which are not translatable into these terms. Non measurable elements exist such as leisure, social welfare amenity, quality of life etc., which may compensate for differences in measurable income. Activity rates, regularity of employment and the incidence of unemployment are not necessarily, in the real world, proportionate to average income levels in a region. Thus a region may have a high average income and at the same time a relatively high unemployment rate (there are examples of this in most countries but the point is also illustrated by reference to differences between countries: e. g. the United States with the highest income per head in the world has consistently had a higher average unemployment rate than some European countries with lower incomes per head).

One of the concepts used in framing or explaining regional policies is that of "more prosperous" and "less prosperous" regions. The terms subsume a whole variety of factors to produce a general picture of the differences between regions and to convey the impression that, on the whole, conditions in certain regions are more "favourable" than those in others. These general terms serve however to hide and obscure the many differences between "more" or "less" "prosperous" regions which in reality are not all one way. *

It would perhaps be better to use in a model a more generalized concept than income, called E (the general state of the economy) to which higher or lower values could be attached. This would subsume all the various factors making for regional differentiations but the model might seem even more abstract and we have chosen concrete, albeit imaginary figures. Nonetheless it may sometimes be easier to think in terms of values of "E" rather than selected indices such as income or capital.

The model is therefore far from reality. But it has its uses, for it enables certain general observations to be made and more readily appreciated. It may also help to interpret some of the facts of the real world by the use of analogy.

We use E in the following section of this chapter as a shorthand device to avoid continual reference to the individual factors which together provide the signs of "regional imbalances" as the differing value, between regions, of E. The value of E in the particular (South) region, Es; can be compared with the average value in the country as a whole,

* See Williamson, op. cit. p. 99.

En, or in other regions Ew, Ex, Ey, etc. "Imbalances" can be seen as divergencies from En or as differences between values of E in different regions, e.g. Es compared with Ey.

1. In a static national economy the equalizing of the values of E in different regions, with those of other regions or with the national average can be effected by a transfer of resources from regions with higher value E to those of lower value "E", population distribution remaining unchanged.

2. Alternatively the same effect could be achieved by a transfer of population from regions of lower "E" values to those of higher, in which case the resource transfer is equivalent to the population which has moved.

3. The smaller the region(s) with the lower "E" in relation to the rest of the country the smaller the resource transfer or population movement required to restore equality of regional "E". (Inversely if the region is larger).

4. The smaller the transfer of resources from regions with higher "E" values to those with the lower the longer the period before equality is reached: conversely with a larger transfer.

5. A policy of raising "E" by a region's "own bootstraps" means expanding on a smaller base than if the resources of the country as a whole or of other regions are called into play. The rate by which parity with other regions can be achieved depends on the effectiveness of measures, the region's potential for growth and the size of the gap to be closed.

6. Dynamic change in the region(s) of lower "E" value or other regions can have repercussive effects. The scale of resources which would have to be transferred, and the time scale needed to achieve equality of "E" values would vary with the nature and direction of these repercussive effects.

7. Disparities between "E" values could widen or narrow according to the movement of "En", resulting from dynamic changes, and the scale of resource or population transfer required to attain equality increase or decrease correspondingly.

8. In a static or no growth economy the removal of disparity between "E" values of different regions requires a redistribution of resources or population, or a combination of both.

9. The use of net additional growth of an economy can reduce the disparity of "E" values according to the proportion devoted to the lower "E" value regions, and the time scale determined accordingly.

10. The effect of special measures to secure a lessening of disparities of "E" depends on whether they generate net growth or are only redistributive in effect.

These observations hold irrespective of the origin of the disparities between the "E" values. These have many causes in the real world. There is no and has never been a pristine state of equality as described at the beginning of this chapter and at any historical point in time a state of imbalance automatically exists. Forces of change are in continuous operation in all respects to alter it further. The fact that change is continuous does not affect the principle that effort to remedy imbalances must be proportionate to its scale. What it does affect is of course the practical problem of assessing and allowing for the forces of change in calculating the scale and nature of the effort required to bring about a greater equality of "E" values.

Nor do the observations by themselves provide a basis for deciding which is the "right" course to adopt in relation to the problem of imbalance. Decisions of this character are essentially political ones and require judgements as to what is desirable and feasible in the particular circumstances. The model only indicates the theoretical choices which may be open: to accept imbalance, to modify or eliminate it in varying time scales, to use redistributive techniques or to base efforts on the utilization of net growth of the economy. These concepts can perhaps help to clarify the issues to be faced and enable the nature of the choices to be defined. But they do not provide any key to preferred choice.

Tools of this kind can only be applied to national situations where the necessary data are available. Since no country has as yet sought to establish a schematic description of its regional problem as a basis for its policies we can only offer some illustrative examples drawn from the data contained in RFED* (and other information supplied to OECD).

A "typical" case of North and South dualism is of course provided by Italy. The "Mezzogiorno", with 40 per cent of the area and 38 per cent population of the country (RFED) contributed 25 per cent of the national income. Its income per head was 68 per cent of the national average and (consequently) about 50 per cent of that of the North. In the absence of other indicators, levels of income are used in our following comments in place of the more general "E" concept.

Original Case A
(South having 40% of population and 25% of national income)

Regional income			Income per head		
N	=	75	Nation	=	1
S	=	25	N	=	1.25
GNP	=	100	S	=	0.625
Population	=	100			

* The Regional Factor in Economic Development, OECD, 1970.

In a situation of no change in national income (no growth or fall) and adopting a policy of retaining its population in the Mezzogiorno we would have an example of Case C as follows.

Case C

Regional income			Income per head		
N	=	60	Nation	=	1
S	=	40	N	=	1
GNP	=	100	S	=	1
Population	=	100			

To achieve this result a transfer of resources from N to S of 15 per cent of the national income must take place, representing a decrease of 20 per cent of Northern income and a growth of $37\frac{1}{2}$ per cent for the South.

An alternative policy based on "special measures" to produce growth sufficient to give the South parity with the North at its existing income level as in Case D would give the following:

Case D

Regional income			Income per head		
N	=	75	Nation	=	1.25
S	=	50	N	=	1.25
GNP	=	125	S	=	1.25

This would therefore require a net increase in the national income of 25 per cent and a doubling of the total regional and per capita income of the Mezzogiorno.

If a national average growth rate of 1 per cent were assumed the task would take 25 years. It would take still longer if the North were to retain a part of the national growth and increase its own income per head, thus widening the income gap to be closed.

It is of course a pure coincidence that RFED estimated that at the existing rate it would take another 20 years to eliminate the "gap" between North and South (p. 30 and p. 93).

The model indicates that a higher rate of national growth than an annual 1 per cent would be required to eliminate the gap in a shorter period. Italy's national rate of growth has indeed been much higher than this, roughly of the order of 5 per cent per annum. However the growth rate has been lower in the South than the North (RFED p. 93) with the consequence that while income per head in the South has been rising substantially the "gap" between N and S has been widening. This fact remains true up to the present time and the Working Party on Regional Policies has drawn attention to it.

Two features have marked the Italian experience which also can be referred to within the framework of the model. The Italian situation is not one of retention of population in the Mezzogiorno. Very substantial migration from the South to the North, and indeed to other countries has taken place. The case is not therefore one in which the solution has been achieved by retaining the existing population however much the necessity for outward migration may be deplored. Secondly no country has a more noteworthy record of "special measures" to secure regional growth than Italy. Yet the special measures, while undoubtedly achieving results in raising regional income levels, have not, as noted, as yet led to a narrowing of the "gap".

At this point it is worth recalling that our model considers the effects of transfer of (income producing) resources as a method of narrowing the gap. Italian measures, while generating net additional growth have an element of resource transfer. The policy of ensuring that a specified proportion of public funds, equivalent to the South's share of population, should be allocated to the South by law is of this nature. The incentives to encourage industrial investment also represent an effort to transfer resources, including resources derived from growth of the northern economy. The sums allocated to regional policies in Italy, as shown in Table 2 p. 66 of RFED, represent a little over 1 per cent of the GNP.

To transfer 15 per cent of the GNP as in the Italian example of Case C would at such a rate take some 15 years. But not all the investment in the South is a true transfer of resources leading to growth of income retained in the South. Some would be generated locally and some income would flow back to the North. The true rate of transfer could therefore well be less than 1 per cent and on our model, the period of equalization take longer than the 15 years in Case C.

The Italian experience, used in conjunction with our model, provides other interesting reflections. We have earlier pointed out that the law of diminishing returns from population growth in a fixed area does not necessarily hold good. It is unlikely, especially, to do so in a situation of rapid technical change and progress. The Italian experience can perhaps be seen as an illustration of the law in reverse, or more technically, as the working of a law of increasing return. The rise of national income already referred to has taken place concomitantly with an expansion of population. In the North population has increased both by natural growth and by inward migration from the South.

In the South, outward migration accompanied by improved land use in certain areas and by the introduction of new industries may have accelerated and in all probability did, the rate of growth beyond what it would have been had there been no outward migration. Compared with the North, with its already advanced industrial society, the South would have been less well equipped to provide for a growth in income producing capacity. Conversely the North could have benefitted by the inward migration adding to its possibilities of larger scale and more modern industries requiring, in toto, a larger labour supply. Unlike the situation in the United Kingdom (see below) the North was the area of modern expansion not the area of inheriting the effects of the 19th century industrial revolution. This is no more than a hypothesis of a kind that (as society is not a controlled laboratory) cannot be conclusively demonstrated. But it serves to illustrate the problem that can face Governments in trying to reach decisions on what policy to pursue in regard to regional imbalances.

In Italy we can see that the magnitude of the gap is such that it would call for a very much larger effort, in the shape of transfer of resources to the South, to reduce it at all and without it the gap will remain a continuing feature of the Italian economy indefinitely. The very considerable effort that has been made, in a climate of national economic growth, has raised the absolute level of income or well being in the South, but not the level relative to the North. An increased effort to transfer more resources for the development of the South could have the effect of diminishing the overall national growth unless it could be shown - contrary to experience (and, the author would say, the evidence) - that a given quantity of resources could provide a higher rate of return than in the North. The question of the "right" policy, as we have pointed out, is not one to be resolved by reference to the various cases provided by the model. All we have sought to do is to show by the Italian example that an analytical approach can throw light on the choices which can be made in pursuance of regional policy. More general conclusions from this example are considered at a later stage.

Some other examples might be used, more briefly. The United Kingdom provides another case of a country which has been concerned with the problem of regional imbalance for a long time and which has pursued vigorous policies to overcome it. In the words of the White Paper published in March 1972:* "The ending of regional imbalance has been an objective of successive Governments in the United Kingdom for nearly four decades. Much has been achieved but no solution is yet in sight". The same White Paper announces new special measures to cope with the problem as "it is clear that the accumulated measures of the years are not enough".

* Cmnd 4942, H. M. Stationery Office, London.

The nature of the problem is not examined in the White Paper but its characteristics have frequently been defined. In RFED it is described as primarily stemming from the different inherited industrial structures of the several regions and more particularly with a higher element of obsolete or declining industries and lower employment possibilities and activity rates. Income levels and social conditions tend also to be lower in these regions though inevitably there is a mixed pattern throughout the country. National unemployment which rose sharply in 1971-1972 has been consistently higher in the declining regions than nationally, with a falling ratio however to the national level. Broadly there is no one single indicator of regional disparity which would enable a particular value to be given to our "E" concept.

The proportion of the country deemed to be less favoured (i. e. with a lower "E" level) and requiring special measures is given in RFED as 55 per cent of the total land surface and 21 per cent of the employed population. Because of large relatively unpopulated mountain areas the former figure would exaggerate the extent of the assisted areas if taken as a proportion of the national economy. The White Paper announced some further additions.

In RFED the expenditures on regional development are given as 552 million US dollars equivalent or roughly one half of 1 per cent of GNP. These are not necessarily the total amounts devoted to regional purposes but as in the previous case they do not necessarily represent a transfer of resources.

The new regional development grants are given in the White Paper as costing £ 300 million to which must be added further selective assistance to particular industries (some of the latter may go to regions outside the assisted areas).

In recent years national growth has been comparatively small and the White Paper itself emphasizes that "A faster rate of national growth is a necessary precondition for effective regional effort" as well as other measures. Since we do not have the means for a precise calculation we posit some arbitrary figures which will serve to illustrate an alternative situation from that in Italy. We stress that they do not necessarily give a correct view of the actual United Kingdom situation.

40 per cent of the population with an average "E" value of 80 per cent of the level of other regions would produce (approximately) a national picture (Case A) as follows: (we use the symbol R_m and R_1 for the "more" and "less" favoured regions, respectively).

Regional "E"		Income per head		
R_m	= 65	R_m	=	1.08
R_1	= 35	R_1	=	0.87
GNP	= 100	Nation	=	1

The "gap" in this case is much narrower than the Italian. On the assumption of no national growth and no national migration from R_1 it would be necessary only to transfer 5 per cent of the national income from R_m to R_1 to bring the proportion to 66 and 40 per cent respectively, and to secure equality of "E". This would represent a decline of 7.7 per cent of the income of R_m and a growth of 14.3 per cent in R_1.

Though a 5 per cent transfer presents in theory a much smaller problem than in the corresponding Italian example it still presents a significant one in conditions in which, as the White Paper indicates, there is insufficient national growth to provide an alternative to transfer. It may also be noted that the case requires a 14 per cent growth in R_1 and it might be surmised that if conditions in the region are not favourable to growth the attainment even of this percentage would take a long time. Since the United Kingdom as a whole is a highly industrialized country and the assisted areas were already essentially industrial areas (unlike the Mezzogiorno before industry was introduced) a policy of transfer from other regions to the assisted areas required a shift of industry from where conditions were favourable to where they were less. In the absence of overall industrial growth the many factors which inhibit industrial movement from one region to another are difficult to overcome and special incentives would have to more than offset the costs of moving. In the depressed areas themselves the conditions which have led to decline, including the environmental problems, were themselves obstacles to the establishment of industry for which there is not an expanding economy to provide a market.

Moreover though the United Kingdom is a highly industrialized economy it is in the services rather than manufacturing industry that expansion has been taking place even during the period of low national economic growth.

In such a situation an industrial expansion of the order of 14 per cent becomes a much more difficult task than the size of the figure seems to suggest.

The achievement of a higher rate of economic growth does not necessarily reduce the disparities of "E". It may perhaps lead to a situation like that of Italy where national growth is accompanied by a continued widening of disparities. This seems the more likely in circumstances in which the main element of growth is in service industries which locate themselves according to their own requirements. The fact that service industries (including a wide range of commercial activities) have tended to expand in the "more prosperous" regions of the South may be one of the reasons why they have been "more prosperous" and tended to attract population.

Migration to the South rather than transfer of resources to the depressed areas may, as in the Italian case, have produced a higher national income than would otherwise have been the case. The United Kingdom may indeed be an illustration of the proposition that imbalances can be a continuing feature of a comparatively stationary economy as Italy may be an illustration of the proposition that higher growth rates do not necessarily reduce imbalances.

If this were true it would suggest that the effort required to eliminate disparities by transfer of resources from "more" to "less" prosperous regions in conditions which are not favourable would have to be very much greater than commonly supposed and that such efforts could be at the expense of overall national growth. The alternatives would appear to be either to accept the continuance of the imbalances or to rely on population movements to reduce or eliminate them. In many countries, including the two used as examples, all three policies appear to coexist, the resultant picture being confused and inconclusive.

There is some evidence that in certain circumstances regional imbalances can be narrowed by population movements from regions or areas with lower to those with higher income. This has been observed in Spain, * a country which, in the years in question, has also had a relatively high growth rate. Richardson has shown that regional income disparities have narrowed due however mainly to population shift. Spanish policy as described to the Working Party accepts some degree of imbalance as "normal" and does not seek to overcome established imbalances as an aim in itself but to direct national growth to where it has greater possibility of achievement. The economy is regarded as in a state a flux and development and the aim is to distribute the national growth in suitable regional locations. In this concept the new regional balance that will occur will be a resultant rather than a motive force in national policy.

* See the article by H. W. Richardson in Urban Studies, p. 43, and "Salient Features of Regional Development Policy in Spain", OECD, 1973.

This does not fit our theoretical model except to the extent that the various alternative courses are discarded. If anything it adopts the policy of allowing economic laws to take the course of (Case B) the movement of population in pursuit of higher income, tempered with a national growth and investment policy in areas, zones or regions considered favourably placed for growth. Since there appears to be no aim to deal with regional imbalances as such calculations of the time it would take or the resources required to be transferred do not arise. Nevertheless there are considerable regional disparities, especially between highly industrialized and major urban areas and the predominantly agricultural regions. The example is perhaps of particular interest in showing a preferred choice in circumstances of dynamic and structural change throughout a country in transition.

The example of the United States is similar in certain respects. RFED remarked (p. 18) that the regional problem in the United States occurs in the context of a highly dynamic economy which, historically, has been marked by great migratory movements. Further considerable movements were predicted as a result of population changes in relation to job opportunities. While median incomes were expected to rise "disparities between rich and poor areas may be greater (by 1975) than today". Higher unemployment in the big cities was also recognized as a potential major problem. The policy was described as implying no attempt to "reverse the economic tide" but to be concerned, in Federal Government programmes, "with the area problems which arise as a residual of the broad economic movements". Here it might be legitimate to bring this example into the framework of Case B: Redistribution of the population is predicated, in response however to economic change rather than to concern about regional imbalance, and resources must be transferred, through Federal funds, to special problem areas.

Italy and the United Kingdom perhaps provide examples of cases in which a considerable effort to reduce certain types of imbalances show no signs of succeeding and in which the gap may widen further in certain conditions of national growth. By contrast Spain and the United States provide examples in which national growth and change are a more dominant feature of basic policy but in the former certain imbalances (of income) may diminish through population movements and in the latter regional disparities may be expected to grow.

We do not propose in this chapter to examine the situation in further OECD countries individually. Our main object is simply to attempt to provide a general framework within which the pattern of changing regional imbalances can be considered. Here we limit ourselves to pointing out certain features in other countries of which account should be taken in reaching any general conclusions.

In France regional policy is partly if not primarily conceived as "aménagement du territoire". The forces of change e. g. the decline of agriculture, the growth of cities, particularly Paris, the development of new resources and the decline of some traditional industries of importance in particular regions, leads to a need for a comprehensive approach to the organisation of the whole country. Special measures, not unlike those in other countries, provide incentives to location of industry in preferred areas or restrain location in unpreferred areas; expenditure on infrastructures is considered in relation to objectives of regional distribution of the population and special attention given to the creation of new centres of activity or nodal points (métropoles d'équilibre). The effort is directed, one might say, not so much to correcting an existing imbalance but to creating a new and better balance between regions in accordance with an overall concept of the strategic planning of the country as a whole. Perhaps a characteristic of this kind of policy is that it seeks, more deliberately than in some other cases, to secure a condition of economic and physical land use planning objectives and to apply methods designed to secure the best results.

This policy however can be brought within our theoretical framework to a certain degree. Redistribution of population is implied in the selection of special growth areas and areas in which growth is to be restrained. Economic activity is to be steered to selected parts of the country rather than left to make its own special pattern. Resources are supplied, through central mechanisms, to areas in accordance with the objectives of the original plan.

The perspective of the operation is a very large one. Something like 50 per cent of the country's area is under the most recent plan* to be the recipient of the special aid measures. In RFED the resources shown as devoted to regional development amounted to no more than about US $ 100 million (equivalent) annually, to perhaps one tenth of 1 per cent of the GNP. Such genuine resource transfer as may be involved in this level of expenditure would clearly be insignificant in relation to a major reshaping of the regional structure of the country and it is not surprising perhaps that the traditional problems which have characterized the French scene have shown little sign of disappearing even though the progress of the economy as a whole has had effects in many parts of the country which were relatively backward.

The new measures in the VIth Plan no doubt take cognisance of the results achieved under previous plans and we do not at this point attempt any assessment of their likely effect. The point that needs to be made

* See "Area Redevelopment and Regional Development Policy in France", OECD, 1973.

in relation to our theoretical framework or model is that, up to the time of RFED, large objectives were being sought by comparatively small means. The time scale for successful results would be accordingly prolonged. Meanwhile dynamic changes in the economy as a whole could be having effects which would quite swamp the efforts to secure the desired regional balance.

The German example as given in RFED again offers some interesting variations in the themes developed so far. It was explicitly defined "in a more restricted sense than in other countries examined" (p. 31). Regional economic policy was seen as an additional effort for the removal of the economic and structural imbalance between the different parts of the country. "Its task is the development of structurally weak regions as well as support for the restructuring of certain industrialized regions".

The "economically weakest" regions were defined in 1968, after the application of specific criteria, to cover one tenth of the population, with an average GDP per capita of two thirds of the Federal average. (This implies that average income in these areas was about 65 per cent of the average in other regions).

On the face of it this would present a relatively small problem, since the transfer of resources required from 90 per cent of the population to raise the level in the distressed areas to the national average i. e. by 50 per cent - would only be of the order of magnitude of 5 per cent of the total - such smaller than in the Italian or United Kingdom cases.

The resources applied to the problem, as shown in RFED, are about US $ 100 million annually, with GNP calculated at 132 thousand million dollars - say one tenth of one per cent. This however, falls far short of what would be required and on our model it would take one thousand years to bridge the gap. Obviously the general progress of the economy would totally swamp any changes which might result from a regional policy on this scale. For this very reason it would seem that the case is one in which, under our model, the problem was not seen as significant.

We note however, that in the most recent plan, as reported to OECD the area of the country affected by special measures has been widened to cover 60 per cent of the Federal territory with about one third of the population. The measures will however only apply to a restricted list of municipalities (312 "key" centres) whose development can have repercussive effects on the surrounding areas.

Possibly Germany might be regarded as a case in which disparity of "E" values in whole regions need not now be regarded as a serious problem. It must however not be overlooked that other means than regional policy have been used to deal with the structural problems in industrial sectors. The post war reconstruction and development in the major industrial areas and cities can only be seen not as an effort to remove imbalances by interregional transfer but as one of complete national reconstruction founded on a phenomenal rate of growth. Since all major concentrations of population and industry were affected by national reconstruction, disparities of "E" values were less important than the need to raise them in all regions.

It will be realized from these few examples that all countries have their special features and it should not be necessary to multiply still further the types of cases which have distinctive features. One point to which reference has not especially been made is that the artificial concept of North/South or simple regional dualism distinguishing between low and high "E" value regions does not place any emphasis on different characteristics of individual regions. Whereas in some countries only one region may be regarded as a special problem region in others, if not in most, regional imbalance is a complex web of differing circumstances, some favourable to economic life and others less favourable. The device of simple dualism can obscure important differences between regions which merit attention being paid to several rather than one for the simple reason, as we have already pointed out, that for each set of indices the regional imbalance is totally different. Thus while unemployment may be distributed in a certain pattern this pattern may not correspond at all to the pattern that is presented by disparities in housing, or health and amenity or indeed to the costs of living and various forms of social costs involved in the provision of basic services such as transport.

It is well known that in some countries neither income disparities nor those in employment are significant, yet a problem of "imbalance" is considered to exist. Compared with the United Kingdom or United States unemployment is not a significant regional problem in Japan, France, Germany or the Scandinavian countries. True there are areas affected by agriculture or forestry run down and a need to provide alternative employment in urban areas with suitable urban activities. In such cases the problem is seen much more as an imbalance between town and country, excessive growth of major central cities and the accompanying problems of social rundown in smaller urban areas. "Congestion" in the large metropolitan areas such as London, Paris, Copenhagen, Tokyo or Milan is often given as a reason for a policy of restraining their growth and fostering the development of alternative urban areas, whether by new or satellite cities or by expanding well placed existing cities as "growth points".

97

A comprehensive analysis of regional imbalance should therefore not ignore this particular aspect of imbalance, nor avoid an attempt to place it within the general framework. The development of alternative urban centres involves resource allocation for regional imbalance purposes, and a geographic transfer of the expenditures required for infrastructures can be determinant of the success or otherwise of policies to correct regional imbalances.

A common way of looking at this problem is to take for granted that cities can be overlarge, can destroy the environment around them and impose intolerable costs on their inhabitants. The obvious solution is seen in alternative development elsewhere and more particularly in creating conditions which deter the inflow of population into them from further afield. More particularly the argument implies that metropolitain cities are located in the "more prosperous regions" and that the logical course is to allocate enough resources to development elsewhere to reduce or even reverse the pressures of population on them. Indeed it is argued that allowing populations to migrate from cities in declining areas with a developed infrastructure is socially wasteful in that the existing infrastructure, housing and services, become underused or even derelict. Regeneration of urban areas whose decline is brought about by the decline in their basic industries is seen as part of the general problem of imbalance.

It would be difficult to apply the simple techniques of our model to this situation since few if any attempts have been made to clothe the concept of urban imbalance with statistics. It is worth asserting however that attempts to restrain the growth of big cities in flourishing areas have historically succeeded in few countries, if anywhere. Throughout the post war period the big cities and urban conglomerations have tended to expand. "Stemming the tide" has proved little more successful than King Canute's command to the waters to recede! In a sense the expansion of the cities and the high costs of living and working in them is of course a reflection of their advantages and their comparative attraction compared with smaller centres less well endowed with the qualities of urban civilisation.

"Rectifying the regional imbalance" by measures designed to overcome the inherent attraction of the metropolitan areas falls, as we see it, within the same category of resource transfer between regions as does the attempt to secure a different regional pattern of employment. It follows that if insufficient resources are applied the same lack of success may result as in that case.

Our method of analysis suggests that the problem can also be looked at in a different way from that traditionally adopted. In the United States, an example we have already taken, the problem of the cities to which people migrate (as at the same time others move out to better environments) has, as is well known, become more acute rather than less and is expected to become still more so in the future unless adequate remedial measures are devised. The same is true of some of the other examples we have quoted. This suggests that the conditions of cities themselves, irrespective of the average level of incomes compared with those of other regions, should properly be regarded as an element in the "E" concept.

What this would mean is that such factors as the higher cost of transport, services (charged to local rates) and the unsatisfactory environment in general is a factor to be set against income levels in the calculation of "E".

If this were done we might get a situation in which a true comparison of "E" values between regions would show a different regional imbalance altogether from that based on other criteria. It is certainly not necessarily so but only the particular study of cases could show where it is so. It could possibly be the case that if proper allowance is made for this factor in the calculation of imbalances the differences between "E" values between so called less and more prosperous regions would be less than appears from taking only the ordinary criteria of income (monetary) or employment. In that case transfer of resources away from cities where problems of congestion, etc. are acute to areas where they are less acute simply creates an imbalance of another kind, usually not recognized.

The apparent reluctance of Governments to devote enough resources to correct imbalance in employment or income levels between regions is perhaps to be seen as a reflection of the pressures which are put on them to remedy the physical and social problems of the big cities in areas outside the official development regions. That these problems are recognized to exist is shown by the special programmes for social development, in housing and welfare, which are devoted to problem cities irrespective of their regional location.

If our method of viewing the problem is correct this is not incompatible with a concept of a regional policy designed to rectify interregional imbalances. It must also cast doubt on the feasibility of diverting substantial resources away from regions which, however "prosperous" in simple income and employment terms, have substantial problems of their own. If such regions happen also to be those most favourably placed for economic growth such a policy may have the effect of lessening the national growth rate and diminishing "E" in them.

It is possible to sum up the conclusions which emerge from this analysis fairly briefly. It has been shown that the problem of "regional imbalance" presents itself in many different ways. Basically policies to overcome imbalance entail either a shift of resources, major or minor according to circumstances, to the less favoured regions or a shift of population from them to the more favoured regions. (Whichever policy is adopted the imbalance could widen or narrow according to circumstances.) If the choice is made of the former by the Government the prospects of success must depend not only on the conditions in the region or regions it is desired to help but also in those of the other regions. Where there is low national growth the shift of resources may be more difficult to make than if there is a high rate. But the closing of the "gap" between regions may not result from a shift of resources based upon a growth economy if the conditions of the less favoured regions are not suited to the kind of growth required by the national economy. The "gap" can be maintained or even widened in the circumstances of either a growing or static national economy. Since all regions are subject to the effects of dynamic change new problems can arise which modify the comparisons between regions. Regional policy can have the objective of securing a certain balance between regions as a primary objective of national policy. But a national policy of growth may involve a deliberate choice of permitting new imbalances to arise as a preferable solution to stultifying national growth by correcting existing imbalances.

We therefore see the urban problem as an integral part of the problem of regional balance and one which poses problems of resource allocation between regions throughout the country.

It would seem important for countries and Governments to examine more deeply the nature of the imbalances with which they are trying to deal and to establish more clearly the reasons for their failure or success. In particular, insofar as it proves impracticable to rely wholly on development in the "less favoured" regions, or on a policy of resource transfer to them it is necessary to recognize the problems that arise in the regions to which population migrates or in which the most favourable conditions for growth may exist. The more intractable the problem of the correction of imbalance by resource transfer to the backward regions the more necessary it would seem to deal effectively with the problems posed by the alternative "solution" - more often imposed by the facts of life than by a deliberate choice of population redistribution. In short, failure to recognize this may result not only in the continuance of imbalance but also in a spread of unsatisfactory conditions into regions where they were hitherto relatively more satisfactory.

Regional policy as a whole is not to be judged solely by reference to its success in remedying imbalances between regions but by its success in achieving the general objective of satisfactory growth and development in all regions. Because regions are interrelated and interdependent an assessment needs to be made of the regional pattern which will emerge after taking account of the policies directed towards correcting imbalance and resource allocations for dealing with regional problems must be tailored to the regional situation as a whole.

Nothing in this way of looking at things should be taken to suggest that a failure in any country to narrow the "gap" in "E" values between regions is a failure of regional policy itself. In, e. g. Italy where regional imbalance has remained and seems likely to remain a continuing problem the condition of the South has been shown to have undergone marked progress as a result of measures taken. Regional policy has had therefore some success even if the aim of correcting imbalance with other regions has not been achieved.

In order to determine the size and nature of the imbalance problem it would seem essential to establish the precise components of "E" for purposes of policies based on comparisons. These statistical differences can obscure the underlying facts, both because of the particular way in which statistical information arises and also because crude comparisons distort and do not necessarily provide a correct interpretation of significant differences between regions. The Spanish concept that there are "normal" imbalances which it is not necessary to correct may be a helpful tool in the process of determining which imbalances need correction and therefore which are the more appropriate and effective methods to be used.

Imbalances between monetary incomes per head do not necessarily reflect imbalances between real incomes if account is taken of price levels, the cost of housing and transport, the nature of the source of income and other variants including the "quality" of the environment in which income is earned. Certainly disparity in incomes is a normal feature of all economies and indeed acceptable to people insofar as the disparity is not judged to result from inequity of treatment. Average incomes per head may be lower in one region or area than in another because of different age and sex composition of the working population, the different proportion in occupations of varying skills, the different way of life, tastes and aspirations of the population. The mere difference in income levels between regions may not therefore present a problem at all unless the differences reflect conditions which are themselves unacceptable. For example in cases where income levels, however equitable in terms of representing the correct price for the values of output, are insufficient to provide an acceptable standard of living the need is to raise the level of skills to permit a higher income earning capacity. The emphasis given in some regional policies to education and training does of course reflect a recognition of this point. It is conceivable that the failure to close the income gap between North and South Italy reflects in part the totally different age, sex and skills composition of the population. To the extent it does so the crude comparison of average income per head exaggerates the true gap.

It follows that a state of interregional equilibrium or "balance" could exist at a satisfactory level for the populations even if a comparison of average levels were to show that they varied. In other words "true" "E's" would be equal but "E" measured by a crude index of income variations would give a false impression. If the latter were used, as perhaps it sometimes is, as a justification for policies to rectify imbalance the result could be to set unnecessary and unattainable targets. The fact that the populations do not migrate in wholescale fashion from regions of lower to regions of higher income may reflect not only the difficulty of migration but also the acceptability of income disparity. The persistence of regional imbalances as commonly described by reference to crude indices such as income per head may be, at least in part, due to their "naturalness" and acceptability.

It seems clear that the concept of regional imbalance is a complex one and that there is a need, if countries pursuing policies of rectifying imbalances are to succeed in their aims, for them to clarify their concepts and adjust their targets and resource use to feasible aims. This is all the more important if "regional imbalance" is used as a justification for the pursuit of policies which call for international understanding and co-operation as, in a separate chapter, we shall be showing.

CONCLUSIONS

A number of positive recommendations to countries seeking to "rectify imbalances" could flow from the acceptance of the foregoing analysis:

1. Countries should conduct regular surveys of the facts of regional disparities and should monitor changes in them.

2. Disparities should be brought together in a generalized concept (of the nature of our "E" concept) which permits valid comparisons to be made of the state of regions as a whole.

3. The underlying causes of the disparities should be identified so that remedial measures deemed necessary should be geared to the causes rather than the symptoms.

4. Distinction should be made between "normal" or "acceptable" disparities and those which give rise to legitimate concern. Indices

of disparities should be carefully chosen to avoid misleading use of crude figures.

5. The forces of change which are operative and could affect the future of each region should be identified and their consequences assessed in terms of their effect on future regional imbalance.

6. The dynamic changes in the national economy through economic, technical, sociological and occupational (or employment structure) change should be appraised and their impact on future regional balance assessed.

7. The factors favourable or unfavourable to growth and development of each region should be examined and their consequences for the future assessed.

8. The scope of and advantages and disadvantages of external transfer of resources to a region and internally generated growth (exogeneous and indigenous growth possibilities) should be compared.

9. The merits of the alternatives of resource transfer or migration policies should be specifically examined.

10. The impact-effect on other regions of the chosen policy for the backward regions (resource diversion or population migration) should be considered and their implications for those regions and for the national economy as a whole assessed.

11. The resources applied to overcoming imbalance, whether internal or external to the particular regions, should be related to their potential effect and the projected time scale by which they could achieve a given target, estimated.

12. The consequences of not eliminating imbalances before the estimated target date should be examined to determine whether a revision of resource allocation or target date would be necessary.

It is recognized that the methodologies for making the kind of calculations suggested in the above recommendations could pose considerable problems since it is safe to say that few countries have as yet approached the whole issue of tackling regional imbalances in a systematical way. There would also be advantage, in a world in which international comparisons may need to be made of the scale and scope of regional policies, for a common method to be employed to standardize the information necessary for such comparisons and to provide countries with a common basis for the presentation of their policies internationally. The OECD might consider that it would be worth appointing a suitably qualified expert to draw up a framework which Governments could use to assemble the necessary data, and make their calculations for a systematic approach to the imbalance problem. In due course the OECD might invite all Member Governments to provide a regular statement based on a standard approach of their policies to effect a better regional balance.

V

UNEMPLOYMENT DISPARITIES

In order to grasp the significance of relative regional disparities in unemployment it may be helpful to take some purely hypothetical figures. What constitutes a "serious" disparity in unemployment is not of course simply a statistical matter. The term "serious" is itself subjective and its use in the circumstances of any country involves essentially a social or political judgement. Particularly in countries which have traditionally - or at least in the post-war decades - regarded "full employment" as a desirable objective of national economic and social policy, any departure from this, either nationally or regionally, tends to be regarded as more of a matter of serious concern than in countries in which a relatively high level of unemployment (including underemployment) is thought to be inescapable or even conducive to a flexible economy. Moreover, even countries which regard anything less than "full" employment as a social and economic evil may feel obliged to accept it, at least temporarily, if it is the result, for example, of attempts to bring other "evils", such as inflation, under control.

In such countries temporary increases in unemployment and in regional disparities may be regarded as less serious than a continuing and persistent high level, with especially persistent disparities between regions. It seems to be a sad fact, but nonetheless true, that the policies open to or pursued by Governments often reflect a choice between evils. We do not, therefore, posit any particular level of unemployment as objectively serious. Our task at this stage is simply to examine some hypothetical situations of regional disparities in unemployment levels.

We can imagine two countries each with a "work force" of 20 million but with total unemployment levels of 2 per cent and 4 per cent respectively, i.e. 400,000 and 800,000. Those in employment would be 98 per cent and 96 per cent or 19.6 million and 19.2 million respectively.

If in each country the "disadvantaged" regions contain 40 per cent of the work force and the rate of unemployment is twice the national average we would have the following situation:

Example 1

		COUNTRY A	COUNTRY B
Total work force ..	number	20, 000, 000	20, 000, 000
Unemployed	number	400, 000	800, 000
40 per cent of work force	number	8, 000, 000	8, 000, 000
Of which Unemployed	number	320, 000	640, 000
Rate	percentage	4	8
60 per cent of work force	number	12, 000, 000	12, 000, 000
Of which Unemployed	number	80, 000	160, 000
Rate	percentage	0. 66	1. 33

National unemployment rates are the same as in Example 1 but in a second example we can imagine that the rate of unemployment in the "disadvantaged" regions is twice that of the other regions. We then have the following figures:

Example 2

		COUNTRY A	COUNTRY B
Total work force ..	number	20, 000, 000	20, 000, 000
Unemployed	number	400, 000	800, 000
40 per cent of work force	number	8, 000, 000	8, 000, 000
Of which Unemployed	number	232, 000	464, 000
Rate	percentage	2. 9	5. 8
60 per cent of work force	number	12, 000, 000	12, 000, 000
Rate	percentage	1. 46 (approx.)	2. 9 (approx.)
Number		168, 000	336, 000

The two examples bring out important differences. In the first example, though the rate of unemployment in the "disadvantaged" regions is twice the national rate, the disparity between them and the other regions is much greater. The rate in the former is six times that in the latter. In the second example the disparity between regions is by definition less (twice) and in consequence the disparity with the national rate is also (and correspondingly) less, 2.9 per cent compared with 2.0 per cent and 5.8 per cent compared with 4 per cent.

The same figures can, of course, be presented in other ways.

In the first example the rate in the "disadvantaged" regions is 500 per cent higher than in the others. In the second it is only 45 per cent higher.

If numbers employed are equated with "jobs" (i.e. one person employed means there is one job) then in Example 1 there are 19.6 million jobs in Country A and 19.2 million in Country B. The percentage increase in "jobs" to secure full (100 per cent) employment nationally would then be .4/19.6 and .8/19.2 or 2.02 per cent and 4.16 per cent respectively. But the percentage increase required in the "disadvantaged" regions is markedly different. In Country A jobs must increase by 32/7.68 or 4.2 per cent (approx.) and in Country B by 64/7.20 or 8.9 per cent.

In Example 2, in respect to the same countries, the required rates of increase would of course be lower, since in both cases unemployment is at a lower rate in the "disadvantaged" regions. But even in this example the rate of increase required for Country B would be higher than required for Country A in Example 1.

In both examples Country A typifies a country with a low national rate of unemployment (2 per cent). It could of course also be regarded as typifing a country with a very high rate of employment. However, to bring the rate of unemployment in the "disadvantaged" regions of Country A in Example 1 to the national level of 2 per cent the number of unemployed would have to fall from 320,000 to 160,000, i.e. be halved. In Country B (in Example 1) to bring it to the national level of 4 per cent it would similarly have to fall from 640,000 to 320,000.

If Country B (in Example 1) sought to reduce its national average to that of Country A it would need to create 400,000 additional jobs. If all these were allocated to the "disadvantaged" regions (leaving the level in the others unchanged at 160,000 or 1.33 per cent) unemployment in them would fall from 640,000 to 240,000 (or 3 per cent of 8 million) representing a drop by $62\frac{1}{2}$ per cent. If it were sought to go further than this and reduce the level in the "disadvantaged" regions to the 1.33 per cent in the others, unemployment would have to fall to 82,640 a drop of 557,360 or 87 per cent. Such figures or calculations give no indication as to the feasibility of measures to reduce unemployment levels by given quantities. All they do is to indicate relative orders of magnitude implicit in the adoption of defined targets.

In some circonstances a drop in total national unemployed from 800,000 to 400,000 is by no means an impossibility and such drops can be found to have occured in some countries in the upswing of the normal trade cycle. In our example 400,000 new jobs represent an increase in numbers employed from 19.2 million to 19.6 million, an increase of 2.0 per cent (approx.). In practice the difficulty lies in allocating extra jobs to particular regions. The same increase of 400,000 if allocated wholly to the disadvantaged regions, would represent an increase of number employed from 7.36 million to 7.76 million or 5.4 per cent.

If the hypothesis were adopted that job numbers expand in proportion to the numbers already available - i.e. the potential of expansion depends on the size of the starting base - then the position would look different. A 2 per cent increase in numbers employed in the disadvantaged regions would produce only 146,000 for them or about 23 per cent of the 640,000 unemployed. The remaining 254,000 jobs would occur in the other regions. Since there were 160,000 unemployed, and if all these were absorbed, the jobs could only be filled by a movement of 94,000 from the disadvantaged regions to the others.

In reverse, a rise in unemployment from 400,000 to 800,000 with the level in the disadvantaged regions remaining at twice the national rate, means, that 60 per cent of the rise occurs in those regions (i.e. 320,000 out of 400,000). The rise would be greater than this if the predisposing conditions of "disadvantage" are such that unemployment rises at a relatively higher rate in the disadvantaged regions compared with the others.

Another approach is to consider the effect on unemployment in the disadvantaged regions of a given fall in the national rate. Thus a drop of one percentage point in the national rate would halve it in Country A and reduce it by a quarter in Country B in each case. Assuming that the rate reduction applied equally to all regions, unemployment would fall in the disadvantaged regions by 160,000 in both cases to 3 per cent and 6 per cent respectively.

If however the drop of one percentage point (200,000) takes place proportionately to the work force, the 200,000 would be differently distributed. In Country A unemployment would fall by two-fifths (80,000) in the disadvantages regions and three-fifths (120,000) in the others. Since there are only 80,000 unemployed in these a shift from the disadvantaged regions would be required.

108

In Country B unemployment would fall by 256,000 in the disadvantaged regions and by 144,000 in the others (leaving 16,000 unemployed).

In countries in which there is already a very high level of employment (or in which potential expansion of the work force is severely limited) an expansion even by a small percentage, such as 1 per cent, could be difficult. In Country A an expansion of employment by 1 per cent would mean an increase of 196,000 cutting unemployment by nearly half. If the whole of this were "allocated" to the disadvantaged regions it would reduce unemployment in them to 124,000 in Example 1 and 36,000 in Example 2. If however it were allocated in proportion to the respective work forces (40/60) the reduction in unemployment in the disadvantaged regions would be only 78,000 the remainder of 122,000 serving to reduce unemployment in the other regions. In Example 1 however, there are only 80,000 unemployed in these so that a shift of work force would be required.

In Country B a one per cent increase in the total employment would produce 192,000 jobs cutting employment by nearly a quarter. In both examples it would not require a shift of population, however it was "allocated".

To bring unemployment in the disadvantaged regions down to the same rate as in the others would require the number to fall in Country A to 52,800 (Example 1) and to 116,000 (Example 2); a drop of five sixths, or 83 per cent and 50 per cent respectively. In Country B the fall would be 534,000 in Example 1 and 232,000 in Example 2 (the percentage falls being as in Country A).

Percentage falls of less than the magnitudes indicated would have correspondingly less effect on disparities. Thus if unemployment in the disadvantaged regions of Country A (Example 1) fell by what would seem a substantial figure of 20 per cent the resulting unemployment rate of 3.2 per cent would still be nearly five times as high as in the other regions.

The assumption can also be made that the unemployment levels are allowed to rise in the regions where it is low to provide a shift in jobs from them to the disadvantaged regions. In Example 1 if unemployment in the former in Country A were raised to the national level of 2 per cent the total would be 240,000 involving an increase of 160,000. If the corresponding jobs were transferred to the disadvantaged regions unemployment would be halved and come down also to 160,000. In other words, in this particular case, the unemployment rate would have to treble in the greater part of the country in order to reduce the level in the disadvantaged regions by half. In Country B the same proportions would hold but the numbers are of course double (corresponding to the national rate of 4 per cent).

109

One or two general propositions corresponding to common sense do however emerge:

1. The use of ratios in describing disparities requires a good deal of circumspection. There is a significant difference if disparities are measured in terms of comparisons with national rates or in terms of comparisons between regions (Example 1 compared with Example 2);

2. A given percentage increase in national job totals presents itself very differently in regions, according to the proportion of the unemployed to the regional total;

3. If the level of employment in the greater part of a country is already so high that it cannot be increased from the existing population, the rate of job increase necessary to eliminate unemployment in the disadvantaged regions can involve either a shift of part of the work force of the disadvantaged regions to the others or a correspondingly high rate of job increase in the disadvantaged regions;

4. Alternatively, a small percentage increase in total jobs needed to eliminate or reduce unemployment in the disadvantaged regions can still require a shift of population if there is no scope for expansion of the work force in the "other" regions;

5. A very large percentage reduction (e.g. one half) in national unemployment can represent a very small percentage increase in employment and diminish unemployment in the disadvantaged regions by much less than the reduction in the national rates;

6. To bring unemployment down in the disadvantaged regions to the lower levels prevailing in the others will involve a fall proportionate to the degree of disparity and the ratios of the unemployed to the total work force. Even in countries with "moderate" disparities and low overall rates of unemployment the percentage fall in the disadvantaged regions may have to be very large to remove the disparity;

7. What might appear to be a substantial percentage fall in the rate of unemployment (such as 20 per cent) would still not significantly reduce disparities which are much larger in relative terms;

8. Shifts of jobs from less to more disadvantaged regions (as an alternative to shifts of people from the latter to the former) can involve a proportionately higher rate of unemployment growth in the former than in the fall of unemployment in the latter.

110

The two Examples which have been given are designed only to illustrate relativities in conditions of a static total work force and static total employment and unemployment. Work forces can however rise and fall, as can the number of jobs available to a given work force. The effect of dynamic change in these factors depends on their regional distribution as well as on their total. The use of dynamic examples however only complicates the picture without adding to understanding of the relativities. Each set of figures resulting from dynamic change can also be examined in terms of a static separate picture for each point in a time series. However the problem of determining how to overcome regional disparities in employment or unemployment requires, for the country concerned, an examination of the dynamic trends, the pattern of distribution and the scope for interregional shifts in job totals or work forces.

Bearing in mind the need to take account of dynamic change, a number of other observations can be made relevent to the determination of the feasibility of overcoming regional disparities.

a) "National" increases in job totals cannot (on the basis of equating one man with one job) exceed the total number of unemployed (and capable of work).

b) If job numbers are increased in proportion to the work force in each region relative disparities will remain the same even though numbers of employed rise in each region.

c) Relative disparities can be diminished only if the rate of job rise in the disadvantaged regions is greater than elsewhere.

d) In conditions of "full" employment in the more favoured regions job numbers in them can be expanded either by an influx of unemployed from the disadvantaged regions or a movement of jobs to them.

e) If neither takes place there can be no increase in job numbers (though there can of course be a substitution of new jobs for old) in the regions of full employment.

f) If conditions are not those of "full employment" (i.e. if there is no upper limit to the expansion of jobs) expansion in the national job total distributed in proportion to the existing work forces brings down the national and regional unemployment without affecting the disparities in relative rates of unemployment.

g) The higher the relative rate of unemployment in the disadvantaged regions the higher must be the relative growth in employment in them to remove disparities if jobs cannot be moved to them or if movement of people to other regions where jobs exist is impracticable for one reason or another.

111

It would follow from these observations that, in order to determine the feasibility of policies designed to deal with imbalances in employ-ment and unemployment the authorities of a country must have some idea of the following entities.

i) The national and regional movement of the total work force.

ii) The scope for increases in the national job totals.

iii) The scope for expansion of jobs totals in particular regions.

iv) The scope for movement of jobs interregionally.

v) The scope for movement of unemployed interregionally.

If a country is unable to identify and quantify these elements in their employment situation then policies seeking to overcome imbal-ances would have something of the quality of shooting arrows at random, or in the dark, in the hope of striking an unspecified target. (Since few, if any countries have as yet sought to examine their employment situation by such methods it is perhaps not surprising that sometimes the impression is, in fact, given that "hit and miss" plays a consider-able part in the policies that have been pursued over recent decades and that this accounts to some degree for the apparent lack of success in overcoming regional employment imbalances.)

These theoretical observations can be pursued a little further by considering in general terms some characteristic features of national economies.

Generally speaking, as is well known, the rate of growth of the "labour force" in most countries is not very large. In periods of rising population due to natural increase and to longer life spans the propor-tion of young and elderly increases: that of the active population dimi-nishes. If we look at the statistics of the total labour force published by OECD, * Table II, the total labour force in all OECD countries rose by only 9.7 per cent in the eleven years from 1957. In the OECD coun-tries of Europe it rose only by 3.0 per cent. [The rise in the civilian labour force was about the same (Table IV)].

There were of course considerable variations between countries. In three cases there was an actual decline (Austria, Ireland and Italy). The rise was greatest in Canada, the United States, Japan and the Netherlands (30.9 per cent, 17.9 per cent, 15.9 per cent and 11.4 per cent respectively). In the large industrialized countries of Europe the rise was of the order 2-4 per cent [Belgium 3 per cent, France 4 per cent, Germany 2 per cent (despite net immigration) and United Kingdom 4 per cent.

* Labour Force Statistics 1957-68, Paris 1970.

In Spain it was 7 per cent]. In the last four years (1965-68) some of these countries saw no growth and even some decline.

It may be rash to generalize but the United States, Japan and Spain (also Canada) are countries with a high internal migration rate. Even in these the rate of growth was much less in the later than the earlier years.

These figures at least suggest that the characteristic feature of many industrialized countries is of a fairly static and, in some cases, declining labour force. They give no indication of the changes in the regional distribution of the work force (which were of course occurring) but they seem to show that, overall, the total work force situation is, in those countries, close to that of our static model.

In such cases the problem of dealing with disparities in regional employment or unemployment is largely one of interregional job shift or work force movement, without the additional complication of a significant growth in the total labour force. While it is possible to invent theoretical levels of employment and unemployment for the purpose of establishing a theoretical framework it would seem that the actual situation in which most countries seek to deal with regional disparities is one in which by far the greater proportion of the populations is employed, very often well over 95 per cent. Statistical definitions of unemployment vary from country to country so that the total of persons defined as unemployed in different countries may not be strictly comparable. It is fairly safe to say however that the figures unemployed may include people who are not in fact available for employment, and they may also exclude some people who might be wishing to work but are unregistered for one reason or another.

As we have seen the significance of a high national level of employment, or a low level of unemployment, is, that the creation of new job opportunities can bring about a diminution in regional disparities either by the new jobs being distributed to the disadvantaged regions or people moving from them to where the new jobs can be provided. Where overall levels of employment are low an increase in jobs nationally can in part still be absorbed in the regions of relatively lower unemployment before the possibility of job shifts or movement of people need arise.

It is therefore useful to consider the actual levels of national unemployment (as the reverse side of the coin to employment) in the world as it exists.

Unemployment percentages (of the Labour Force) are given as yearly averages for each of the years 1957-68 in the OECD publication already quoted "Labour Force Statistics 1957-68, Paris 1970. In what

follows possible differences of definition are ignored. We give only
figures, for the terminal years and intermediate highest and lowest
points.

UNEMPLOYMENT PERCENTAGES

	1957	1968	HIGHEST	LOWEST
Canada	4.5	4.8	7.0 (1961)	3.5 (1966)
United States ..	4.1	3.4	6.5 (1958) (1961)	3.6 (1966)
Japan	1.9	1.2	2.2 (1959)	1.1 (1964)
Belgium	2.3	2.9	3.9 (1959)	1.5 (1964)
France	0.8	2.1	2.1 (1968)	0.8 (1957)
Germany	2.9	1.2	3.0 (1958)	0.5 (1965)
Italy	6.9	3.5	6.9 (1957)	2.5 (1963)
Netherlands ..	1.3	1.8	2.4 (1958)	0.7 (1963)
Spain	1.5 (1960)	1.9	1.9 (1967) (1968)	1.2 (1962)
Sweden	1.8 (1960)	2.2	2.2 (1968)	1.2 (1965)
United Kingdom	1.1	2.1	1.9 (1963)	1.1 (1957) (1961) (1965) (1966)

Only Canada, United States and Italy had a rate in excess of 4 per
cent at any time. The lowest rates in all the other countries were below
2 per cent - mostly markedly so. In Canada, United States and Italy
the lowest rates were below 4 per cent and very much below the highest.

As has been seen from Examples 1 and 2 of "Country A" even a national
rate as low as 2 per cent can still involve considerable regional disparities. In the countries listed and for the year quoted the scope for an
overall national increase of jobs was clearly very limited and the reduction of disparities would clearly have depended on the degree to
which job expansion in the disadvantaged regions or job shift to them or
migration from them was feasible.

(It can be noted en passant that this was a period of continual rise
in GNP).

The question whether job expansion can take place in disadvantaged
regions is not one to be answered by purely theoretical reasoning. We
have seen that the lower the starting base (in terms of employment) the

114

higher the proportionate increase must be to remove the disparity with other parts of a country. This cannot be ruled out a priori. The rate of potential job expansion in any region depends on the suitability and availability of the work force, the suitability of local conditions for particular activities or industries from which job expansion is possible and the readiness or ability of the State or private enterprise to make use of the potential - itself of course depending on the general economic climate and the competition of other regions for the available investment resources. The question is always how far these conditions can in fact be satisfied in particular circumstances. The fact that, in periods of growth of GNP and despite considerable efforts made by Governments to encourage investment in disadvantaged regions, there is a persistence of regional employment disparities suggests that these conditions are not easily fulfilled.

To take only the example of the United Kingdom, a country in which employment disparities have been a key feature of the regional economic problem, in which there is a long history of attempts to overcome them and where overall national unemployment has been comparatively small, the following figures provide some evidence of the inherent difficulty in bringing about a significant improvement in the situation of imbalance (and also of the problem of correct interpretation of changing ratios).

PERCENTAGE RATE OF WHOLLY UNEMPLOYED

	GREAT BRITAIN	NORTH	N.W.	SCOTLAND	WALES
1954	2.3	2.1	1.4	2.6	2.3
1955	1.0	1.6	1.0	2.2	1.7
1956	1.0	1.4	1.2	2.2	1.9
1957	1.3	1.6	1.5	2.4	2.4
1958	1.9	2.2	2.1	3.4	3.4
1959	2.0	3.0	2.4	4.0	3.4
1960	1.5	2.7	1.8	3.4	2.5
1961	1.3	2.3	1.5	2.9	2.2
1962	1.8	3.3	2.2	3.5	2.9
1963	2.2	4.3	2.7	4.4	3.2
1964	1.6	3.2	2.0	3.5	2.4
1965	1.3	2.4	1.5	2.8	2.5
1966	1.4	2.4	1.4	2.7	2.7
1967	2.2	3.8	2.3	3.7	3.9
1968	2.3	4.5	2.4	3.7	3.9
1969	2.3	4.6	2.4	3.6	3.9
1970	2.5	4.6	2.6	4.1	3.8
1971	3.2	5.5	3.7	5.6	4.5

We examine the situation as illustrated by the above annual figures of the percentage rate of "wholly unemployed", (i.e. males and females, excluding school leavers) taking seasonally adjusted monthly averages. (The wholly unemployed also exclude those "temporarily stopped" i.e. out of employment for a short time). For convenience figures for Great Britain are contrasted with those of selected "disadvantaged" regions, viz. Scotland, North England, North West England and Wales.*

In September 1967 the four regions specified had a total of 6.8 million "employees in employment" out of a total for Great Britain of 22.0 million, i.e. 31 per cent approximately. In september 1970 they had a total of 7.2 million out of a total for Great Britain of 22.4 million, i.e. 30 per cent.

A simple comparison between the first and last years produces the following result.

REGIONAL UNEMPLOYMENT
AS A PERCENTAGE
OF THE GREAT BRITAIN RATE

	1954	1971	1970
North	175	170	184
N.W.	116	115	104
Scotland	217	175	164
Wales	191	140	152
Great Britain ...	100	100	100

The latter figures show that while unemployment was much higher in 1971 than 1954, in all the specified regions the unemployment rate as a percentage of the Great Britain rate had declined. Nonetheless it was still substantially higher than the Great Britain rate. The same appears to be true of other periods. Between 1964 and 1971 unemployment in Great Britain doubled but the rise in the specified regions was less than double. The Great Britain rate also doubled between 1955 and 1959 and the rise was less than this in the North, Scotland and Wales.

* Department of Employment Gazette, March 1972.

On the other hand, if 1958 is compared with 1968 the Great Britain rate increased by 21 per cent whereas in the North it more than doubled, in the North West it rose by 60 per cent, in Scotland by 9 per cent and in Wales by 14 per cent.

In the period 1959-61 in which Great Britain rates declined by 54 per cent they declined by less in the specified regions. It would be something of a paradox if the "cure" for regional unemployment disparities were to be found in increasing unemployment, or if it were the case that disparities change inversely to the change in unemployment. This impression is created by the comparisons quoted for 1954-71, 1958-68, 1955-59, 1964-71 and, inversely, 1959-61. This inference is sometimes drawn or implied, for example, when it is suggested (as it has been in the United Kingdom) that the apparent narrowing of relative rates in favour of the disadvantaged regions in the period from 1964 could at least be taken as an indication of some success of intensified regional policy measures. The fact that there was a narrowing of the disparity in other earlier periods of comparison, such as 1955-59, when weaker measures were in operation, casts doubt on the validity of any such explanation.

The use of ratios calls, as has been said, for circumspection and this is a true in the regional as in any other field. The changes in the ratio of unemployment in the specified regions to that of Great Britain are also mirrored in corresponding changes in relation to the other regions. It is therefore just as possible that the causes can be found in the other regions as in those for which figures have been quoted.

In the United Kingdom the period 1964-71 was subject to the dominant influences of national measures to secure a solution to the balance of payments problem and the adjustments required as a result of the devaluation of sterling in 1967. The conditions of employment themselves changed as adjustments were made in the private sector of the economy, including a more rigorous attitude to the use of labour (contributing to the so-called "shake out"). In such circumstances the effects could be expected to bear particularly on the "buoyant" regions. Thus from 1966-71 the unemployment rate (wholly unemployed, excluding school leavers, seasonally adjusted) rose from 0.8 per cent to 2.9 per cent in the West Midlands, from 0.8 per cent to 2.8 per cent in the East Midlands, from 1.1 per cent to 3.7 per cent in the Yorkshire and Humberside region, from 1.4 per cent to 3 per cent in East Anglia and from 1.7 per cent to 3.4 per cent in the South West.

In terms of numbers the Great Britain total increased in the same period by 420,000, in the South East by 77,000, in the West Midlands by 47,000, in the East Midlands by 26,000, in Yorkshire and Humberside by 52,000, in East Anglia by 11,000, and in the South West by 23,000. In the North West they rose by 67,000, in the North by 40,000, in Scotland by 67,000 and in Wales by 16,000.

It is difficult to conceive that in such circumstances there could have been any progress towards removing the "deep seated and persistent" disparities which have constituted the underlying regional employment problem for many decades. It is more possible to conceive that as the process of recovery takes place the situation in the greater part of the country will improve while the problem of securing net increases in employment in the disadvantaged regions remains.

In general terms the responsiveness of a region to broad changes affecting the economy as a whole, such as the upswing or downswing of the trade cycle or the contraction and expansion resulting from monetary policies depends on how close its own economic structure corresponds to that of the country. In a country, such as the United Kingdom, in which most regions are fairly well integrated into the national economy there may be a closer correspondence than in say, Italy, where the structural differences between North and South are much greater. Major upswings or downswings of the economy occurring over a relatively short period can do little to change the structural pattern of the regions. Consequently the change in relative employment disparities which are bound to occur in periods of boom or slump can have little significance as a measure of progress or otherwise in the problem of the deep seated continuing imbalances.

The question still remains, therefore, of what is implied in attempts to overcome regional disparities in employment by exceptionally high rates of employment growth in disadvantaged regions, such as avoid the necessity for migration to regions where employment opportunities are greater.

A point to make is that the full measure of the problem is not given by taking the existing situation as a starting point. "Disadvantaged" regions are normally those in which conditions operate to produce a decline in employment in the industries which already exist - e.g. agriculture in Southern Italy and most countries, coal, ship building, steel, textiles in the United Kingdom and some other advanced industrialized countries. Depending on the scale in the rundown of the staple industries of a region there is a problem in simply keeping pace with this. If efforts to do so are successful but limited to this they may still leave the position relative to other regions one of substantial disparity. The effort required is therefore two-fold - to overcome the "backlog" and also to counteract future decline insofar as the run down of existing industries continues.

From the information available we have seen little evidence that most countries seek to measure their problem in such terms. Unless they do however, it seems unlikely that they can correctly assess the scale of the effort required to produce an acceptable employment balance between regions, or the costs involved and results, in terms of achievement.

The second point that we would make is that it is necessary to appraise the reasons why some regions are disadvantaged for without this appropriate remedies cannot be devised. In some countries the reasons are primarily demographic - population growth disproportionate to the opportunities for employment that can be created. In some the main reason may be sectoral, the fact that particular industries, such as those already mentioned, have become obsolescent, or lessening users of manpower or have failed to keep abreast with the times. Other reasons may also apply, such as the resources available in capital, skilled manpower, or the deficiencies in infrastructure and environment. These factors must not only be seen as absolutes. If other regions suffer less from such disabilities they are automatically more attractive to the new industries which are set up in response to technological change, change in supply and market conditions.

The description that is given by most countries of their problem regions suggests that the reasons for disparities are not to be found only in sectoral problems but in many other factors as well. If this is so it may go some way to account for the fact that the regional problem appears so intractable. It would certainly lead to some scepticism about the possibilities of the very exceptional rate of employment growth that would be needed to eliminate situations of serious disparity. It is obviously not possible, on purely theoretical grounds, to dismiss the possibility that exceptional rates of employment growth can be achieved. Prima facie one must doubt it on a realistic view, since the very conditions which have brought about the disparity have been conducive to exceptional rates of decline rather than growth. A more optimistic view would only seem, however, to be justified if it is possible to point to new factors capable of radically transforming a regional situation so that it becomes one of potential growth rather than decline.

Such new factors would be represented by a determined effort on the part of a Government to shift the distribution of investment resources from better placed to less well placed regions to the degree necessary to achieve the objective. The willingness to do so may however - and if the disadvantaged regions form a large part of a country, is likely - to be limited by the repercussion effects on the other regions. Again there is little evidence to suggest that countries are willing to shift investment to the degree which would cause unfavourable repercussions in other regions. It is of course sometimes argued in countries, such as the United Kingdom, that restraints on growth in the better off regions or discriminatory investment policies are pursued to the point where some danger exists that new regions of depression can emerge. (This argument has been put forward many times in the region in which the author has worked). Governments may deny that their measures have this effect, and it is no part of this study to determine how far there is any truth in such allegations.* The denials, however, suggest that Governments would be unwilling - and indeed could see good reasons against - to press transfer of resources to the point of producing new problems in other regions. All that can be said is that in certain circumstances this could in fact be necessary to achieve a sufficient injection of new resources in the disadvantaged regions to secure exceptionally high rates of growth in employment.

Since the resources devoted to regional policies are in most countries only a marginal fraction of national resources (see RFED and Chapter IV) it would seem unlikely that the rate of expansion required in the disadvantaged regions can be achieved in practive by this means.

New factors which provide a net addition to national resources can obviously help to secure exceptional growth rates without detriment to other regions. Such new factors do emerge, vide North Sea gas and oil, new technological industries etc. We have dealt with such matters in the chapter on "National Factors". Their effect on regional disparities in employment depends on the conditions required for their development and the part that individual regions may be able to play. Without such new factors operating to the especial benefit of disadvantaged regions the scales would still remain weighted against securing exceptionally high rates of growth in disadvantaged regions.

A further point that might be made is that interregional economic relations can be a determinant of the rate of growth in employment which is feasible in any particular region. Many industrial functions and operations are complementary and the development of industry in any particular part of a conntry may call for complementary development elsewhere. The growth of industry (whether manufacturing, service industry or commerce) is itself dependent on a whole host of factors which need not be enumerated in the present context. Very little work has been done (with the notable exception of Japan) to establish the input

* The influence of restraints can of course be to prevent or hold back the growth in the restained regions without necessarily resulting in an equivalent transfer of jobs to the disadvantaged regions (since firms which are refused permission to expand have other choices open to them besides expansion in the assisted areas). Insofar as this was so in the United Kingdom the apparent relative improvement in the ratios of unemployment in the period after 1964 could have in part reflected the intensification of restraints rather than benefit from the positive incentives. It is not possible to be certain since there is no way of telling what would have been the employment position if there had been no restraints.

-output relations between regional economies. Generally speaking, however, regions are not self contained independent economies (nor indeed,
in the modern world, are whole countries) and the effect of this is that
growth in employment in one region through industrial expansion may
call for complementary growth elsewhere. Insofar as this is so the
problem of securing relatively exceptionally high rates of employment
growth in particular regions is made more acute. As has been seen,
so long as there is a capacity for expansion of employment in all regions
national growth in number of jobs may draw on all regions. It may also
posit either a movement of people to regions of low unemployment or a
movement of jobs to the regions of higher unemployment. The feasibility in either case must depend on the circumstances. If it is borne in
mind that much modern industrial development is capital rather than
labour intensive, production aims can be achieved with relatively less
employment for a given capital investment.

Unless conditions in the disadvantaged regions are most favourable
for new investment (and prima facie they are not) it would follow that
in economies with a high degree of interregional complementarity the
problems of securing an exceptional increase in employment opportunities in disadvantaged regions must be one of special difficulty. In economies in which development is increasingly through capital intensive
undertakings the argument is a fortiori.

If securing an exceptionally high rate of employment growth in the
disadvantaged regions has to be regarded as a specially difficult and
intractable problem and unlikely to be solved by deliberate transfer of
resources on the required scale to the detriment of other regions, can
the same be said of the other theoretical solution, namely movement of
people from the disadvantaged regions to the others?

In purely economic terms the answer is simply the reverse side of
the same coin. The potential for expansion tends to be higher in regions
in which the industrial sectors are the more flourishing ones, in which
problems of obsolescence, outdated techniques or foreign competition
may be less severe. The same basic factors which have encouraged
growth in them, relative advantage in infrastructure or environment,
the presence of a higher proportion of the work force with the skills of
modern industry, are conducive to further growth. Whereas in the disadvantaged regions the problem of securing exceptionally high rates of
growth is the intractable one, in the other regions the problem of reducing the structural factors predisposing to growth in the more favoured
regions equally typifies the difficulty of changing imbalances by this
means. The inflationary pressures in these regions may be seen as
the counterpart of the deflationary conditions in declining regions.

Such theoretical considerations do not provide the answer as to the right solution in any country, any more than theoretical considerations show the degree of expansion required in hypothetical disadvantaged regions. The right solution always depends on the actual facts and circumstances in particular countries.

We can only note how the facts do present themselves in a limited number of examples. Undoubtedly regional redistribution of working population and job opportunities has taken place on a great scale in most countries, a feature which is discussed in the chapter on regional imbalance as such. Interregional shifts were considerable not only in the United Kingdom in the early post war decade (and in earlier times). It has been marked in the United States, Japan, Canada, Italy, Spain and France. It may be noted also that many of the countries with high internal mobility have also had relatively high growth rates in GNP and that in the United Kingdom where mobility has tended to decline in recent years the rise in GNP has been relatively slow. Too much should not be deduced from such limited data. Nonetheless they do lend some support to the common sense view that, in purely economic terms (and this is stressed) the problem of expansion of employment in the more favoured regions of a country does not present the kind of difficulties inherent in seeking exceptionally high growth in declining regions.

That there are difficulties is clear from the reluctance of some, though not all, countries to accept interregional migration as a solution. Partly this reluctance reflects a judgement of the social, psychological and political disadvantages of migration. There are also real costs to a country in providing for the necessary infrastructure and services in areas of incoming population where the existing level is already inadequate. How far such costs outweigh the loss to the economy of retaining people in areas where they have less, or less satisfactory, opportunities for gainful employment, or how far costs must be incurred in providing infrastructure and services in such areas is a matter of calculation in particular circumstances. There is no universal rule, since adaptability to population movement varies from country to country and within countries between regions, areas and cities. What is clear is that the right solution to the regional employment problem requires a weighing, not only of the special factors in the disadvantaged regions but also of the significance of the special factors in the others. The feasibility of any solution to the employment imbalance problem depends on how well account is taken of the relevant factors in all regions rather than of the disadvantaged regions alone.

122

CONCLUSION

This chapter has sought to bring out some of the implications of the concept of imbalance in employment and unemployment. It has perhaps shown the need to evaluate precisely the degree of imbalance which may exist and the interregional relationships which determine the possibility of alternative methods of overcoming these in particular circumstances. Some of the reasoning at least would suggest that the very factors which lead to the imbalances can account for the recognized difficulty in overcoming them. It would also suggest that measures to overcome them cannot be successful if they are not attuned to a correct appraisal of their origins and scale.

VI

EFFECTIVENESS
OF FINANCIAL INCENTIVES TO FIRMS

An "effective" incentive is, by definition, one which works, i.e. brings about a different decision from the one a firm would have taken in the absence of the incentive. The wide range of incentives offered by individual Governments and the frequent changes which are made indicate that there is no concensus as to the most effective types or to the scale needed to make a given type effective. Since the economic conditions in which firms operate in different countries are often totally different, similar types of incentives applied on a similar scale can have quite different effects. Simple comparisons between incentives offered by different countries can therefore by themselves throw little light on why in some cases they are effective and in others not.

A useful way to approach the subject is to consider, initially, the way in which incentives work in general terms. The question that has to be asked first and foremost is "what turns the scale in the mind of an enterprise when considering the value to it of a given incentive?"

The studies already made by the Working Party have shown that many factors influence an enterprise in determining the location for a new establishment, or the expansion of an existing establishment: e.g. the general profitability of an enterprise, the prospects of meeting its requirements for various types of labour, buildings and land, the suitability of an area in terms of communications with sources of material and equipment, supply, markets and services, the availability of infrastructure, housing and social services for staff, the attractiveness or otherwise of an area in terms of its amenities and recreation. In addition the firm may be influenced by its judgement of the future prospects of the economy as a whole, the confidence it feels in its own future and the time scale over which an investment has to be amortized. It may be influenced by uncertainties due to such factors as instability in world currencies or in the development of new competition, whether at home

125

or abroad. Its attitude to risk taking of all kinds, including the risk of establishing plants in new areas rather than expanding in situ may be conditioned by its judgement of the relevance of all these factors in its own particular circumstances.

In exercising its judgement between alternative locations, the bearing of all these factors has to be weighed before a rational decision can be taken.

Because the process of weighing so many possibilities is often very complicated it has to be recognized that firms do not always take rational decisions. This is in itself a factor to be borne in mind in considering the effectiveness of a given incentive. It can of course work both ways: a firm may irrationally underestimate or overestimate the value of a given incentive in coming to its decision.

To isolate the effects of incentives it could be assumed that the total effect of the other factors on a location decision is neutral. The incentive could then be considered as the marginal factor which would "turn the scale" according to its nature and size or its general "aptness" to the circumstances of the firm. This would however be an unrealistic assumption. In the real world it is not a single marginal factor which turns the scale but the marginal effect of the totality of factors which are weighed together.

It would be more logical, and realistic, to assert that an incentive can only turn the scale in favour of a given location if the other factors, in their totality, do not outweigh the effect of the incentive.

It follows that a small incentive can turn the scale in circumstances in which the other factors are neutral: and that a large incentive cannot do so if the other factors outweigh it.

A second general point, following from the first, is that "largeness" or "smallness" are relative terms. The incentive has to be measured against something, in order to determine whether it is large or small. The obvious element against which a rational firm can measure an incentive is the profitability of the enterprise. Whatever method it adopts, whether it uses simple or discounted returns on capital, it is only if an incentive affects profitability that it can "turn the scale" from one decision to another.

It follows that an incentive has no effect (a) if the profitability is already sufficient to turn the scale in favour of the desired location rather than another and (b) if profitability, even with the incentive, is insufficient to justify the investment or (c) if the conditions for profitable operation do not exist anyway.

A third general point is that a rational firm seeks the highest profitability of which it is capable, from a given investment. It follows that if profitability is higher in one location than another an incentive can only work in favour of the latter if it sufficiently changes the ratio of profitability between the two locations. The question of what is sufficient cannot be answered theoretically. As in other fields, there is an element of "inertia" to be overcome before any movement takes place. In the economic world if "normal" calculations predispose in favour of one location a small marginal change in profitability due to an incentive may not be sufficient to overcome the predisposing features of the first choice location. Thus in two different circumstances an incentive of the same relative effect on profitability can produce different results in terms of willingness to move to the location in which the incentive applies.

Fourthly, because the economic world is one of dynamic change the effectiveness of given incentives, or range of incentives, must vary over time. The significance of the "other factors" on investment decisions, such as general profitability of industry, greater or less confidence in the future, the relative attraction of different locations as communications or market patterns change etc., may become larger or smaller and reduce or increase the relative importance of a given incentive. An incentive that could be sufficient in period I may become less or more than sufficient in period II.

Fifthy, incentives bear differently on a firm according to its structure, and the relevance of an incentive to its needs. Thus a tax relief is significant only if tax burden is important. A 100 per cent remission of customs or exercise duties on commodities not used by a firm has no effect. A reduction in a tax on profits cannot help a firm which cannot operate profitably in the location to which the incentive applies. A reduction in taxes or social security charges on employment does not affect a fully automated enterprise with no employees. Grants for new plant and equipment help only to the extent that the costs of these items are significant in the total cost picture. A saving of interest on loans helps a firm with a need for additional capital, or, if it is self-financing, to the degree to which it is prepared and able to substitute new loan capital in its capital structure.

Finally an incentive can only influence a firm to choose one location rather than another if it is sufficient to outweigh the benefits it can obtain in the location of its first choice. Thus the effects of any incentive can be reduced by changes in the financial conditions in which it could operate in the location of its choice. A general reduction in taxation lessens the effects on firms of regional tax reliefs. Increased general profitability due to monetary or fiscal policies or improved marketing conditions reduces the differential benefit of incentives affecting enterprises located in particular regions.

The fact that many conditions have to be satisfied before an enterprise can function in a given location means that the effectiveness of a financial incentive can only be judged in the context of the firm's needs as a whole. No financial incentive, however large, can enable an undertaking to operate when, for example, the energy or water supplies needed are lacking. The size of an incentive necessary to affect a firm's decision on location depends therefore on the need for and the scale of the complementary inducements which may not be directed towards the individual firm but to the generality. In circumstances in which the main obstacle is the deficiency in infrastructure and public services it is not until steps are taken to remedy these that financial incentives to a firm can have any effect at all. It follows too that small financial incentives - if any are needed at all - may be quite sufficient to turn the scale in some cases whereas large financial incentives to firms may have little or no effect in others in which insufficient attention is paid to the provision of needed infrastructure etc. Thus where there is a combination of factors which deter firms from establishing themselves or expanding in locations which are desirable from a public policy point of view it is the "package" of measures rather than any single one that matters.

The foregoing has been concerned with the effect of incentives on the decisions of firms in choosing between locations. The effectiveness of incentives can also be considered in terms of the influence they have on the areas or regions which they are designed to help by encouraging firms to move to or expand in them. The question here is: "how do incentives to firms provide economic expansion in one region rather than another, to a particular degree?"

Here also the effectiveness of incentives is not determined by their absolute size but their relevance to the conditions in the region concerned and to the way they compare with those in other regions. It is also determined by the number and scale and nature of firms which may be influenced by the incentives.

The term "footloose" can be applied to those firms which are not for one reason or another, tied to a particular area or location. The number of footloose firms is of course not static but varies with the general state of the economy and changes in the technical factors of operation which bear on location decisions. In an expanding economy, or one in which technical conditions alter, the needs of firms for different combinations of equipment, manpower and services of various kinds and the number of footloose firms may change rapidly. In a stagnant or unchanging economy the number may be small or declining. A given set of incentives can consequently have quite different effects in terms of securing movement towards the areas or regions in which the incentives apply. Since regions may of course not be dependent for their expansion on the attraction of footloose industry from other regions but have an indigenous industry capable of expansion, the effectiveness of incentives can also be judged by the degree to which they encourage such expansion.

Always bearing in mind that incentives can only influence location decisions if they sufficiently affect the totality of determining factors, a number of principles can be adduced in considering the effectiveness of incentives from the point of view, not of the firm, but of the region they are designed to assist.

Incentives may have little net effect on footloose industry (a) if conditions are already favourable to a sufficient movement of footloose industry to a region, (b) if conditions are so unfavourable that incentives are insufficient to outweigh them and (c) and if there is no footloose industry anyway. Alternatively both small and large incentives may have large effects on the movement of footloose industry if conditions are so closely similar that a marginal change in profitability could be decisive. Conversely, large incentives may have a small effect on movement (a) if conditions are so disadvantageous in the region in which the incentives apply as to outweigh the effect on profitability of the incentives, or (b) if operation still remains unprofitable, or (c) - again - if there is no footloose industry anyway.

The expansion in the economy of a region depending on the attraction of footloose industry is, of course, proportionate to the amount of footloose industry it attracts. If small incentives are sufficient to attract a large amount of footloose industry they can be described as "effective". Similarly large incentives which are insufficient to do so in the given circumstances can be described as "ineffective". The effectiveness or otherwise of incentives in attracting footloose industry into a region is therefore a function of the prevailing conditions and not only of the scale of the incentives. The fixing of incentives without reference to the disparities in conditions between regions may therefore make them less or more effective than they need be. It can also be observed that the effectiveness of given incentives varies over time as the disparities between regions vary. It can also vary with changes in their real value, as monetary or other circumstances change.

The same sort of arguments apply to the expansion of industry indigenous to a region. Large incentives may be needed in some cases, small in others, or small incentives may turn the scale in some cases, while large incentives may fail to do so in others.

The effectiveness of financial incentives of a given size in bringing new industry into a region, or in expanding existing industry within a region, also depends on whether they are automatically available to all firms meeting defined criteria or whether they are available only on a "selective" basis. The effects depend in both cases on the number and size of firms which would benefit. Small financial incentives influencing a large number of firms in an "automatic" system may have considerably larger effects than large incentives affecting only a small number of firms. It is also the case that relatively large "automatic" incentives may have little effect if the general circumstances of a region are not conducive to expansion, while comparatively large "selective" incentives may have a bigger effect if the selected enterprises are well chosen, in the circumstances of a region, to produce a general stimulus to the growth of other enterprises even though they may not be eligible for any direct financial incentive.

A further observation that may be made is that the effectiveness of incentives in bringing about expansion in regions through the attraction of "footloose" industry is a function not only of the scale and nature of the incentives and the disparities between regions but also of the size of the regions in which they apply compared with the rest of the country. A given amount of footloose industry can produce only a given amount of expansion in the regions to which it moves. The wider the area covered by the incentives the less footloose industry there is for each part of the region. Alternatively it may be stated that the widening of the areas covered by given incentives reduces the effective expansion possible in each region from a given supply of footloose industry.

All those propositions – both those relating to the effectiveness of incentives in influencing individual firms, or their effectiveness in securing expansion of economic activity in regions they are designed to assist are, or should be, self evident logical propositions. They can provide no answer to the question of what would be the right incentives in the particular circumstances of different countries. They can however assist to interpret situations which arise and also point to the principles to be observed if desired objectives are to be achieved in given circumstances.

A number of surveys have been made in OECD countries of the preferences of firms for different types of incentive.* All of these show, as is to be expected, that preferences vary between countries. If the above analysis is correct the reason is to be found, not in the arithmetic of incentives of different scale or nature, but in the circumstances of the economy in which they operate.

A clear understanding of the criteria for determining the effectiveness of financial incentives is necessary not only to help the choice of the right ones to fit particular circumstances. It is necessary also if the proper conclusions are to be drawn when comparing incentives offered by Governments. The belief or fear that "competitive" bidding in incentives can be harmful in leading to an undesirable degree of subsidization and to "distortions" of normal production and trade patterns gives rise to the making of such comparisons.

---

* "The Effects of Government Incentives on the Location Attitudes of Entrepreneurs", OECD (unpublished report).

The Working Party itself has suggested that incentives should be of similar magnitude in areas suffering from the same kind of disadvantages; that care should be taken to avoid giving disguised sectoral aids to uneconomic enterprises and that the problem of competitive bidding between countries requires consideration. In the EEC rules have been adopted specifying that the rate of investment support should not exceed a certain level in the central areas of the Community. What has been said so far suggests that the adoption of simple rules of comparison of financial incentives can have unintended results, since their relative effects or effectiveness cannot be measured by simple comparisons of percentage rates and the effectiveness of financial incentives given to firms, whether from the point of view of the firms themselves or from that of regional development, cannot be judged simply by considering the size of the incentive. It can only be judged within the total context of the economy of firms and regions.

Nonetheless some comments may be made on the way different types of financial incentives to firms can affect them individually. The "rational" firm in considering whether to locate its operations where it can take advantage of incentives would need to work out the "balance sheet" value as one at least of the elements which will influence the final decision.

The considerable variety of incentives and the many changes that have been made in most countries make it impracticable within the framework of this report to attempt an evaluation of actual incentives. (In the writer's opinion however it could well be useful if a detailed factual assessment could be made by a qualified international accountant into the balance sheet effects of the various financial incentives, which have been offered to enterprises in different countries over the years). All that can be done is to look into the matter in a general way.

For this purpose it may be sufficient to distinguish between the following main categories of financial incentives designed to improve a firm's "balance sheet":

1. Reliefs, concessions or modifications of direct taxes on company profits or revenues;

2. Grants for the purchase of equipment, machinery and plant;

3. Remissions or reductions of indirect taxes;

4. Grants or favourable terms for the acquisition of buildings;

5. Rebates or reduction of charges;

6. Grants or assistance towards running costs (operational grants);

7. Employment support grants or assistance;

8. Assistance for workers training and removal expanses;

9. Loans on favourable terms;

10. Guarantees of loan interest and/or repayments;

11. Special sectoral subsidies.

The list is not exhaustive and the individual terms may not entirely match the forms in which incentives may be offered in different countries. The list however shows the considerable variety of types of incentives that exist, each of which will have quite different effects on the balance sheets of individual firms according to their structure and the relative importance of the various elements within it. The incentives are not mutually exclusive and the total effect on a balance sheet depends on the eligibility of a firm for any or all of the range.

It has been noted that a financial incentive to a firm can only "turn the scale", i.e. induce a firm to choose a certain location if the differential advantage it gains, compared with the alternative locations, is large enough. It has also been noted that unless other conditions are satisfied even the most favourable financial incentives may serve no purpose. The aim at this point is therefore only to consider the differential benefit to the balance sheet involved in different types of incentives, without regard to whether the incentive provides an inducement to a firm to choose a given location.

1. Direct Taxes

Relief of direct taxes on profits can in theory take various forms, varying in general from applying different rates of tax (including exemption) on taxable profits, or providing differential allowances to reduce the taxable profit while maintaining common rates of tax. In practice the most common form is the provision of differential allowances for depreciation of capital equipment. In principle the effect is to leave a higher proportion of the net profits in the hands of the enterprise and thus enhance the return on the capital invested.

A number of points can be made about this method.

First, it only provides an incentive if the conditions for profitable operation exist in the incentive-location. This can be seen as having the merit of giving less or no encouragement to enterprises which are basically unprofitable or unsound. Conversely it can have the disadvantage that there is little or no encouragement to the establishment of firms which, if initially unprofitable, may become profitable at a later stage. (In illustration of the different views which it is possible to hold about this type of incentive it may be noted that, in the United Kingdom it was replaced by investment grants in 1965 because these had a more direct effect not related to profitability whereas in 1970 (vide Cmnd 4516) the new Government reverted to it for, inter alia, the same reasons).

Second, the effect of the tax relief, in whatever form, depends on the importance of the tax burden to a company and on the rate of return on capital necessary to justify (in its own eyes) an investment. If the difference between high initial allowances or "free depreciation" on the one hand and "normal" depreciation on the other is only to provide for an earlier write off against tax, the differential effect over the life time of the equipment can be marginal; since a "rational" firm will have regard not only to profitability in the early years but in the future as well. The value of high initial allowances or free depreciation is in providing an earlier return on capital rather than significantly to increase the total return over the whole life (though it can do this). The effect on the total balance sheet of the company also depends on the ratio of the capital equipment to the total capital. It may serve to show the effect in a purely hypothetical case in which a 100 per cent initial allowance is contrasted with a 60 per cent initial allowance followed by equal annual writeoff to the outstanding balance over five years.

Assume the purchase of a piece of machinery costing 100 units and yielding a net return on capital after tax of 15 per cent. In the case of 100 per cent initial writeoff we may say that the net return is 15 per cent. In the second case it would be 60 per cent of 15 in the first year and 8 per cent of 15 in each of the remaining years: say $9 + (1 \times 5) = 14$ per cent. The difference is 1 per cent of the return on the capital invested in the equipment. If the equipment represents only half of the total capital invested the difference to the balance sheet is only one half of one per cent.

It has already been observed that the influence of any benefit received on a company's decision on location cannot be judged only by reference to the size of the benefit.

But it is clear that large differentials in depreciation allowances do not produce correspondingly large benefits to the balance sheet and can in some cases be so small as to have little significant effect at all.

The margin of benefit is of course narrowed still more if the return on capital is lower in the incentive location than in the alternative (owing for example to the need to incur extra costs in removal, training, etc.). Moreover, reductions in the rate of tax on profits can reduce the saving from tax benefits. Since tax rates on company profits do change, such effects as differential allowances may have will change although no change be made in the differential.

It is not suggested that "generous" systems of depreciation allowances do not provide an incentive to investment. They do so but they necessarily operate only on the margin of profitability (since there are very few if any tax systems which do not provide for the ultimate charging of the cost of capital equipment as a tax deductable expense). "Generosity" lies in the time over which the charging is permitted. The effect of the regional differential system is simply to act marginally on a margin. It would seem logical not to expect too much benefit in the shape of influencing a firm's location decisions.

2. Investment Grants

The system of investment grants contrasts with that of tax allowances in that it is an outright subsidy which does not depend on the tax position of a company. As has been noted it can represent a subsidy to profitable and unprofitable firms alike. Its influence as an incentive is, prima facie, directly proportionate to the amount of the subsidy in relation to the overall investment required for the enterprise. Even a large grant may still have no effect on a company's decision if it is not large enough to outweigh other costs or disadvantages in moving to the location to which the incentive applies.

Though a grant for the purchase of machinery or equipment is an outright subsidy the amount of the subsidy still depends on the tax treatment accorded to the purchase. If the cost of the purchase cannot be charged to tax, i.e. does not enjoy the benefit of depreciation allowances, the loss of the latter must be set against the grant in calculating the net benefit. It is of course open to Governments to decide to give depreciation allowances as well as a grant on the same machinery. (In the United Kingdom the new measures announced in March 1972 for the first time provided that tax allowances would be given on the full capital expenditure even when part of the expenditure is financed by regional development grants*.)

The regional incentive effect of a system of cash grants for purchase of equipment lies in the differential and the effect this has on comparative rates of return on capital. We take another hypothetical example, as illustration, in which the purchase costs 100 units and produces a return on the tax of 15 per cent.

In the case in which <u>no</u> grant is given and depreciation allowances are given on the basis of 60 per cent in the first year, followed by even

---

*   Cmnd 4942, para. 9.

allowances in the next five years (without a full 100 per cent write off)
the rate of return was reduced to 14 per cent.

A grant of 20 units would reduce the notional cost to 80. However
this should be raised by the loss of the depreciation allowance on the
20. If the system had been one of 100 per cent depreciation allowances
the firm would be in the same position. If the system had produced an
overall depreciation allowance on 20 of 19 (95 per cent) the notional
cost would be 99. The rate of return would be 115/99 or 16.2 per cent,
an improvement of 2.2 per cent. If, in addition, to the grant of 20 units
the firm was allowed to write off 95 per cent of the 20 the unrecouped
depreciation would be 1, and the notional cost of the purchase would be
81 instead of 80. The rate of return would be 15/81 or 18.5 per cent.

Exact comparisons between the systems of depreciation allowances
and investment grants are difficult to make not only because the terms
and conditions on which allowances and grants are made are not necessarily comparable, but also because results are different on different
assumptions regarding the life of an asset, the period over which it is
amortized for tax purposes, and the rate at which future revenues are
discounted. A study made of the effects of changing from investment
grants back to a depreciation allowance system in the United Kingdom
shows very different results in cases in which a five year life of an
asset is compared with a 20 year life.* The new system is shown to be
marginally beneficial in non development areas in the case of a longer
life and disadvantageous in the case of a shorter life. In the development areas it is disadvantageous in both cases but less so in respect
of the longer life.

Our particular example serves to show (a) that differences can be
marginal and (b) that a given percentage differential can mean quite
different things. It serves also to show (c) that tax treatment of an
investment grant can significantly affect the differential effect. These
conclusions may be deemed to be of some importance, particularly when
international comparisons are made of rates of grant or allowances,
and they call into question the validity of the assumption that two countries whose differential rates are the same are necessarily offering the
same incentives.

It remains true that the improvement of a firm's balance sheet
over a relevant period is a measure of the incentive effect to the firm
of the system. It is not possible from this however to deduce that one
system is necessarily more effective than another from the point of view
of encouraging development in backward regions. The important thing

* Scholefield and Frank, published in the Quarterly Review of the National
Westminster Bank, February, 1972.

here is both the number of firms which may be influenced to move to or expand in those regions and the degree to which their operations become self-sustaining in the longer term. If it were the case that, in the longer term, self-sustaining growth requires profitable operation, a system which is geared to such operation may produce more and better founded results in terms of regional development than one which initially produces a marginally better balance sheet in firms which have less possibility of profitable operations. The choice is in practice made as much on the basis of economic and political philosophy as on a single comparison of marginal differences between systems.

The relevance of this kind of analysis to the real world is that it seems to demonstrate that the incentive effects of these two types of incentives are not constant even when the differentials in rates remain unvaried. Other variables which determine the incentive effects include:

1. The general level of tax on company profits and revenues;

2. The tax allowance system as it affects firms in the regions to which the incentives do not apply;

3. The degree to which installation of plant and equipment is required;

4. The relative levels of profitability in the incentive and other regions;

5. The general economic "climate" as it affects interpreneurs' decisions to move or expand;

6. The extent of the areas to which the incentives apply;

7. The global value of the incentive;

8. The impact of other measures.

To ascertain what influence the use of the two types of incentives so far discussed has had it would be necessary to examine the situation as it has developed in each country in which they have been applied. This is a task for continuous survey and research. However the example of one country - the United Kingdom - can provide an illustration of the context in which the basic principles outlined above can operate.

In 1965 the system of incentives based on differential depreciation allowances was replaced by one of investment grants. (One reason for doing so was the findings of the National Economic Development Office that firms did not take sufficiently into account the effect of depreciation allowances on their balance sheets - see the report "Investment Appraisal", HMSO 1965).

In the same year the areas to which the incentives applied were widened to the "Development areas". Subsequently they were widened still further by the addition of "Special Development" and "Intermediate" areas.

In 1966 and 1967 severe fiscal measures were adopted, prior and subsequent to devaluation, which affected the buoyancy of the economy and the availability of mobile or footloose industry. These measures had a continuing effect in later years.

In 1970 the new administration replaced the system of investment grants by a new system of differential depreciation allowances. As a temporary measure to encourage investment generally the initial allowance in non development areas was raised to 80 per cent. The total aid programme to the assisted areas was kept at broadly the same level but there was an increased emphasis on expenditure on infrastructure in the assisted areas. (The implication of this was that there was a fall in the global value of the incentives to firms). In addition the intention to "phase out" the Regional Employment Premium was announced.

The new administration also reduced the rate of Corporation Tax from 45 per cent, first to $42\frac{1}{2}$ per cent and subsequently to 40 per cent. Other fiscal measures were also adopted in the 1971 budget to increase the growth rate of the economy.

In 1972 further budgetary measures designed to revitalize the economy and encourage consumption as well as investment were introduced. A new organisation was set up to promote development in the depressed regions. The areas for assistance were further widened. Initial depreciation allowances were raised to 100 per cent for the whole country, more emphasis was placed on "selective" measures and regional development grants, not to be offset by withholding of depreciation allowances, were introduced with varying applications to the different types of assisted area.

It would require a study in depth to evaluate over the period 1966-71, the precise contribution that investment grants and depreciation allowances made to regional development. The writer can only express the personal opinion that during the period neither system had more than a marginal influence on decisions to invest in the assisted regions and that the impact of the other factors was far greater.

The period was also one of uncertainty about the future of the economy, of low profitability and increasingly of cost push inflation. While profitability showed some improvement in 1971 this was, at least in part, due to economies made in the use of labour and was not accompanied by any marked resurgence in investment. Against this background and with the numerous changes made in the incentive system it would seem not only that its influence was marginal but that it was also declining. In all these circumstances the difficulties facing the enterpreneur in calculating the benefits to his balance sheet from the incentives, especially long term benefits, will have been accentuated. It is perhaps not surprising that by early 1972 the Government concluded that new measures to stimulate industrial growth and to create confidence were needed and that they would have to be "as clear, simple and certain in the impact as possible" (Cmnd 4942, HMSO 1972).

Turning now to the other types of incentive listed many of the general remarks that have been made apply equally to these when considered individually. The remission of indirect taxes, customs and excise duties or local charges, assistance towards buildings, act variously according to the size of the incentive, the importance of the particular item to the firm, the economic climate in a country generally or in the regions for which special stimuli are deemed necessary. Since the cost of buildings may represent a considerable proportion of the investment capital of a new project a more significant reduction in their costs to the entrepreneur may be more effective than a reduction in local charges or indirect taxes. Taken by themselves the effect of the latter would seem more often to be of a symbolic character, indicating the general attitude of the authorities to investment in certain localities rather than a substantial relief to the entrepreneur's balance sheet. Nonetheless if the various incentives are given together their influence must depend on the size of the "package" taken as a whole and, if other circumstances are favourable, the total effect of the "package" may be greater than the sum of the individual items might suggest. As the practice of countries varies considerably it is not possible to generalize about the effectiveness of these types of incentive, other than to point out that "packages" which are limited to a few minor reliefs can not be expected to have a significant influence on entrepreneurs' major long term location decisions.

Some further observations can however be made on the remaining types of assistance listed as (6) (7) (9) (10) (11).

6. Operational Grants

An example of operational grants is provided by the United Kingdom following the creation in 1968 of the "Special Development Areas". Under the local Employment Act grants could be made to new incoming industry of 30 per cent of eligible wage and salary costs during the first three years of operation. This was an additional benefit to those already available for development areas, but a limiting condition was that the incoming industry should provide sufficient new employment to

justify the assistance sought.* These operational grants were super-
seded by the new system of regional incentives announced in March 1972
(Cmnd 4942).

It would be interesting if the United Kingdom authorities could make
available an analysis of the actual effects of these grants. In the absence
of such an analysis it is only possible to make some theoretical observations. A 30 per cent grant towards wage and salary costs can obviously
mean significantly different things to firms with different proportions
of personnel to other costs and varying build-up periods to the full
development of the employment potential. If an hypothetical proportion
were taken of say 40 per cent a grant of 30 per cent would reduce costs
by 12 per cent. This would be more than marginal over the period in
which the incentive was available. Under the conditions in which it
was available however it could only be expected to have a significant
effect (a) if prospects of profitable operation after the expiry of the
three years were sufficient to outweight the disadvantages of the location and (b) if the proportion of personnel to other costs attracted a
sufficient amount of grant. As has already been noted conditions regarding future prospects were uncertain and this alone might have mitigated
against the effectiveness of the incentive in the prevailing conditions.
The stated view of the United Kingdom Government (Cmnd 4942 paragraph 13) was that the limitation to projects providing employment ruled
out this form of assistance for many modernization projects. The regional grants under the new system are therefore not limited in this
way and are to apply also to firms already established in the assisted
areas. A conclusion that can be drawn is that operational grants designed to lower current costs are more effective if they continue for an
adequate period, if they are not tied to restrictive conditions and if
there are sufficient numbers of firms willing and able to benefit by them.

7.   Employment Support Grants

The "classical" form of employment support grants is the Regional
Employment Premium in the United Kingdom payable to manufacturers.
Other methods of relieving an employer's wages bill are also possible
e.g. by reduction or elimination of social security charges in designated
areas (Italy). The effect of this on a firm's balance sheet depends on
the proportion of wages costs to the total. It can have little effect on
highly "capital intensive" undertakings. Its effects on the demand for
labour depends also on the elasticity of demand. In conditions of overall
depression or in which labour demand is reduced by technological change
and increasing capital intensiveness or more economic use of labour

---

*   See official Brochure of the Department for Trade and Industry: Incentives for
Industry in the Assisted Areas December 1971, summary p. 6).

the effect may not be noticeable even if it results in more labour being employed than would otherwise be the case. In the United Kingdom unemployment continued to rise in the development areas even after the introduction of the Premium but this is no proof that it may not have had some effect. As has been noted however the effect of an incentive on footloose industry is likely to be larger the more it alters the comparative advantage of the incentive area over the long term life of the enterprise.

In the United Kingdom the rate of grant payable per adult male employee was £ 1. 50 weekly, perhaps 8-10 per cent of the wages bill. On a hypothetical proportion of wages to other costs of 40 per cent this could have meant a subsidy of 3-4 per cent of total costs in each year. However the initial period for which the Premium was assured was seven years. This meant that its gross discounted value declined year by year. By the fourth year manufacturers could count upon it only for another three years and the decision announced in late 1970 to phase it out by 1974 without any indication that anything would take its place virtually eliminated it as a long term incentive. In the prevailing circumstances of the United Kingdom economy from 1967 onwards it is difficult to believe that the incentive could have played a significant part in steering manufacturing industry to the assisted areas; insofar as it did the effect would have continuously declined as time moved towards the terminal year.

It would however be wrong to deduce from this one example that employment support grants could have no significant effects in any circumstances. They obviously could do so (a) if the rate and duration are significant, (b) if demand for labour is elastic in the areas or regions in which the grant is available (c) if shortage of labour is a limiting factor on the expansion of industry, or supply is inelastic in the non-assisted regions and (d) if other factors are conducive to the expansion of labour intensive industry, (e) if the grant applies to those industries which have the capacity to expand labour demand. It may be noted, en passant, that at the time the REP was proposed in the United Kingdom conditions still reflected the post war shortage of manpower (see Green Paper "The Development Areas: a Proposal for a Regional Employment Premium" paragraph 24). The considerable change in the national economy in the years following the introduction of the REP rather than the validity of the theory on which it was based, may have been the explanation of its apparent lack of effect.

It may be useful at this point to refer to an argument that has been used in favour of employment support grants, namely that, because it applies to areas of labour surplus it can bring about an increase in total demand for labour without inflationary consequences. This assumed that no upward pressure on wage levels is exerted by the workers to take advantage of the higher incomes of firms due to the grants and that there is no spill over of the grant revenue by higher spending by the recipient firms in other regions. Neither of these assumptions necessarily hold in all circumstances.

9. and 10. Loans and Guarantees

The advantages and disadvantages of State financed loan and guarantee schemes must turn in the first place on the availability of capital and the terms on which it is available from the commercial market. In countries with a highly developed capital market extending to all parts of the economy any firm launching a commercially viable project can obtain capital, whether equity or loan on current market terms. If the project is otherwise viable the fact that it is undertaken in a declining or backward region does not necessarily mitigate against its chances of raising capital on the open market. On the other hand even in countries with well developed capital markets there may be scope for State loan schemes to meet particular needs or to assist undertakings which, for a variety of reasons, may not have access to the market, e. g. some State industries or firms in which the State may have a controlling interest. In countries with less developed capital markets State loan schemes may be the only or main way in which new enterprises can hope to raise capital for projects in areas suffering from special disabilities.

The simple difference in interest rate chargeable on a market and a State loan is not necessarily a measure of the incentive effect of a State loan, if a firm is unable to raise a market loan. The provision of a State loan may make all the difference between going ahead with a project and giving it up altogether. Where there is a choice, a marginal difference in the rate of interest may not be a decisive factor in inducing a firm to operate in one region rather than another unless it is accompanied by other inducements (as it often is). To take a hypothetical case, if a firm is able to earn a 15 per cent rate of return on capital in an investment in a region of first choice and only a 12 per cent rate of return in an investment in a region of the Government's choice a difference of 1 or 2 per cent in the rate at which it can obtain capital may not be decisive in encouraging it to choose the Government's preferred location. On the other hand it could turn the scale if rates of return were approximately equal.

The influence of interest rates could also be different for firms of different sizes and according to the other conditions which may accompany a State loan, such as the repayment terms, the degree of supervision or State participation and the extent to which the loan may be linked with other benefits such as the provision of local or State services, infrastructure etc.

141

It may be noted that State loans play a very small part in the incentive armoury of the United Kingdom and a larger part in those of Italy, Japan (and Germany). Yet it would appear that only in Italy are they regarded by firms as being a significant part of the package of incentives obtained by firms which have been induced to develop in the Mezzogiorno.

Very few countries use the system of loan guarantees as an alternative to direct loans. In essence it enables a firm to raise a loan from a commercial source, such as a bank, while transferring the risk from the source to the guarantor. The benefit to the firm is that it is enabled to raise capital when it could not otherwise do so. The benefit from the point of view of a region depends on the opportunities it can offer to earn the required return and the number and size of the additional firms that would be influenced by their ability to obtain guarantees, and who would not be able to raise capital on equal terms in the open market. If, as is often the case, the conditions for guarantees are as stringent as those imposed by the capital market itself, the effectiveness of the guarantee system as a means of encouraging development in selected areas would be correspondingly limited. We consider that the disadvantage of the guarantee system is that it substitutes the judgement of the guarantor for that of market institutions and can only be really effective if it is applied so leniently as to encourage "unsound" enterprises. It would seem more straight-forward and less open to this objection to provide capital at favourable rates to enterprises which could pass the test of viability.

The effectiveness of loans and guarantees on regional development depends not only on the term and conditions but on the amount of additional capital provided through either system. Their effectiveness can also be limited by the need for selective administration if each application has to be carefully scrutinized and by the type of accompanying conditions, such as a requirement that the borrower or guarantor raises a given proportion of the total capital. On the other hand if loans can be made available on a large scale to enterprises which can make a significant impact on development they can have a more marked influence in a region than automatic forms of assistance which may be beneficial to a firm yet not produce, in the prevailing circumstances, any new development.

11. Special Sectoral Subsidies

All the incentives discussed so far, whether they are automatic or selective, are of a type which apply to firms meeting certain defined criteria. Thus investment grants or depreciation allowances are given to firms installing machinery or equipment, building grants for buildings for certain types of enterprise, labour support grants to employers of labour and loans to selected enterprises contributing to development. Many apply only to manufacturing industry and though selective in this sense are not confined to particular branches of such industry. There is however another form of incentive, namely grants and loans or other forms of assistance, to particular sectors of industry.

Some sectoral subsidies are given nationally to provide support for particular industries facing special problems and though they may have diverse effects in different regions according to the importance of the industry concerned, they are not specifically designed as regional incentives. On the other hand it is recognized in some countries that support schemes for particular industries may be an effective means for coping with regional problems where, for example, a region may depend to a large extent on a declining industry and other alternative industry is unlikely, despite general incentives, to develop to a sufficient degree. Schemes of financial support for particular agricultural crops provide one example. Another example are schemes for selective assistance to the shipbuilding industries in a number of countries.

Since the United Kingdom has been among the countries in the vanguard of those pursuing vigorous regional policies it is of some interest to note that early in 1972 the Government reached the conclusion, following a review of regional policy, that there was a need to supplement the many general or basic incentives by broadening the scope for schemes of selective assistance to particular industries. It had already conducted a special "rescue" operation (after several earlier unsuccessful attempts) for the particular case of Upper Clyde Shipbuilders, in the development area of Scotland. Further general measures to assist the shipbuilding industry were however considered necessary since "the short term difficulties of the shipbuilding industry are urgent and immediate help is needed". Since over 90 per cent of the employment provided by the main merchant shipbuilding firms were in the development areas the aids proposed for this sector can therefore be regarded as regional policy measures. Temporary assistance was to be provided in the shape of tapering grants in the period 1972-74 in respect of the construction and equipment of new ships over 100 gross tons. The grants were to be at the rate of 10 per cent on the contract value of work carried out in 1972 and at the rates of 4 per cent and 3 per cent in 1973 and 1974 respectively. A necessary requirement for the success of this short term assistance was an improvement in the conduct of industrial relations (Cmnd 4942 paragraph 38).

How far these measures will succeed in their purpose remains to be seen. It is not our purpose to examine their merits per se but to cite them as a particular example of sectoral aids with a regional purpose. The difference between this type of incentive and the more general types is that it is specifically geared to the problem of an industry important in the context of regions in which the possibilities of alternative employment - despite the general incentives available - are very limited. The adoption of this type of incentive also implies that, for a given amount of State aid, more results can be achieved in terms of employment and industrial recovery than in other ways.

A further important feature of sectoral assistance is that it cannot necessarily be confined to industries located in the regions with special difficulties. In countries in which a particular industry may be spread over many regions and constitutes an integrated whole the most appropriate form of assistance may be of an industry-wide character, irrespective of the location of particular plants or enterprises. Regional and national economic growth are closely interlinked and the logic of this is to look at the needs of whole industrial sectors to maximize the effects of any assistance deemed necessary. This principle appears to be recognized by the specific statement in the United Kingdom White Paper, paragraph 36, which says "On occasion ... it may be necessary to consider the wider structure of an industry or major project beyond the boundaries of the assisted areas. The Government will seek new power also to provide selective assistance more widely in such cases."

It could be useful to examine the systems of sectoral support which exist in many OECD countries to determine how far they lend themselves, or are intended, to bring special benefit to particular regions. Without a detailed study it would be unsafe to generalize. However it might well be found that some systems of sectoral support, e. g. in agriculture, may be so designed as to give more help to certain disadvantaged regions. On the other hand they are not necessarily confined to such regions and in some cases may give very little assistance to regions whose basic problem is the decline of agriculture as a source of employment and income. It could well be therefore that some advantage would be gained by a specific study of the marginal effects of schemes of sectoral support to determine how they could lend themselves more to achieving certain of the objectives of regional policy.

So far we have listed and discussed the various types of incentives and the discussion has perhaps served to show the difficulty of reaching any clear conclusions as to their effectiveness, whether taken individually or as a "package", either on the balance sheets of firms or on the degree of regional growth which they can occasion. Perhaps one of the more important conclusions is that the degree of effectiveness can be assessed only in the context of the general situation of the regional and national economies, and as this changes, so does the effectiveness of particular incentives.

There is one further point to be added for completeness and that is the multiplier or "trigger" effect of a system of incentives within the regions in which they are applied. Insofar as incentives do in fact work

144

to encourage firms to establish themselves, or, if already established, to expand in designated regions their effects may well be spread beyond the firms themselves. An obvious point is that incentives which success-fully generate growth in manufacturing industry may stimulate, as a secondary effect, the growth of service industries in the surrounding areas. How far this happens is again dependent on the general econ-omic climate as well as the particular circumstances of a region, the nature of the industries benefitting from the incentives, and the degree of confidence in the longer term future. It may also depend on the degree to which complementary or conflicting policies are adopted which especially on the non assisted sectors.

In this connection it may be noted from the Italian experience that while there was considerable success in establishing in parts of Southern Italy some major basic industries the growth of secondary and tertiary industries was comparatively limited, a fact which has been commented on by many observers, official and academic. How far this was due to the nature of local circumstances, e. g. the lack of commercially advanc-ed population, the insufficiency of markets for secondary industries or the difficulty of securing capital for unassisted enterprises it would be impracticable for one with no intimate knowledge of the region to judge. As a general proposition it might however be asserted that unless adequate attention is given to the problem involved in the growth of the secondary and tertiary sectors the effectiveness of incentives confined to basic or major industries can be less than it would otherwise be. It may also be noted that, in the United Kingdom, the intensification of incentive measures from 1965, designed to encourage manufacturing industry in the development areas was accompanied by a measure for the restraint of employment in the service industries, noteably through the imposition of the Selective Employment Tax. To the extent that this did in fact discourage employment (on which no opinion is offered) in the services field it could have operated to reduce the multiplier or trigger effect of the manufacturing incentives. This example is cited, not as a comment on the suitability of the measure in the general economic climate of the time but as a possible further illus-tration of the thesis that the secondary effects of the incentives depend on the existence, or absence, of complementary policies relating to the unassisted sectors. It might also reasonably be suggested that the im-position of any measure of restraint on the secondary and tertiary sector, for whatever good reason, tends to reduce the beneficial effects of incentives on the other sectors.

OTHER CONSEQUENCES OF INCENTIVES

So far the question that has been considered is the effectiveness of various types of incentives as they influence firms and as they influence the regions in which they operate. It is desirable to consider also what other consequences they have in the context of national economic policies and their international setting and how far they may be compatible with other objectives of economic policy besides those of regional development. The Working Party itself has identified a number of questions which reflect a concern that they can have what might be termed "side effects" such as possible "distortions" of international competitive conditions, the fostering or encouragement of uneconomic enterprises and competitive overbidding for international capital investment. A systematic examination of the other consequences of incentive systems may provide a perspective within which such questions can be fruitfully considered.

Perhaps the first point to be made is that all incentives constitute a claim on resources which, in the economic sense, are always scarce, for there are always alternative uses to which they can be put. It has to be recognized that the motives for incentive schemes are often of a political character, reflecting the need for political purposes, to show that some action is being taken to deal, for example, with acute problems of regional imbalance. In a technical report it can only be noted that such motives may underly the choice and scale of some incentive schemes and that such political advantage as may be gained is not necessarily matched by economic benefit. The suggestion has been made in the Working Party that the criteria for applying incentives should be economic rather than political. Though it is not to be expected that a proposition of this kind would be acceptable to Governments faced with political problems arising from disparities in the social and economic life of different regions it nonetheless remains true that if the economic benefits from incentives are not commensurate with the resources devoted to them they constitute a net burden on the economy as a whole. How far any net burden is acceptable is essentially a matter for political judgement and how far particular incentive schemes constitutes a burden is a matter for factual determination in individual cases rather than for theory.

There is nothing illegitimate in a country being willing to pay a price for regional development. If the price is lower national economic growth than could have been obtained by a different use of the same resources it may well be worth paying in return for the benefit of a more balanced distribution of what economic growth there is. What is less legitimate is to assume that incentives which aim to steer development to particular regions contribute to national growth in all circumstances. This is clearly not valid when incentives succeed in diverting resources from areas of high return to those of lower, or when they are misapplied to industries with no capacity for self sustaining growth or long term survival or when they are absorbed by the beneficiaries with no effect at all on economic growth. The previous sections of this chapter have shown how difficult it can be to assess the effectiveness of various types of incentive. Few countries, including relatively wealthy countries, can meet all the claims on their resources and really afford to waste those they have. In such circumstances there would seem to be no case for exempting regional incentives from close scrutiny of their effectiveness to ensure that the resources devoted to them are not in fact wasted.

The problem may not as yet be a very serious one since in many countries the proportion of total resources applied to regional objectuves remains relatively small. However as the weight given to them increases, and the range, scope and scale of incentives widens and becomes more sophisticated the need for safeguards against the danger of wasteful use of resources becomes more important. The answer does not lie in abandoning incentives but in attempting to ensure that they are properly attuned to their objectives and to the situations on which they operate. In the writer's view the available evidence suggests that this has not always been sufficiently recognized and that this has resulted, in some countries, not only in a wasteful use of resources but also in a recognized lack of success in achieving objectives of regional policy.

The question of whether incentives encourage uneconomic enterprises is linked to the one discussed in the preceding paragraphs in that the maintenance of uneconomic enterprises may well constitute a waste of resources or a net burden on the national economy without commensurate economic benefit. It would go beyond the scope of a work devoted to the issues of regional policy to consider the merits or otherwise of State subvention or support of industries in a general way. Though Adam Smith may well be turning unceasingly in his grave as his spirit contemplates the degree to which the State intervenes in the economic affairs of nations, the fact remains that the subsidization of industry of one kind or another is a feature of the modern economic scene. The use of incentives for purposes of regional policies is only one species of a widely prevalent genus. There is no reason to single them out for special criticism based on a general belief that subsidies as such are harmful, or to maintain that they are in their nature so special that they cannot have the same sort of consequences, for better or worse, than subsidies for other purposes. What is more useful is to consider whether some forms of regional incentives are more likely than others to produce harmful consequences such as the promotion of uneconomic enterprises.

It should be noted that the country studies and examinations conducted by the Working Party have revealed that most, if not all Governments have been conscious of the need to avoid the creation of uneconomic enterprises by the use of incentives. Where grants or loans are made on a selective basis to individual industries the overt aim has been to

147

create enterprises which have, at least after the initial years, a chance of independent survival on a commercial basis. The concept is that of "infant" industries applied regionally. As with infant industries general- ly the question is always when will the infant grow up and what happens if the period of adolescence is over prolonged? Even when incentives are automatic i.e. grants or tax reliefs for the installation of plant and equipment, or employment premiums, their "once for all" nature, the limited duration of availability and their marginal influence on profitability may be held to limit the danger of promoting unviable projects.

The danger nonetheless exists and varies from one type of incentive to another and according to the circumstances of the particular industry or industries which may benefit from them.

An existing industry or enterprise may be uneconomic for a variety of reasons. It may be subject to severe competition from lower cost (or higher productivity) producers. Its products may be ill-suited to the market, its equipment and buildings obsolete, its labour productivity low, its location unfavourable and its organisation and management inefficient. Such industries may need radical change and reorganisation before they become permanently viable. If they are able to benefit by financial incentives their short term profitability may be improved; but unless they use the breathing space so afforded to make the radical changes necessary, and are in fact able to do so the incentives may act as a palliative rather than a cure and can indeed help an enterprise to postpone the effort to remedy its basic disabilities. In the longer term it may remain as before, incapable of economic operation in a competi- tive world and the resources used as incentives are largely wasted.

The same may apply when incentives encourage the establishment of new undertakings on the wrong scale for long term viability, in un- favourable locations producing higher operational costs or where there is insufficient scope for adjustment. The incentives may cause such disabilities to be discounted but as their effects wear off, or cease to be available, the undertaking finishes up in less favourable circumstances than those of its competitors operating in conditions with fewer disabil- ities.

It may of course be said that none of these dangers exist if new or expanding firms correctly calculate and allow for all the hazards. This is true, but it is also true that firms which are struggling for existence in adverse conditions may grasp at any life line that is thrown out to them or, like individuals, may prefer to keep their heads above water for as long as possible rather than attempt a long swim to distant shores offering better chance of ultimate survival.

Incentives which encourage firms to maintain a larger labour force than they would otherwise do, may be beneficial in terms of employment. Insofar as they are effective they may mitigate against the most economic use of labour. When, or if the incentive ceases the firm may be less competitive than other firms elsewhere which have had no labour subsidies and may therefore have economized on labour costs. Since the "regional problem" in many countries is a surplus of labour in disadvantaged regions, the use of temporary labour-oriented incentives may produce a short term solution at the cost of creating enterprises which may become unviable when the incentives ceases. Whether the price is worth paying is a matter for political judgement. Uneconomic industries may be better than no industries at all; but they may be very disadvantageous if they stand in the way of the development of alternative, more economic industries. If no such alternatives exist the prolongation of the period over which labour incentives are available may be preferable to cutting them off and leaving the industries less capable of facing competition.

There is little information available to enable a judgement to be made of how far the use of regional incentives has in practice led to the maintenance or establishment of uneconomic industries. It would certainly not be true to assert that all the industries which have been supported or benefitted by incentives of various kinds in the South of Italy, the development areas of the United Kingdom, the expansion zones in Spain and France or in the maritime industrial areas of Japan are uneconomic. Many of them, especially perhaps the newer industries are modern, well equipped and favourably located. Other factors, besides direct financeial incentives have played their part in creating the necessary conditions for economic operation. The attention that is paid in Italy, as evidenced by the system of "planned negotiations", to the overall conditions in which industry is encouraged, or in the United Kingdom to the need for fundamental reorganisation of such industries as shipbuildings before financial support is provided suggests that safeguards against the development of uneconomic enterprises are recognized to be necessary. The fact remains that many incentives are available without any safeguards and the Working Party's concern that they may lead to the maintenance or creation of uneconomic enterprises would seem to be not entirely without foundation.

A further consequence of regional financial incentives is the repercussions they can have on regions outside those in which they apply. The repercussions are of three kinds. Incentive money is not necessarily wholly spent in the region in which it is received. It may be used for equipment obtainable from other regions (or from abroad) or for specialized labour which may be required to be brought into the region e.g. for construction, installation or operation of buildings and equipment. Secondly firms which have integrated operations in several regions may be able to use some incentives to free their own resources for use in other regions than those in which the incentives supply. Thirdly the income benefit from the investment generated by the incentive does not necessarily accrue to the region. It may also be added that the income from administration of incentive schemes - which sometimes can represent a substantial proportion of an incentive - accrues in the region in which the administration is centred. The decentralization of administration can of course help to reduce this effect.

Again there is very little information available to show the interregional distribution of the expenditure of incentive funds or the income flows which they may generate. The distribution will be very different according to the types of incentives, the interregional pattern of production, and ownership of the created assets. The short term and long term repercussions will also be different; the purchase of equipment may provide only a short term boost outside a region while a new asset within a region will have effects over its life time.

Grants or investment allowances are normally spent where the plant and machinery is available. In concrete terms the installation of steel-making or manufacturing equipment in Southern Italy may have to be preceded by the manufacture of equipment in Northern Italy. The development of a manufacturing industry in the "polygon" of development of Seville creates a demand for equipment from possibly, Bilbao, Barcelona - or Birmingham. The highly automated steel plant in, say, Mizushima may increase employment in the plant manufacturing areas of Japan without adding much employment in Mizushima. The modernization, with State assistance, of the shipyards of Northern Ireland or Scotland may involve subcontracting throughout Britain.

The long term effect on the non incentive regions depends on how sustained the demand for their product is likely to be. In conditions in which existing capacity is utilized to the full, a sustained additional demand may require new capacity to be created or lead to inflationary pressures on existing capacity. Paradoxical as it may seem, policies which seek to overcome inflationary pressures by transferring demand to non pressure regions may still lead to inflationary conditions in the pressure areas through the repercussion effect of incentive expenditure.

Employment grants, given on the basis of numbers already employed can encourage or enable some firms to expand their labour force. On the other hand firms which can meet the demand for their products without any expansion of the labour force may find it more advantageous to use the incentive money received for other purposes and elsewhere than in the incentive region. It may be noted that some criticism was made of the Regional Employment Premium in the United Kingdom on this score.

Whatever form incentives may take the income generated by an investment is in the profits, interest and dividends received by the owner of the asset, the wages and salaries of the employed personnel and the net profit earned by suppliers to the enterprise and staff. It follows that the regional income benefits from an external investment brought about by incentives may be less in the case of capital intensive than of labour intensive projects. The fact that in Southern Italy much of the investment in the early years of the development programme was of this nature emphasizes the importance of this point. To illustrate it by a hypothetical example; a project costing, say, $ 100 million and yielding 15 per cent on capital produces an annual income to the owner of $ 15 million. At an assumed "cost per job" of $ 20,000 it would provide 5,000 jobs requiring an average wage or salary of $ 3,000 to produce as much local income as the return on the capital invested. The local benefit would be greater insofar as there is local participation in the capital investment or smaller if the project is still more capital intensive and wages and salaries are lower in total. Such hypothetical figures do no more than illustrate how important external repercussions can be. (They do not of course mean that the incentives which produce large benefits outside the region are not worthwhile. The incentive normally forms only a part of the total capital investment, and the benefit in terms of local employment and income may be deemed worthwhile return).

The point is of some importance also in considering the way in which regional policies can influence the problem of "imbalance" - a problem which is discussed at some length in another chapter. It serves to show that while a capital intensive investment may, if successful, increase the income of a disadvantaged or incentive region it can also increase the income of other regions. Insofar as it does so the "disparity" or imbalance may remain, or not diminish in proportion to the investment (especially, also, if the return on the investment is higher than it would be if made in the non incentive regions). The fact, noted elsewhere, that the high and discriminatory level of investment in Southern Italy has not brought about a narrowing of the income disparity with the North may possibly be partly explained by the capital intensive nature of much of the development assisted by incentives of various kinds and the external source of the capital inflow.

"Distortion of competition" is, in principle, as much a consequence of regional incentives as it is of other forms of financial support given for other purposes deemed by Governments to be in the public interest. Those who believe that all forms of support of industry lead to "distortion" of a harmful kind would have no reasons to exempt regional incentives from fundamental criticism of the whole principle. How far it is a "good" or "bad" thing to cause distortions is a basic controversial issue that has existed since economics became a respectable subject in its own right, or since that classic clash between mercantilism and laissez-faire began to define the economic issues which ultimately are only resolved according to the weight of political forces and the political philosophies they express. Arguments, pro and con, about distortions of competition brought about by incentives underly equally the division between those who believe that the State should intervene as little as possible in the conduct of economic affairs and those whose belief is that the State has a positive duty to guide or plan the economy, to correct the ill effects of competition and to substitute other principles than free competition as the directing force of economic development and change. In modern times the wide range of intervention in the economy made by all States indicates that the issue nowadays is not whether the State should intervene at all but how far it should intervene and what are the advantages and disadvantages of particular forms of intervention in given circumstances.

International agreements exist to regulate the use of practices which distort and frustrate competition. They do not prevent the use of incentives for defined purposes recognized by the participants in the agreements to be desirable. The test for rejecting or accepting particular incentives is the pragmatic one of whether it can be reconciled with the general objective of the agreement, such as, for example, the furtherance of international trade, or, if it is not reconcilable, whether a case exists for a derogation from the general objective. It is no part of the task of this report to examine how far regional incentives constitute departures from the principles of international agreements, since this is a matter for the participants. The aim here is the limited one of considering the ways in which incentives for regional policy purposes produce "distortions" and how far the consequences can be said to be beneficial or otherwise.

It should be said boldly at the outset that the purpose of regional incentives is actually to create "distortions" i.e. to bring about situations different from those that would result from the free play of competition or unfettered "natural" economic forces. It is because the free play of economic forces may lead to the decline of industries important to whole regions and their populations or to the retardation of development of "backward" regions that incentives are offered at all. The whole object is to correct, adjust or modify the regional distribution of economic activity to achieve a more acceptable situation. To prove that incentives bring about distortions is not to prove that they are undesirable or unnecessary. That is their very raison d'être. It can also be said that the more successful incentives are the greater the "distortion" they may entail. The practical question is whether any limits should be placed on incentives to avoid excessive or harmful distortions. This can be approached from both the internal and external (international) aspects of a country's economy and in relation to the different types and levels of incentive.

152

Internally, the granting of financial assistance to firms in certain regions places them in a more favourable position vis-a-vis their competitors in other regions than they would otherwise be. The benefit reinforces their financial position and enables them to withstand competition much more successfully. If the benefit is not large enough to offset their disabilities compared with those of their competitors in other regions the incentive is insufficient - a large "distortion" is required to offset large disparities. If the benefit more than offsets the disabilities it places their recipients in a more favourable competitive position than their rivals in other regions, even to the extent of reducing the latter's own capacity to survive.

The same is true in relation to external competition. If the incentives are large enough the beneficiaries can better withstand foreign competition or indeed weaken the foreign competitor.

The ultimate effect on the national economy internally depends not only on the response to the incentives in the beneficiary region. It depends also on the response of those affected in the other regions. They may be able or willing to accept a lower level of profitability for example by cutting prices in order to maintain their competitive position, so nullifying the incentive. If they are not willing or able to do so they may contract or close down, or, alternatively seek to obtain the benefit of the incentives by transferring operations to the beneficiary region. Since firms are affected differently some may react one way, others another. The same applies of course to firms within the beneficiary region.

In all these cases the "distortion" effect is in the change of the relative competitive position of producers in different locations. This may not produce any growth in national output and insofar as it leads to a shift from favourably to unfavourably placed - lower cost to higher cost - locations there can even be a net loss to the national economy. Since the objective of the incentive is to bring about such a shift there can be no complaint on this score. If however, there is no shift, but an offsetting reduction of profitability, the regional objective is not achieved but the terms on which producers compete have nonetheless been altered - the beneficiary possible being the consumer of the products, who may, at home and abroad, get them at lower cost.

There is however an essential difference between the internal and external effects of such "distortions". In the former the decision is made by the Government of the country concerned on the basis of its concept of the national interest. If it decides that it is in the national interest to bring about an interregional shift in profitability of producers in non incentive regions, the "distortion effects", such as they are, represent a price willingly paid. In the latter however the Government of a country affected by the "distortion" of competition has a different national interest which it may consider is adversely affected. Since the benefit from distortions of competition to the regions of another country is of no direct concern to it, it does not have to take this into account in deciding what remedial action, if any, is called for.

If the foregoing analysis is correct the conclusion that would follow is that "distortions" of competition are inherent in any system of regional incentives and that any benefits or disbenefits (such as the creation of uneconomic enterprises, as discussed previously) are those which stem from the use of incentives themselves. It would not be logical to assert that distortions of competition are in themselves harmful domestically if they result in the regional benefits the distortions - or the incentives giving rise to them - are designed to bring about. The position is different in the international field because it is open to other countries to respond to distortions of competition affecting their own trade by countervailing measures which, if pursued far enough, may not only nullify regional policies of the countries against which they are directed but could hamper the development of international trade, bringing mutual loss all round.

While there have been instances of disputes between individual countries over the effect of regional incentives in special cases, no evidence has been supplied to the Working Party which suggests that the danger of widespread adoption of measures to countervail regional incentives is more than a theoretical one at the present time. Most countries pursue regional policies involving the use of incentives of one kind or another, and in the total perspective of factors affecting international trade the level of incentives offered by most countries is statistically very small. Both factors are conducive to mutual tolerance of such distortions of competition as have occured. As however systems of regional incentives are strengthened in order to make regional policies more effective the international effects of distortions of competition could become more noticeable. It would well be advantageous for countries to attempt to agree in advance on the limits to be set to incentive systems before they create distortions which prove unacceptable and lead to a round of countervailing restrictions. The OECD might be well suited to take the lead in promoting the examination of this question in conjunction with other international bodies concerned.

COMPETITIVE OVERBIDDING

Regional incentive systems, can, like any other attempts to induce people to do something else than they would otherwise do, give rise to the problem known as "overbidding". While the Working Party have

154

identified the problem as existing particularly in the field of attraction of foreign investment it is not confined to this, nor is it specially related to particular types of incentives.

The prototype of an overbidding situation is that of an auction in which the price finally paid as a result of competitive bidding, assuming it is above the reserve price, is higher than necessary to induce the seller to part with the object of sale. A private sale between one seller and one buyer may result in a bargin satisfactory to both sides: but in the auction the object goes to the highest bidder.

Regional incentive systems may be different from an auction if the incentive "bids" are published in advance. The seller (or investor) then chooses the highest incentive bid. It is more like an auction when there is a high degree of discretion allowed to the authority offering incentives. The seller (investor) can make the best of this situation by negotiation in which he draws attention to the most favourable terms he can obtain elsewhere - and "squeezes" the buyer as far as he can.

The seller's joy can be diminished of course if the auction is "rigged" i.e. the buyers agree beforehand between themselves on what they will bid. The bargain may still be a satisfactory one to the seller but not as much as if the auction were genuine.

The key to an auction is that there are several independent buyers with no collusion between them. The degree of overbidding - the difference between the price necessary to get the seller to part with the object and the actual price reached - reflects the intensity of the ultimate buyer's desire for it.

Regional incentive systems correspond to an auction if there are several independent competing authorities offering incentives; and they agree between themselves on the limits to which they should go.

While a "rigged" auction is usually illegal and certainly immoral, agreement between public authorities offering incentives can be regarded as prudent administration and a legitimate defence of the taxpayer's interests. It is not necessarily desirable, even if justifiable, when authorities believe they can gain more for their constituents by rivalry rather than co-operation.

Internally, regional incentives can give rise to overbidding when several authorities have powers and means to offer different levels of incentive as in Federal States or States in which there are sufficient large and financially powerful local authorities. Where incentives are administered by single central authorities the problem can hardly arise, though centralized or unitary States can still of course create and endow regional organisations with incentive funds which may be used in competition.

"Overbidding" resulting from internal competition between authorities can spill over into the international field if the authorities are empowered to offer their incentives to foreign as well as domestic investors.

The fact that regional incentives are offered by independant authorities at different levels does not of itself constitute "overbidding". The essence of overbidding is in the deliberate raising of the price in order to defeat the previous bid. In the regional field this would mean one authority deliberately fixing the level of incentives at a higher level than that of another authority in order to attract the same investor or class of investors. Competitive "overbidding" then occurs if the second authority responds by raising the level of its incentives. Depending on awareness of and interest or determination of authorities to overcome the competing incentives, the process can become an escalating one of bid and counterbid, resulting in an ultimate level of incentives higher than is in fact needed to attract investment to the regions concerned.

There is nothing inherent in systems of regional incentives which leads automatically to competitive overbidding. Throughout the past two or three decades the main systems of regional incentives have been those administered by central authorities with the object of making certain regions more attractive to investment than they would otherwise be. The effort has been directed towards internal adjustment of the investment pattern. In scale and impact the incentives offered by local or subordinate authorities have rarely been significant compared with those under central direction. The central incentives have been primarily directed towards influencing the decisions of the domestic investor and producer even though, if they are not discriminatory, they also influence the foreign investor. In these circumstances the external factors, such as incentives offered by other countries, appear to have played little part hitherto in determining the level of incentives in most countries.

The possibility that they may do so in the future cannot however be ruled out. As the international economic climate increasingly favours the flow of capital between countries and efforts are made to reduce discriminatory barriers between domestic and foreign capital, and as at the same time more weight is given to regional policies and to devising stronger and more effective incentives, they provide countries with opportunities for killing two birds with one stone. Capital inflows may be seen as a means not only to contribute to national growth but also to the problem of overcoming regional disparities and imbalances. The more important this factor becomes, the more likely it is that some countries will see advantage in attuning their systems of incentives to make them particularly attractive to those sources of international capital that they wish to encourage. The many cross flows of international capital make it difficult to generalize or point to

156

specific cases where this is likely to happen. Capital flows, for examples in both directions across the Atlantic, between Europe and North America. It flows from North America to Japan, and vice versa. It flows between Europe and Japan and between European countries themselves. Regional incentives can provide a stimulus not only to flows to particular regions but to a country as a whole. The removal of barriers between European countries which are members of the EEC will be widened as the membership of the EEC is extended by the admission of the United Kingdom, Ireland and Denmark. The member countries offering the strongest regional incentives such as Italy and the United Kingdom even if they do not specifically discriminate between foreign and domestic investors, can offer stronger "carrots" to foreign investment than those countries whose regional problems call for less in the way of regional incentives.

The fact that EEC countries are seeking to limit incentives in central areas suggests that the danger of competitive and overbidding is seen to be a real one. If no steps of this kind were taken there would not only be a danger that systems of regional incentives could be used as a device to make one country more attractive than another to foreign investors from third countries. It would also carry with it the danger that incentives would be so strengthened as to place beneficiary industries or regions in a position to compete to the severe disadvantage of industries in other countries in which there was not so strong a case for regional incentives. Moreover the "lure" of permitted incentives may also be strong enough to divert international capital movements away from countries in which the real net return on capital is higher than in countries granting regional incentives.

It would seem to follow that if the danger of overbidding is a real one between EEC countries it can also be a real one between members and non members of EEC alike and that there could be a case in the general interest of all OECD countries, for an attempt to regulate the level of those incentives which are important enough to influence the flow of international capital. Failure to do so could lead either to competition between countries in their regional incentives to ensure that they each secure the international investment that they may need, or to countries not requiring strong regional incentives offering counteracting inducements to offset those in other countries.

The case for scrutinizing carefully the influence of regional incentives on international investment rests also on another foundation. It has been suggested above that "overbidding" implies paying a higher price than is really necessary to effect a sale by a willing seller. If a country pays a higher price for foreign capital than is necessary the consequences are different than for domestic capital. In the former case there is an extra direct charge on the balance of payments. In the latter the effect is primarily redistributive within the country. In times in which foreign investment played a small part in regional development there was little need for countries to give much thought to possible adverse effects on the balance of payments. However foreign investment can and does play a very large part in individual major projects in some countries e. g. where the special expertise of a foreign concern may be needed for a major development or where a region offers an opportunity to a foreign concern for the extension of its operations.

The growth of multinational companies has its own motive force but systems of regional incentives can well play a part in influencing the location decisions taken by such companies. It is not possible to say in general terms what such companies would do in the absence of regional incentives. It could well be that in such cases they would choose a particular region in another country even if there were no special incentives. Foreign investment has, after all, been a normal feature of international commerce over decades, long before regional incentives were first thought of. It is perhaps a new feature of modern times that many countries which were, and still are, a source of international capital are now, in effect, paying a special price in the shape of regional incentives, which is over and above the "normal" market price and has the effect of attracting foreign capital to them. Regional incentives which are designed primarily to divert or steer internal investment to problem regions may, in the absence of discrimination have the unintended effect of giving foreign investors a bonus which may not be required.

There is some foundation for the view that the EEC and its prospective enlargement has significantly increased the incentive to United States firms to establish themselves in EEC countries in order to take full advantage of the unified market. In some EEC countries the "problem" regions may well be the ones best able to meet the requirements of such firms for labour, communications and services. If that is so the regional incentives represent an additional and possibly unnecessary and costly bonus. The more that countries compete among themselves in the matter of incentives the larger and more costly the bonus and the less the difference it makes to the final location decision which will be governed by the firm's assessment of the total advantages and disadvantages of the alternative locations.

All this is hypothetical and individual countries may still consider that the risk of paying an excessive price for foreign investment in problem regions is outweighed by the advantages to them of securing investment which might otherwise go to other countries. It suggests two things however. First, that there could be scope for international agreement which imposes some limits on the escalation of competitive incentives. Secondly, that countries anxious to secure the participation of foreign capital in regional development should examine carefully what other factors besides financial incentives are relevant and seek to deal with those in order to lessen the danger of giving unnecessary bonuses. Since such bonuses constitute more of a burden on weaker than on stronger economies the reduction or elimination of unnecessary bonuses would free resources for use where they are most needed.

GENERAL CONCLUSION

In the earlier part of this chapter it has been shown that the effectiveness of regional incentives cannot be gauged by reference to their nature, size or scale in isolation from the context in which they operate. Changes in the context such as occur all the time as economic conditions change, can render given incentives ineffective or produce results which are not intended. Simple arithmetical comparisons of incentives provide no indication of their comparative effectiveness. Incentives which may seem quite substantial when expressed as differentials may have marginal or negligible effects on beneficiary firms or on development in regions they are designed to benefit. The time-scale over which incentives are available can be a material factor in determining their usefulness. No one kind or set of incentives is necessarily superior to another; whether it is or not can only be determined in the light of all the accompanying circumstances. It follows that incentive systems can only be expected to work if they are correctly attuned to the prevailing circumstances. Since few, if any, countries have done more than experiment pragmatically with a wide range of incentives it is difficult to escape the impression that incentive policies up to now have had a large element of "hit and miss" in them. A precondition of successful policies would be a careful analysis of the nature of the problem they are supposed to deal with and then the maintenance of such policies over a sufficient period of time to enable them to achieve the desired results. We would venture to recommend that all Governments should devote more effort to a systematic analysis and appraisal of the relative conditions in their "incentive" and "non incentive" regions, and to the likely response to incentives inside and outside the regions affected before deciding on their incentive policies. The frequency with which incentive systems are changed, even by the same Governments, would seem to highlight the need for a much more rigorous appraisal of this kind, than has been attempted hitherto. An organisation like the OECD might well be able to assist Governments by the preparation of model incentive schemes to fit varying circumstances.

In the latter part of the chapter consideration has also been given to repercussion and "side effects" of incentive systems, some of which can be shown to be in conflict with other criteria, such as efficiency, economic operation, or the economic use of resources. Some of these effects may be detrimental and avoidable. Others, even if detrimental, may be a necessary part of the price to pay for regional development or rehabilitation. Regional incentives cannot properly be rejected on the grounds that they create "distortions" of competition but the distortions can have effects which go beyond those intended and can be detrimental. In the international field the free use of regional incentives can give rise to a process of competitive bidding the results of which may outweight the benefits. There would seem to be scope for international agreement to regulate or limit such competitive bidding in a common interest which extends beyond that of members of any one organisation. Here again there might be scope for positive action by OECD to join with other organisations to avoid regional incentive systems going beyond what is strictly necessary and placing unnecessary burdens on economies which may be weak or under strain.

VII

RESTRAINT SYSTEMS FOR REGIONAL POLICY

The converse of an incentive system is a system of restraint. A
system is one of "national" regional policy when it is designed to influence
the location of economic activity towards, or away from, selected regions. Systems of restraint can also be used to influence the location
of economic activity within a region. They can also be used for purposes
of local planning, to protect the environment, to enforce conformity
with zoning regulations for residential, industrial and other uses, or to
secure local development in accordance with an area plan.

This chapter will be primarily concerned with the "implications" of
the first two systems, since they are specifically designed for purposes
of regional policy. The third system, important in itself, is essentially concerned with the sitting of establishments to suit local conditions.
In so far as local planning takes account of wider regional planning its
implications for regional policy can be dealt with in that context. It may
however be noted that local planning restraints can be used to prevent
development in certain areas within a region to conform with a regional plan. Since local planning is usually the responsibility of the local
authority concerned its willingness to use local planning powers for
regional planning purposes will depend on the pressures within its area
affecting the availability of alternative sites and its readiness or obliga-
tion to co-operate in the regional planning system. Regional restraint
systems can, in theory, take several different forms, including licencing systems, differential penalties taxes and charges, and support withholding arrangements. It is necessary to stress the words "in theory"
since the vast majority of OECD countries have hitherto chosen, as a
matter of policy, to rely on inducements and encouragements, rather
than restraint systems as the main instrument for "steering" economic
activities towards disadvantaged regions.

As will be seen from "The Regional Factor in Economic Development" (p. 88) it is only in the United Kingdom that there has been for

any length of time, a comprehensive country wide licencing system. In France licensing has been applied to the Paris area only, leaving industrialists with the free choice of the whole of the rest of the country subject to building controls (which are of the nature of local planning restrictions). In Japan restraints have been imposed (RFED p. 120) on development in the densely populated areas of Tokyo and Osaka. While these serve the purposes of regional policy, the lessening of congestion and environmental pollution in overcrowded cities, the controls, though exercised by the central authority, can be considered as local rather than country wide regional policy restraint systems. In Italy powers have recently been taken by the Central Government to require permission to be granted for new industrial plants or expansions involving large investments (exceeding 7 billion lire), with penalties (fines) for proceeding without permission.* In Sweden there is a compulsory consultation procedure whereby firms wishing to make investments in the major cities have to have prior consultations with the Labour Market Board.

So far as differential taxes are concerned no actual cases have been notified to the Working Party of such taxes in operation, though the idea of a "congestion tax" has been mooted from time to time in some countries. By "withholding support arrangements" is meant the use by a Government of those powers it has to provide support to industry, to withhold it unless the assisted project is located in accordance with regional policy. The powers possessed by many Governments to support industry are of course very wide and it may be that some Governments exercise them in this way. In Italy the system of "planned negotiations" or "contractual programming" permits the Government to use its powers for assistance selectively between different locations in accordance with the plans for regional development in the Mezzogiorno. Similarly, in the United Kingdom the dependence of nationalized industries on Government finance may provide an opportunity to restrain development in non-preferred areas. In Japan the policy of positive development of new areas to reduce the overloading of the great centres implies restraint in Government supported development in the congested regions. While such opportunities exist we would hesitate to use the examples as evidence of the use of restraint systems per se. The primarily purpose of all support schemes is assistance of projects meeting certain criteria. The avoidance of support in some cases where it conflicts with regional policy aims does not constitute a generalized system of restraint of development.

Inevitably, therefore, discussion of generalized systems of restraint must be based largely on the "model" provided by the United Kingdom. This is the only country in which such systems have been

* Banco di Roma, Review of Economic Conditions in Italy.

sufficiently comprehensive, and in force long enough to permit some observations to be made on the basis of experience. It may be of some importance to draw some conclusions from that experience. Though no other member countries have used the licensing system to the same extent as the United Kingdom and may have no intention to do so, an appraisal of its advantages and disadvantages is clearly a necessary part of any discussion of the instruments of regional policy.

The main features of the controls operating in the United Kingdom are well known and can be briefly summarized. The principal control system is that over industrial buildings in operation since 1945. A second system, of control over office building, was introduced in 1965. The basic principle is that a certificate [Industrial Development Certificate (IDC)] in the case of industrial building or a permit [Office Development Permit (ODP)] in the case of office building had to be obtained before building could proceed, or any necessary authority could be granted by local planning authorities. In each case the certificate or permit was required for new buildings, extension or change of use of existing buildings, when the floor space involved exceeded a stated minimum.

The minima have varied from time to time, and different minima have been fixed for different regions, through 3,000 sq. ft. in the regions of most stringent control to 5,000, 10,000 and 15,000 sq. ft. in others and to complete exemption in some cases. In March 1972 the limit for IDCs was raised selectively; in the South East from 5,000 sq. ft. to 10,000 sq. ft.; in East Anglia and the two Midland regions (East and West) from 5,000 sq. ft. to 15,000 sq. ft., in others outside the assisted areas, from 10,000 sq. ft. to 15,000 sq. fit.; and in the assisted areas the minimum of 10,000 sq. ft. was replaced by exemption.

In the case of ODPs the control applied originally only to the South East, was later extended to the Midlands from which it was removed in stages and altogether in late 1970. At the time the minimum for Greater London was 3,000 sq. ft. and that for the South East region 10,000 ft. In late 1970 the minimum for Greater London was raised to the South East level and the control in the South East region was retained in the measures announced in March 1972.

In the case of IDCs the applicant is required to state the use to which a building or extension will be put. The regulations apply to industrial use - generally speaking manufacturing and processing. The control therefore in principle does not apply to other uses, storage, warehousing or to non industrial buildings. The control on office buildings applies in general irrespective of the nature of the business to be carried out in the offices.

The purpose of the IDC control has been defined as to secure a better economic balance between the different parts of the country. In its practical interpretation this meant encouraging the expansion of industry in the development and intermediate areas and moderating expansion, particularly the demand for labour, in areas liable to pressure on available resources. In issuing the IDC the responsible Minister certifies "that the development in question can be carried out consistently with the proper distribution of industry". In considering whether any development can be carried out consistently with this requirement he has to "have particular regard to the need for providing appropriate employment in development areas". Subject to this overriding requirement special consideration is also given to the employment needs of intermediate areas and the industrial needs of the new and expanding towns are also borne in mind. ("Trade and Industry", July 1971). Thus in effect the system enables priority to be given, in descending order, to the development areas, the intermediate areas, the new and expanding towns and, finally, the rest with some preference for areas where there are special local "pockets" of unemployment and inadequate alternative employment within reach.

The original purpose of the office control, though broadly consistent with the same aims, was both to lessen the pressure on building resources in favour of housing, and to influence the location of office employment away from Central London and "congested" areas elsewhere. The fact that it had little effect on the interregional distribution of office employment led to the progressive dismantling of the control. It is now retained in the South East only on the specific ground of "planning pressures in the South East". It is left to local planning authorities to control office development in their areas according to their own planning criteria.

Throughout the lifetime of the IDC control it has been insisted by successive Governments that the control is operated "flexibly" allowing account to be taken, within its overall purpose of changes in the employment and unemployment situation and of the merits of each, individual application. In the official statement of July 1971, it was pointed out that while IDCs were generally freely available in development and intermediate areas the Department might wish to discuss in which particular location an applicant's needs for labour can best be met. In other areas the Department could take account of the problems created for individual managements if they had to undertake industrial development at locations distant from their existing establishments, and of benefits to efficiency from new building. Generally speaking the system enabled certificates to be granted even in the "prosperous" regions where necessary for the viability of an enterprise, the criteria being however more stringent if any substantial increase in employment was involved.

The system therefore in no sense involved a ban on industrial development outside the assisted areas. That this is so is evidenced by the statistics of areas (floor space) of industrial buildings approved. The total approved floor space has of course fluctuated considerably with economic circumstances, as the following figures shows.

INDUSTRIAL BUILDING IN GREAT BRITAIN
(OVER 10,000 SQ. FT.) APPROVED

million sq. ft.

1960	91.3	1966	67.6
1961	50.8	1967	76.5
1962	32.7	1968	98.0
1963	33.8	1969	103.0
1964	52.1	1970	88.9
1965	54.5		

For the South East and the West Midlands (two "prosperous" regions) and for the North (a development area) the figures were as follows:

MILLION SQ. FT. APPROVED

	SOUTH EAST	WEST MIDLANDS	NORTH
1960	24.6	9.8	3.8
1961	16.5	4.3	6.2
1962	10.3	3.0	2.7
1963	7.9	2.8	3.9
1964	10.1	3.9	7.7
1965	9.2	4.0	5.7
1966	10.5	5.3	7.7
1967	17.8	5.6	7.0
1968	18.1	9.9	11.4
1969	22.8	8.6	9.2
1970	19.5	7.7	7.8

SOURCE: Abstract of Regional Statistics No. 7, 1971 HMSO.

The South East has about 32 per cent, the West Midlands about 9.5 per cent and the North 6.2 per cent of the population of Great Britain. The figures show not only that, since 1965, the North received a higher proportion of the approvals than its population (not of course more than a rough guide to relativities) but also that the rate of increase was much higher in the South East and the West Midlands than in the North.

While they are sufficient to demonstrate that the controls permitted approvals to be given on a substantial scale outside the development areas they do not indicate the amount of industrial building that actually took place. Firms do not necessarily proceed with a development for which they have obtained a certificate, postponing or putting off the development altogether if intentions or circumstances change. Actual completions have continuously been well below approvals. Thus in 1969 only 43.8 mn sq. ft. were completed in Great Britain, of which 4.6 mn (over 10 per cent) in the North, 8.6 mn (20 per cent) in the South East and 2.9 mn (6 per cent) in the West Midlands.

By its nature the control operates to discriminate against the regions outside the assisted areas, refusals of certificates being the means by which pressure can be exerted on firms to consider location in them. While figures of refusal are published from time to time they provide no indication of the way the system operates. Firms may apply more than once, may secure approval for modified schemes or may be deterred from applying if they consider there is little or no chance of an application being approved in the prevailing circumstances; they may apply without necessarily having decided to proceed with a development if approval is granted or they may withdraw an application before a formal refusal becomes necessary. Neither the way the system operates, nor its efficacy can therefore be judged from figures of refusals. It may be added that, since all applications are dealt with as a confidential matter between the applicant and the Government department concerned no reasons are normally given or published for a refusal. The statements of general principles, together with the figures of approvals, are sufficient to substantiate the view that the system is operated flexibly but with a deliberate bias in favour of the assisted areas and against the remainder.

Some further general features should be noted. First, the system is one of negative control. It does not contain within it any power to direct a firm to locate its enterprise in an area or region of the Government's choice. Secondly, it has always operated concurrently with the complementary system of financial incentives or other inducements. A firm which is refused (or expects a refusal of) an application has a number of choices open to it: to move to an assisted area; to move to existing already certificated buildings in its own area or else where it deems it can best meet its requirements; to reorganise its use of its existing building; or to give up or modify its plan for development altogether. Its choice will be affected by its knowledge and evaluation of the incentives but is its own choice, not that of the Government. The control operates as an instrument of persuasion, obliging a firm to consider the alternatives.

Thirdly, the system permits a firm to expand freely within the minimum limits. Thus, if the minimum for which a certificate is required is X. 000 sq. ft. the firm that is granted a certificate can add another X. 000 - 1 sq. ft. without an additional certificate. The possibility that a firm may wish to undertake subsequent expansion is however one of the factors which can be foreseen and taken into account by the authority. This in-built flexibility is however more important to the smaller firms rather than large undertakings requiring buildings well above the minimum for which certificates are required.

The use of IDC controls to foster the growth of new expanding towns, as an alternative to the major existing cities is basically a "physical" planning, rather than an "economic" use. It postulates a planning philosophy, that the existing cities are over large, that they cannot cope with their environmental problems and that in some senses they are costly and inefficient. The assumption is implied that new and carefully planned expanding cities are more efficient and economical and that it is preferable that economic development should take place in them rather than in existing over large conurbations.

There are however counter considerations. The large cities offer a wider market, closer association and better linkages between suppliers, greater choice of work for labour, and are often strategically better placed in relation to national communications. Their larger scale enables common services, in higher education, large hospitals, cultural and other amenities, to be provided for larger "catchment" areas, and hence more economocally, the financing of common services, organised from the revenues of the large city or city region is more easily achieved than in smaller centres. The pressure on firms to move away from the larger centres, if successful, can reduce the ability of the cities to finance their needs. The use of IDC controls can prevent manufacturers establishing themselves or expanding where their own needs can best be met. The use of IDC controls for the purposes of better physical planning may run contrary to the policy of developing industry where it can operate most efficiently.

The conflict is less easily resolvable and calls for close coordination when different authorities, central Ministries, local authorities and Development Corporations are responsible for the physical and economic policies and administration. The need to make a "success" of a new or expanding town and to secure an adequate return on the capital invested in its infrastructure postulates a degree of priority over existing cities which calls for a delicate judgement in deciding on applications for IDC's in the latter. Again, a refusal may restrain development in them without necessarily leading to a firm moving to or establising itself in the new town. Firms may prefer to remain in a location, even if this means continuing to operate in unsatisfactory or obsolete buildings. Unless carefully operated with an eye to productive efficiency, a control system designed to steer industry to preferred locations from an internal regional planning point of view can prevent necessary adaptation to change and the attainment of the most efficient scale, organisation and location of individual industries. Studies have shown that many firms are reluctant to more more than short distances when they are dependant on local linkages and sources of supply. Systems of priorities for selected locations may contain an in-built pressure to disregard or underestimate the importance of such factors, since too much regard for them can involve accepting a slower rate of development of the new towns than that predicted by the planning policy.

At times of rapid economic growth when there is an abundance of firms seeking to expand substantially or more new enterprises, the existence of new well planned towns with adequate space for development may be an attraction in itself and the control operates as an effective means of ensuring that firms give proper consideration to their advantages. At times of slow growth the volume of potentially "mobile" industry may be smaller and a rigorous application or control may help to restrain redevelopment of existing industry without leading to any marked movement to the new centres. A constant monitoring of economic conditions and their implications for industrial mobility and efficiency is therefore necessary if the control system is not to constitute a hindrance to economic progress.

APPRAISAL OF THE IDC SYSTEM

Any appraisal of the system must begin with the observation that it is extremely difficult to make one objectively. There is ample room for legitimate differences of opinion on the virtues of control as such or on the comparative merits of systems of inducements as opposed to controls. There are those who believe on principle that the State should be armed with strong powers to intervene in the decisions of the private sector and those who believe, equally on principle, that the exercise of such powers can only be detrimental to economic progress.

Throughout its long history - nearly three decades - the system has given rise to controversy. There have been those who have argued that it should be retained for all but the smallest developments and those who consider that the system is a useful instrument but should be confined to major projects of real importance for the industrial growth of the disadvantaged regions. Some have criticised its administration for being over lenient towards the prosperous areas, and others who have criticised it for being too stringently administered. While most might agree that the system is not rigid and inflexible, there are differences of view as to the degree of flexibility called for.

Views also change as economic circumstances change. In periods of high inflationary pressure on labour, or low unemployment, industrialists who may be opposed to the system in principle welcome its operation in practice, insofar as it lessens the pressures on the labour force in areas of high demand. In times of relative stagnation or intensified external competition the same industrialists may criticise it for hampering their efforts to modernize and re-equip in locations of their own choice. There have been times when public criticism has been abated by the relative ease with which certificates have apparently been obtainable and other times when criticism has been strongly directed towards the alleged over severity with which the system is operated.

The views expressed by responsible bodies in the regions, such as the Economic Planning Councils and large local authorities are equally varied. Those in the assisted areas are the natural protagonists of a system ostensibly and clearly designed for their benefit and tend to oppose the raising of the minimum limits or relaxation in the stringency of administration. Those in other regions in which the system is intended to restrain development that might be diverted to the disadvantaged regions are more apt to express concern that the system operates to the disadvantage of their region and to the growth of the country as a whole and hence of the disadvantaged regions.

Since there is strength in all these conflicting arguments and views the disinterested observer or competent student may well feel relieved that the only body that is required to come to a definite conclusion is the Government of the day.

The difficulty for those outside Government (and perhaps inside as well) in reaching a firm conclusion is accentuated by the lack of authoritative information on the way the system has actually operated and its effects. Despite numerous reviews of regional policies conducted by Governments, there is no authoritative survey of the operation of the system over close on thirty years. To some extent this is inescapable. Publication of all the considerations which Governments have taken into account in literally thousands of cases would not only require massive and sustained research, much of which would be of little relevance to the current situation. It could lessen the effectiveness of the system itself by revealing loopholes or ways to "get around" the system. Though the confidential nature of the individual applications could be generally safeguarded, publication of all the circumstances taken into account in dealing with major projects could entail risks of breaches of confidence detrimental to the enterprise concerned.

Moreover there is no objective way of telling how far firms' decisions are due to the working of the control system or of inducements or other factors. A considerable degree of follow up would be necessary to ascertain what a firm does after its application for a certificate has been dealt with and the factors involved. Statistics of numbers and scale of firms which have located themselves in the assisted regions, or of their subsequent growth provide no evidence of the reasons for their decisions, nor can they show what would have happened if they had remained in a non assisted region.

Though the necessary information is lacking to permit an accurate assessment to be made of the amount of industry that has moved to the disadvantaged regions because of the IDC system there is no reason to doubt that the system has in fact played an important part. It is unlikely that the system would have been retained for so long if it had not. One of the ways in which the system works effectively is that it obliges industrialists to consider thoroughly the possibility of moving. This may be particularly important when they are not fully cognizant either of the value to them of the incentives or of the advantages which another location can offer. The need to secure an IDC provides an opportunity for the Government to ensure that all such factors do in fact get taken into account. Secondly, the system does sometimes compel an industrialist to choose a location in an assisted region if this is the best choice among the alternatives from which he can choose or being refused an IDC in the area of his first preference. Certainly the IDC system serves to reinforce the incentive system, though that is not to say that it would be effective without it.

There are some facts that are well known and can be used in evidence of the effectiveness of the system in securing the movement of some large industries to the assisted regions. The location of some large motor vehicle plants in the North West and Scotland are perhaps the best known examples. Even in such cases however it is difficult to reach a conclusion on whether the total effects of the system have been beneficial or otherwise. The assisted regions concerned may be deemed to have benefited by receiving an important industry; and some would argue that the change of location was beneficial also to the exporting region through the reduced pressure on its labour force. Against this it is argued by some that the "splitting" of the vehicle industry between regions distant from each other made the industry less efficient, reduced the unity of its manufacturing process and produced inverse transport

170

flows in both directions, raising costs and lessening ability to compete with the vehicle industry in other countries where manufacture is permitted in the way it best suits the manufacturer.

It is not possible to be dogmatic over such an issue, either in particular cases or in general. The justification for regional policy in most countries is based on the belief that private and social costs differ and that action to counteract the social disbenefits from private profit motivated decisions is necessary. The possibility that costs may be raised is not a conclusive objection to the user of a particular instrument of the policy, if it is considered the price is worth paying. The risk that the IDC system (as the system of incentives also) may carry with it some loss of efficiency is one that can be deliberately accepted. It has been accepted in the United Kingdom. * The use of the IDC system calls for a considered judgement in each case of where the balance of cost and benefit lies.

It may be noted that despite the considerable growth in unemployment in the United Kingdom in 1971, which affected such regions as the West Midlands as well as the assisted regions, and despite the recognized need for an acceleration of industrial investment the IDC system was retained and was not explicitly relaxed. Following the review of regional policy conducted over the turn of the years the policy was modified by the raising of the minimum limits and by exempting the development and special development areas from the operation of the system. Outside the exempted areas IDCs were to be "more readily granted than hitherto for schemes of factory modification which involve some increase in the number of employees. These changes will provide greater flexibility and scope for modernization while still retaining the essential purposes of the IDC control which is to seek to divert potentially mobile industrial projects to the areas of greatest employment need". (White Paper on Industrial and Regional Development. Cmnd 4942).

The change of IDC policy thus lessened the control over smaller developments while maintaining the apparatus of control for larger developments outside the exempted areas. How far the remaining controls will be relaxed in practice cannot be assessed from the statement itself. The accompanying changes in the whole system of national and regional investment incentives (see Chapter VI) suggests however that the balance of United Kingdom regional policy has shifted to some degree,

---

* In a speech to the Birmingham Chamber of Commerce on 17th March, 1972 the Secretary of State for Trade and Industry stated "I have little doubt that in the short-term the abandonment of controls and incentives for regional purposes would probably enhance the national product and would on balance, improve industrial performance. In the long term I am sure it would not".

away from direct controls towards enhanced incentives. As this followed a comprehensive review of regional policy it presumably represents
a carefully considered judgement by the United Kingdom Government
about the merits of the system in the prevailing circumstances and in
the light of its own experience.

While the United Kingdom provides the main experimental "test-
bed" for restraint systems used for regional policy purposes, any
appraisal of such systems relevant to the widely varying circumstances
of other countries can only be in general terms.

Perhaps the most important feature of the system, underlying all
others, is that it operates negatively. It can prevent a development
taking place in a given area but does not of itself cause a development
to take place in an alternative area. What actually happens in an individual case as a result of a refusal of a licence (or of an anticipated
refusal) depends on the alternatives open to the applicant and the choice
he makes.

The usefulness of a system cannot be judged only by reference to
what happens in individual cases. Responses of individual firms will
be different. The test of the usefulness of a system as a wnole is
whether it leads to a response from firms generally in the desired direction.

As with positive incentives, the usefulness or efficacy of the system will therefore depend on the context in which the system is operated. The context in which firms operate and which conditions their response to a control system is a complex one, that of an individual firm's
own viability and the varying degree to which it can meet its requirements in alternative locations; and the context which affects firms generally, i.e. the national economic climate, the differential advantages
and disadvantages of alternative regional locations and the influence of
external factors, including competition from sources not subjected to
restraint policies.

The most favourable conditions for the operation of a restraint system would appear to include:

a) An expanding national economy which encourages firms to
develop.

b) The lack of space for expansion in the areas or regions in which
the restraints operates.

c) Availability of space for expansion in areas or regions favoured
by the control system.

d) The lack in the regions of restraint, of the complementary factors required for expansion, e. g. labour supply, services and a relatively higher capacity for satisfaction of these requirements in the regions favoured by the control.

e) The ability of industry to sustain, against competition, any extra cost which may be entailed in the alternative location.

Conditions less favourable to the operation of a control system would appear to include:

a) A stagnant economy throwing up fewer needs for physical expansion of existing firms, or fewer "new" firms requiring new locations.

b) An adequacy of space or complementary factors for economic operation within the regions in which the control is applied; and an inadequacy of space or complementary factors in the regions favoured by the control system.

c) Highly competitive conditions in which marginal cost differences can affect viability of industry to an important degree.

It may perhaps be assorted that during the period in which the control system has operated in the United Kingdom most of these factors have changed considerably, in absolute and relative importance. In the early post war years reconstruction and recovery afforded a climate of rapid economic expansion, less susceptible than in later years to the pressures of international competition. Such conditions were favourable to the creation of "footloose" or "mobile" industry leading, as official studies show, to something like 100,000 jobs being "moved" to the development regions. During these years the pressures on the "congested" regions were such as to encourage industrialists to consider the advantages of the less congested regions, a process assisted both by the incentives and by the controls. In the later years the supply of "mobile" industry tended to diminish as the economic climate became less favourable while the influence of international competition necessitated continual attention to cost factors. It must however remain an open question, at least in the present writer's view, whether such changes in the distribution of industry as occurred were due to the system of control or would have taken place even if it had not existed or had been operated with less stringency.

The second feature of a licencing or control system worth noting is that it is an administrative system and one that affords a high degree of administrative discretion. It is selective rather than automatic. A firm cannot tell, until it has had discussions with the administering authority, what decision will be made in its own case. The general aim of the control may be made known through the legislation and public statements by the Government. Since each decision is however made after the consideration of the "merits" of each individual case, the general principles behind the legislation or statements can serve as no more than a guide to individual firms. The built-in "flexibility" of the system enables the administering authority not only to deal with each individual case "on its merits" but also to change from time to time the ground rules which it observes as general conditions change.

Flexibility clearly has an advantage, in that the stringency with which the control is operated can be varied as economic circumstances change. It can also have the disadvantage of creating some uncertainty among applicants as to the likely outcome of their application. The absence of any system of public "case law" prevents comparisons being made of the reasons which have led to applications being granted in some cases and refusals in others.

The inevitable uncertainty created by any such system can be mitigated, but not altogether eliminated, by speedy and efficient handling of applications to reduce delays in reaching decisions to a minimum. There is no reason to doubt that in the United Kingdom the authorities have always been aware of the need to avoid undue delays. Though there have been criticisms of the system on this score there is, inevitably, no firm evidence to suggest that the delays are more than those which are inescapable in any administrative system. Since administrative systems vary a great deal between countries, consideration of the degree to which uncertainty and delay would be inevitable would no doubt be a factor to be taken into account in deciding whether to introduce a licencing system.

The third feature of the system, which arises from its discretionary nature, is that it calls for a judgement to be made, by the administering authority, of where the balance of advantage lies. This is one of the reasons why there can be no single view as to whether licencing systems are a good or bad thing, since opinions differ on the ability of Governments or "bureaucrats" to exercise their judgement correctly. What can be said is that the judgement called for is often a delicate one. Both the considerations which Governments have to take into account, and the evidence on which the decision must be based, can lead to conflicting conclusions. The administering authority has to weigh the need to secure the objectives of regional policy with the need for an efficient national economy; it has to judge what the effect of its decisions will be on the applicant firm's final choice of location; it has to assess the evidence provided by the firm against its own knowledge of the firm itself and the prevailing economic conditions. A firm which is anxious to expand in an area of its own choice will be anxious to demonstrate that it cannot operate efficiently elsewhere. A Government which seeks to persuade or if necessary oblige the firm to consider a region of the

174

Government's choice has an opposite interest which can influence its judgement on the merits of the case, as presented to it by the applicant.

The ability of a Government to operate a licensing system without detriment to its several policy objectives must turn therefore on the range and validity of the knowledge it possesses of the economics of a firm or an industry in the context in which it has to operate. The more complex the situation and the greater the number of variables or uncertainties involved the more problematic the chances of assessing correctly the effects of its decisions. One need only list some of the matters which may fall to be considered before reaching a decision whether or not to grant a license, to show just how difficult the task must be of reaching a judgement on the basis of any but the simplest criteria, viz:

1. How urgent, from the firm's point of view, is the need for the expansion it proposes?

2. How far can its requirements in fact be met elsewhere than in its own chosen location?

3. What would be the need in the future for further expansion, once the initial expansion takes place and is successful from the firm's point of view?

4. What alternatives are open to the firm if it is refused a license to expand in its chosen location, and which alternative is it likely to choose?

5. What effects will a decision to refuse a license have on a firm's costs and competitive ability, taking account of the situation of competitive undertakings within and outside the region, including abroad?

6. How far will the inability of a firm to develop according to its own location preferences inhibit its adaptability to future changes in the conditions governing the industry and the economy ?

7. What are the trends in operation affecting competing firms in the industry, at home and abroad, and how far can they be taken into account, or ignored in reaching a decision?

A licencing authority can decide how far such questions may be relevant in particular cases and the amount of information it will be satisfied with before reaching its decisions. The onus of proof is not on the administering authority but on the applicant firms. The system is designed for the specific purpose of putting restraint on development in certain regions and it is the applicant that must show cause for exemption from that restraint. There is no corresponding onus of proof on the authority to demonstrate that it has correctly assessed all the possible advantages and disadvantages of its decision. Because the difficulties of knowing the answers to such questions as those listed are obviously very great, an authority may have to be content with making broad rather than detailed judgements. Unless however, the broad judgement is based on a fairly correct assessment of the actual and prospective conditions, the licensing system may still have consequences for individual industries, and for the economy as a whole, which are not necessarily intended.

Thus a license may be withheld in the belief that the planned expansion pf a firm will none the less take place, but in an area or region preferred by the Government. If the facts and possibilities have not been correctly assessed the outcome may be different from that intended, i.e. no expansion; or expansion in other ways than that desired.

A licensing authority may have no intention of weakening the competitive capacity of an industry, yet may do so if it incorrectly assesses the forces of competition that are at work. The example of the motor vehicles industry in the United Kingdom to which reference has been made above, is sometimes quoted in evidence for the view that the licensing system can operate adversely to the efficiency of an industry by compelling the "splitting" of establishments. We offer no opinion on this and doubt whether it is susceptible of proof anyway.

What might be said however is that, at the time the decision was made the influence of the foreign motor industry was less strong than it is today. If it had been possible to foresee the development of foreign competition a different decision might have been taken. There is no way of telling. The fact remains that much of the United Kingdom car industry must now operate as best it can within a location structure determined by the licensing system rather than by its own assessment of the most efficient geographical structure. Perhaps a conclusion to be drawn is that, in determining the way in which a licensing system is to be operated, regard must be had not only to past and present conditions but also to those which may operate in the future.

Licensing systems can also have different effects from those intended if development does not take place in a region in accordance with expectations. In the United Kingdom an underlying assumption during much of the period in which the system operated was that, without it, the development that would take place would be deleterious in the "prosperous" or congested regions - creating inflationary pressures, overloading etc. A further assumption was that, if the development could be steered away from these regions to the assisted areas, not only to their benefit but also to the benefit of the national economy as a whole, those resources, particularly manpower, would be brought into use and the social costs of economic development lessened.

This too must be deemed to be improbable. During much of the period the United Kingdom economy was characterized by at best, slow growth and sometimes by contraction or stagnation. It can be legitimately doubted whether, in such periods, the licensing system was anything but an additional curb on the economy rather than a means of providing a stimulus to its overall growth. It is also open to question whether in periods in which the economic climate was unfavourable to growth and expansion the lifting of licensing restrictions would, at least in the short term, have had a noticeable effect on the total growth of the "more prosperous" regions.

A further difficulty that confronts licensing authorities is that of assessing correctly the influence of the licensing systems on the location decision of foreign firms. The growth of foreign investment which has taken place in recent years as well as the development of multinational concerns with integrated organisations embracing many countries poses additional problems.

Whereas a domestic concern - or one that has no external option - has only a choice of locations that is permitted under the licensing system the foreign concern has the wider choice presented by the several countries offering alternative possibilities of meeting its needs. A licensing authority can impose on domestic concerns the need to consult with it. It can only have consultations with those foreign concerns that seek to develop in its country. Insofar as licensing is operated in a non discriminatory manner between domestic and foreign enterprises a country which has a licensing system may place itself at a disadvantage, in regard to the attraction of foreign firms, viv-à-vis countries without licensing systems. While a country may be able to make some broad judgement of the likely reaction of foreign firms to its licensing system it is unlikely to have as much knowledge of their motivations as of domestic firms obliged to conform with the licensing system. The possibility of incorrect assessments is likely to be greater in the international field than domestically.

The problem may gain in importance in the context of the developing European Economic Community. The creation of the larger market that is implied and the progressive harmonization of trading systems and institutions opens up wider ranges of location choices to enterprises seeking to obtain the full benefit of the larger market. The way in which these choices are made can have very important implications for the regional pattern of production throughout Europe. It remains to be seen whether central rather than peripheral locations will be favoured. A licensing system operating in a single country can do little, beyond providing an obstacle to development in certain areas within the country, to affect the international pattern which may result.

CONCLUSION

The observations in the foregoing do not lead to any conclusion that licensing or restraint systems are in themselves a satisfactory instrument of regional policy. So much depends on the way they operate and the conditions in which they operate that such generalizations cannot be made a priori. Since they are intended to operate through restraint they can only be consistent with growth policies in conditions which are generally favourable to growth, and they can present an obstacle or deterrent to growth. They cannot create growth but can help to divert it to regions which the system is designed to foster. They are selective rather than automatic, in operation and pose numerous problems of administration and of judgement in matters in which the necessary know-ledge for objective and correct assessment may be lacking. They can have important implications for international investment, especially within inter-state organisations. All these considerations would need to be weighed before any conclusions could be reached on the desirability of the system in any country or group of countries.

VIII

THE ROLE OF INFRASTRUCTURE
IN REGIONAL ECONOMIC PLANNING

The Working Party have identified the role of infrastructure as one of the important questions which arise in the formulation of regional policies. One of the few safe generalizations that can be made about the practice of countries pursuing regional policies is that all use at least two main instruments to secure policy objectives. These are the financial incentives which bear directly on firms' balance sheets, the "soft" loans, grants, subsidies, tax relief and the like; and the development of the infrastructure in the areas in which, for one reason or another, a special regional promotion effort is required.

The Working Party have been clear that there can be no single formula by which to determine the balance between the two methods. The regional problem differs too much between countries to permit this. There is, of course, also an interdependence between the two methods. In the regions of some countries the deficiencies of the infrastructure are such that it is not until they have been remedied that incentives to firms can have much effect. In others the inherited infrastructure may be comparatively adequate. The causes of backwardness or decline will be due to other factors, and the most effective policy will be the one which deals with those factors, for example by overcoming the weaknesses of existing industries or introducing new industries to replace them. In such cases incentives to firms may have a more significant role than improvements in the infrastructure and be required to enable the infrastructure to be valorized.

A particular situation may call for either or both instruments to be used. The answer to the question of when it is wise to concentrate on infrastructure and when on incentives to industry must depend on the circumstances. Only if these are carefully and properly surveyed is the "right" balance between the two likely to be struck. The very fact, however, that the two methods represent alternatives reinforces the general case for basing regional policies on such careful surveys rather than on any general view of the efficiency of one method or the other. The experimental nature of many regional policies means that "trial and error" cannot be altogether avoided. Since the provision of infrastructure is both costly and long term in effect error has to be kept to a minimum if resources are not to be wasted. The fact that regional policies are necessary does not of itself justify wasteful expenditure. How to shape infrastructure policies so as to avoid wasteful expenditure is therefore one of the issues of regional policy with which a report of this kind must seek to deal. By wasteful expenditure is meant not only the technical misapplication of resources, so that they do not achieve their intended direct return, but also expenditure in ways which do not lead to the achievement of the ultimate purpose. To put it in more concrete terms, expenditure on a road, if applied with technical efficiency, will produce a road of a desired specific capacity. It nonetheless is wasteful expenditure if the purpose of the road is to bring about a given level of regional development and it fails to do so on the scale which is required to justify the diversion of resources to the construction of the road. Here again, the possibility of wasteful expenditure can only be avoided if preliminary survey shows that a road can be constructed within given cost limits and also that the complementary conditions exist which, with the help of the road, lead to development of the region or area in question sufficient to justify the investment in the road.

The term "infrastructure" can be used, broadly, to denote the complementary equipment which a society needs and possesses to enable the individuals, organisations and enterprises of which it is composed to function and carry out their activities. There are many ways in which it can be classified and sub-divided, according to the purposes in hand. It comprehends physical equipment, land, buildings, plant and machinery and the manpower which operate them and enable them to serve the population at large. It can be broken down into categories describing purposes, such as "social" infrastructure providing education and health services, housing amenity and recreation; "economic" infrastructure providing the communications, power, water, drainage and irrigation etc., i.e. equipment necessary for economic activity; and the "administrative" infrastructure which provides the legal framework and the apparatus for law enforcement, administrative control and coordination.

Each form of infrastructure can serve a wide variety of purposes. "Economic" infrastructure, power, water works and the like is needed not only for factories but for hospitals, schools, houses and environmental needs. The "education" infrastructure is necessary also to provide technical and vocational training for industry. The "administrative" infrastructure does not provide administrative direction as an end in itself but to further all types of activity in which a community must be engaged.

A distinction can also be made between "external" and "internal" infrastructure. Some of the forms of infrastructure mentioned above can be provided by enterprises to meet their own particular requirements. The great bulk of a society's infrastructure is however provided not by or for individual enterprises but externally, serving the community, the users and beneficiaries, at large. The supply of infrastructure is thus largely provided on a collective rather than individual basis. Roads, hospitals, schools, power installations and so on serve the needs of the community collectively and cannot in most cases be economically provided except to meet the needs of a multiplicity of users.

This is not to say that, because infrastructure largely serves the collective needs of society, it necessarily has to be provided by public authorities. The range of alternative systems varies considerably from country to country, from private enterprise at the one end to wholly State-owned and run at the other. In between, the variety of owned and controlled organisations providing different elements of the infrastructure may range from local authorities to State agencies and public utility corporations which are expected to observe commercial principles, deriving their capital from market as well as public sources. Even in the social fields, health and education institutions can be, and sometimes are, provided by private enterprise, with or without forms of State support and control.

These features deserve to be mentioned because they remind us that the development of infrastructures does not necessarily take place in accordance with the desires, policies and plans of Governments, regional or otherwise. It will be the outcome of both the relevant legislative framework, which will be determined by Government policies, and the actions of the bodies which provide infrastructure. Unless Governments enforce a specific regional policy on those bodies the resultant regional distribution of the infrastructure will simply reflect the general criteria that govern their operations. The regional distribution of economic activity is the outcome of the decisions of individuals and organisations operating, within the framework of law, according to their judgements of what is worth doing. There is no basic difference in regard to infrastructure development. Private enterprise providing infrastructure will be influenced by similar considerations to those which influence private enterprise engaged in economic development. State enterprises which are required to follow commercial principles make their decisions on scale and location accordingly, and there need be no correlation between these and any preconceived regional pattern.

Nor do the facts that the provision of infrastructure meets needs of society which can best be satisfied collectively and includes "social" needs, such as education and health, mean that principles of economic accountancy are irrelevant or automatically incapable of application.

This is clearly not the case when an infrastructure service can be provided in measurable quantities and the cost per unit calculated and charged to the consumer, in proportion to his consumption as, for example, with electricity supplies or railway services. In such cases the economic calculus can be applied irrespective of whether the enterprise is private or owned by a State authority, agency or public utility. Even where consumption cannot be metered, except at excessive cost, as for example with domestic water supplies in most countries, the economic calculus can be applied to costs and prices to secure an equilibrium level between expenditure and revenue. Finally social services can be charged for, directly or through taxes. The scale of the service to be provided can still be determined according to economic principles of matching marginal cost with marginal benefit, however assessed.

What the application of economic principles to infrastructure development means is that, no more than in other fields is it possible or, for that matter, desirable to ignore costs and benefits in determining the nature, scale and location of infrastructure development. Since resources are not infinite the line has to be drawn somewhere. The question for regional policy makers is in what ways and how far the line should be drawn differently because of regional needs, and what the effects of so doing could be in terms of given regional policy objectives. The question of the role of infrastructure in regional policies is not an academic one but a major practical issue.

All development, whether economic or social, requires or brings about development in the various forms of infrastructure, and the way in which development takes place regionally affects both the needs for and possibilities of infrastructure development in the regions of a country. The greater part of public expenditure, is expenditure on the various forms of infrastructure and public expenditure accounts for a high and increasing proportion of the national product in most countries. For example in the six Member countries (1972) of the EEC the proportion of GNP constituted by public expenditure ranged in 1957 from around 30 per cent to around 40 per cent and by 1967 the range was of the order of 40 per cent to 50 per cent. (Source: Industrie et Société dans la Communauté Européenne, Rapport No. 7, p. 23).

In their studies the Working Party have noted that many countries have devoted, and are increasingly devoting, resources to developing or improving infrastructure as part and parcel of their regional policies. This is a common feature of regional policies, even though the policies themselves have different characteristics. In the United Kingdom, where the primary problem has been the persistence of relatively high unemployment in declining regions greater emphasis has been given, in recent years, to remedying deficiencies in infrastructure. In Italy comprehensive development in the Mezzogiorno involves a massive

182

effort to provide the infrastructure which is seen as a concomitant of economic growth. In France the policy of "aménagement du territoire" or planned territorial growth involves a concerted effort to provide the necessary infrastructures. In the United States much of the financial assistance to promote development in the poverty areas is applied to infrastructure problems in the locations concerned. In the rapidly growing economies in countries such as Japan and Spain, the steering of economic growth to chosen areas requires large investments in communications, power and water supplies, ports and harbours, housing and social service in accordance with the pattern of regional growth that is being sought. Similar observations can be made in other countries.

The importance of infrastructure in regional development cannot however be gauged by reference only to these special efforts which, as has been noted elsewhere, in many cases only represent a marginal shift of resources. The greater part of public expenditure on infrastructure stems from the normal and continuing process of development and improvement and adaptation to change. The rate at which it proceeds is governed by area and sectoral needs and potential, the scale and manner by which resources can be provided and the criteria by which their use is determined. The extent to which infrastructure policies can influence the regional situation of a country will depend not only on the scale of the "special" and marginal policies but also on the extent to which regional considerations enter the normal criteria which determine the bulk of the expenditure on infrastructure. Part of the problem of striking the right balance, between regional and other needs such as national growth, in the field of infrastructure, is in fact that of determining how far regional requirements should influence the "normal" criteria by which the bulk of expenditure on infrastructure is governed.

The problem is not an easy one, not only because of the limited powers of Governments to influence the expenditure of many of the organisations and bodies that make the decisions on infrastructure, but also because of the conflicts between policy objectives which prevent any one objective - such as regional balance - having an overriding say over all others. Thus, to take a familiar example, the needs of a country for rapid industrial growth may require the concentration of infrastructure development on, say, roads, in those regions which have the greatest scope for the needed industrial development. Conversely, the need to secure a relatively higher rate of economic development in backward or declining regions than in the rest of the country may call for such a substantial diversion of resources for the infrastructure that the infrastructure development elsewhere may not keep pace with the requirements of the economy. Whatever policy decision is made it may, in either case, involve some modification of "normal" criteria by which investment in infrastructure is determined, such as the earning of the minimum rate of return, or preference to projects earning higher rates of return over those earning a lower one.

It is difficult to escape the impression, from the studies that have been made by the Working Party, that these and similar conflicts are resolved somewhat arbitrarily in many countries. Political pressures clearly play their inevitable part in securing preferential treatment for some regions or areas. There is however also very little by way of an accepted corpus of knowledge and theory on the way infrastructure is related to general development so that many decisions are inevitably taken on an "ad hoc" or experimental basis. It would not be possible to fill this gap in the theory of regional development without a considerable and sustained research effort which is, fortunately, under way in some countries. Attention can however be drawn to a few basic considerations, some of which have been touched upon in the Working Party's own studies.

First, there is a reciprocal relation between the general growth of a society and infrastructure. As with the chicken and the egg, neither comes first. Without communications, energy and water, education and health etc. a community cannot live and work, or can do so only to the degree permitted by the state of the infrastructure. On the other hands, unless there is an economic surplus there are no means to provide the infrastructure on the requisite scale. But there is no fixed proportion, or any given level of infrastructure development, which is appropriate to a given level of general development. The level of infrastructure is the outcome of the choices that are made, and the priorities allotted to the expenditure of the social product. Nor is there a direct, one way, relationship between the marginal change in infrastructure and general economic development. An expansion of the infrastructure may serve other than economic purposes and some economic development may be possible without a corresponding expansion of all forms of infrastructure.

Second, there is a degree of complementarity, not only between the infrastructure and general development but between the various kinds of infrastructure. Roads, hospitals, schools, power and water supplies etc. will produce different results, in terms of the development of industry, if provided in different combinations at different times. Conversely, however, the ratio of needs for different kinds of infrastructure is not a constant function of general development but depends on the nature and scale of development and the demands it makes for particular types of infrastructure.

Third, the regional pattern of a country's general development implies, or requires, a corresponding regional pattern of its infrastructure, but there can be no direct or even close correlation between that development and any one kind of infrastructure. Regions can differ widely in terms of population size, age and sex composition and skills, in economic structure and social needs, in state of development and in the potential for development. Investment on different kinds of infrastructure will in consequence produce different degrees of development from region to region. The adoption of fixed criteria for required direct returns on investment even differentiated between regions, will have therefore different results in the growth of infrastructure according to the way in which both needs and potential for development are distributed.

Fourth, there is no "fixed fund" which can be applied at will to the development of regional infrastructures, such that decisions not to develop infrastructure in one direction, in one region, automatically free equivalent resources for use in another. This is implied in the chicken and the egg relationship between infrastructure and resource growth. Thus the effect of not meeting infrastructure needs in one region may be to deter its growth and the generation of resources for development, without providing additional resources elsewhere. Alternatively it may provide additional resources, but the scope for their use elsewhere may be limited by required rates of return concepts or, more broadly, by the lack of potential development. By the same token, the effect of adopting lower rates of return may be to reduce the total supply of resources available for infrastructure development.

Fifth, the technical efficiency or success of regional infrastructure development projects does not measure their efficiency or success in achieving the objectives of regional policy. As has been noted a road may be built efficiently and to design capacity and not produce any results in terms of regional economic development if the requisite complementary factors (such as skilled labour, water supplies, social amenities etc) are not available. Even where such factors are present, however, the effect these and the road may have on the location decisions of industrial or commercial enterprises will turn on comparative advantage in relation to other potential locations. To secure a higher rate of growth in a selected region it is not only necessary to remedy infrastructure deficiencies but to ensure an advantage over competing locations. If these are equally well or better provided with infrastructure, this may require concomitant application of other measures, such as subsidies and financial inducements to firms. The role of infrastructure in regional policy can therefore only be correctly assessed by considering the totality of conditions affecting the regional distribution of economic activity.

Sixth, it would seem to follow from these considerations that the "normal" regional pattern of distribution of infrastructure and its growth is closely geared to the regional distribution of the activities of the society as a whole. On this basis the bulk of the development of infrastructure is more or less bound to take place where the bulk of the economic and social life of the community occurs. Infrastructure expenditure is not an independent instrument which can be used to bring about any desired shift in the regional pattern of activity but a concomitant result of the totality of the forces at work which together determine the regional distribution of a country's life. Since the bulk of the regional structure of a country is more or less predetermined, and a large proportion of its marginal growth is a development of existing activities it would seem inevitable that the influence of infrastructure policies on regional development can only be a slow and long term one.

Finally, one other general observation may be made, and that is that the development of the national pattern of infrastructure is constantly influencing the regional problem itself, by altering the relative balance of advantage and disadvantage between regions. This has been referred to in the chapter on the impact of national factors and needs therefore only a brief mention in the present context. Thus the development of a national network of motorways in the United Kingdom is beneficial to the more remote regions and development areas but is also beneficial to the other regions. It is difficult to establish which regions may have gained the greater benefit, but there is strong presumption that the benefit will be greater in the more densely populated and developed regions, in particular in the capital and central regions. It has been suggested in the Working Party that developments such as the Appalachian highway in the United States, the north-south highways in Sweden and Italy and the construction of improved communications in Japan and Spain can contribute as much, if not more, to the development of the areas of concentration as of the more distant areas which they are designed to open up. Similarly the development of major international airports close to the big centres of population, as in London or Paris, may create new foci of development which work against the policy of regional decentralization. It obviously doesn't follow that infrastructure developments which are necessary in different regions for both local and national reasons should be abandoned if they do not harmonize with regional policy. What such facts may suggest is that the role of infrastructure in regional planning is at least as much to provide the social equipment in the regions according to their requirements and their scope to meet national needs, as to secure a predetermined regional growth pattern.

The foregoing description of the meaning of infrastructure and its relation to general and regional development points to a number of principles which could help in determining the role of infrastructure in regional policy. It also suggests the sort of questions, relating to aims and methods, which need to be asked when considering the development or improvement of infrastructure as a means of promoting regional policies.

First, there is in all countries, what can be termed a "normal" rate of development of infrastructure in all regions, reflecting the application, throughout a country, of established codes and policies. Such codes, which can be regionally differentiated, include the provision of infra-structure in response to effective demand, requirements regarding rate of return on or benefit from investment and the adoption of standards of provision. The normal codes may also permit the provision of some forms of infrastructure on a basis of subsidization from local or central authorities in order to achieve prescribed minimum standards, for example of housing accomodation, education, health and amenities. These codes may be prescribed in national and local laws and regula-tions, and in the rules of the organisations which are concerned with the provision of infrastructure.

The application of these "normal" codes leads to differential rates of development in different regions because of the variations in their circumstances, e. g. the size, skills, customs and needs of the popula-tion, their economic structure and the capacity of the resources and in-dustries to utilize and benefit from infrastructure development. The rate at which the infrastructure develops will depend not only on the codes themselves but on the ability of the organisations concerned to recognize and appraise the needs and possibilities, and to devise and implement projects within the constraints of the codes.

The first question for a regional policy on infrastructure is therefore whether the outcome of the application of the normal codes is likely to be satisfactory in terms of given regional policy objectives. If not, the problem then arises of whether to modify the codes (or national pol-icies which produce unsatisfactory results), or introduce "special" codes as a corrective to bring about a different regional situation than would otherwise be the case.

Second, either method can only effectively change the regional situation in the desired direction if it is based on an adequate assess-ment of the role that infrastructure development plays, or can play in that situation. Diagnosis must always precede cure. The questions to be asked fall, broadly, into two categories: (a) What are the particular infrastructure deficiencies which account for the regional situation which it is deemed necessary to modify? and (b) What would be the effect on that regional situation of proposed special codes and measures?

It will be clear from what has been said in the earlier part of this chapter that not all infrastructure deficiencies have the same signifi-cance, so that the identification of those which can be effectively and fruitfully tackled is a key problem in devising suitable regional poli-cies. Thus no amount of provision of infrastructure will promote econ-omic or other development in areas in which the necessary complemen-tary preconditions do not exist. The "top of the mountain" is the extreme classical illustration but many of the actual regional problem areas afford illustration of the point. Areas previously built up to exploit

187

natural resources, minerals, forestry, fishing, and which had a suitable infrastructure can lose their raison d'être when the resources are exhausted. Development of a new infrastructure will be of little help if the conditions for alternative industries cannot be satisfied. On the other hand backward or declining areas, including those previously dependent on primary production, may have a scope for development or conversion. They will not necessarily be deficient in all types of infrastructure but their progress may depend on a proper identification of the relevant deficiencies. In some backward or declining areas the deficiencies may be in roads, in others in water supplies and drainage facilities, in technical skills, lack of amenities or any other of a wide range in different combinations. In these, as in growth regions, the identification of the relevant infrastructure deficiencies and needs is an essential preliminary to an effective infrastructure policy.

As has been noted, a particular deficiency in infrastructure may altogether rule out some types of economic development, primary, secondary or tertiary. The converse, that the remedying of the deficiency will bring about those types of development is not true, however, unless the deficiency is the only significant obstacle. The effect of remedying the deficiency when other obstacles are not removed can be nil, and the expenditure would fall within the definition of wasteful.

Third, the essence of all "special" regional codes for infrastructure development is the provision of the needed capital or revenue resources on specially favourable conditions compared with those in which they are available elsewhere. There are many different practices which amount to the granting of more favourable conditions. In countries in which there is controlled access to capital markets infrastructure authorities in selected regions can be given access to them in cases in which it is denied to others; infrastructure authorities, both public and private, can be furnished with public capital at lower rates of interest than normal market rates at which it is available to others; direct grants and subsidies may be made to infrastructure organisations in the selected regions on a more favourable basis than elsewhere; organisations may be encouraged, authorized or directed, as the constitutional and legal situation permits, to undertake developments by relaxation of normal conditions, from variations in standards of provisions to earning a lower than a customary rate of return.

All such favourable terms and conditions can be regarded in the same light as the inducements or incentives and restraints which are provided to encourage private industry in selected regions and the effectiveness of such measures can be considered in broadly the same way. Inducements work only if, in the prevailing conditions, they are sufficient to "turn the scale" and make a project worth while when it would not otherwise be so. The provision of capital to an electricity undertaking at, say 5 per cent instead of a "normal" 10 per cent will not turn the scale and cause it to construct a power station if market conditions for electricity will not ensure a minimum return of 5 per cent. The offering of subsidies and grants to local authorities to improve their environment will have no effect if the local authorities have neither the will nor the technical capacity to make use of the aid. The erection of hospitals and schools will not provide an educational and health infrastructure if teachers and doctors are not available to staff them.

There is of course one important difference in the working of incentive policies for industry and those for infrastructure. The former work on the balance sheet of the firms, and, if the impact is sufficient, have a direct expansionary effect on the industries concerned. The latter, however, only work indirectly on the economy of a region. The effects of a given expansion of the infrastructure, brought about by the inducement measures, are not directly correlated with the size of the expansion. In considering whether an infrastructure policy is desirable it is necessary therefore to calculate the indirect effects as well as the capacity of a project to secure the prescribed direct, if lower than normal, return on the capital directed to the region.

Fourth, the remedying of infrastructure deficiencies, or the effective use of infrastructure policies to promote regional development, poses special institutional and organisational problems. As has been noted, much of the infrastructure is the responsibility of the public sector but the same reasons which occasion the backwardness or decline of a region, or give rise to the need for growth, bear also on the capacity of the institutions of a region to promote the development of the infrastructure. Public sector infrastructure in most countries is provided by both central and local authorities. The institutional problem arises mainly when the local authorities are too small, or ill equipped with the necessary technical expertise and development is required on an unaccustomed scale. This is likely to happen, for example, when the infrastructure must be designed to service a region rather than individual local areas, when a new and technically advanced service has to be developed, for which local experience is no guide, or when resources and expertise may have to be brought in from outside the region on a scale which is large in relation to the normal.

The tasks involved are several and often complex and difficult. They include identifying and appraising the need and scope for different kinds of infrastructure and the contribution they can make to the region, the design and specification of projects, the mobilization of financial resources from within and outside the region and the attraction and selection of competent personnel or organisations to build, maintain and run the projects. In many instances the tasks require a combined or coordinated effort of central and local bodies working on complementary projects. The variety of infrastructure projects which may be necessary to make a significant impact on a region's problems may be wide and disparate, from roads, irrigation and power to social institutions such as hospitals and colleges of higher education and universities. The ability to take initiatives, to administer and coordinate a multifarious range of activities is consequently a prerequisite for regional development policies in which significant changes in social equipment or infrastructure are required.

Examples could be quoted to show that this principle is recognized and applied in most countries which are pursuing regional infrastructure policies. It is only necessary here however to emphasize that regional policies involving the substantial development of a wide range of infrastructure calls for appropriate organisation, without which many of the centrally provided inducements cannot be effective. The efficacy of an infrastructure policy can therefore be judged in part by the way in which it provides for the tackling of the organisation problem.

Fifth, individual infrastructure projects may produce benefits to a region, according to their nature and scale, but the use of infrastructure policies to transform a region's productive capacity or its relative position in the interregional scale may need a comprehensive approach to infrastructure deficiencies as a whole.

This principle derives from a number of the features of infrastructure already noted, viz that the interregional distribution of a country's infrastructure is a result of as well as an influence on the problem of its economic life; that the effects of various forms of infrastructure are interdependent and interrelated and that, because only marginal shifts can be made in the short term, major transformation in the regional location of a country's infrastructure is a long term task.

The same principle and considerations imply that comprehensive strategic planning is needed to make a regional infrastructure policy effective, strategic planning at both national and local regional levels. What has to be determined is the way in which future prospective development of a country's economic and social life will produce needs for change in its infrastructure and where; what priorities and time scales for the development of infrastructure will best fit the prospective development; what new regional problems and needs will result from the disparate rates of change or progress in different regions; and how alternative patterns of infrastructure can shape progress in the regions, to prevent or reduce the emergence of new and unacceptable regional disparities. These are some of the questions for central strategic planning but strategic planning questions arise also at the regional level. What will be the effect on a region of the major changes in national economic policies and development?; how far will the existing infrastructure

190

need to be changed to adjust to these factors?; which kinds of infrastructure should have priority to permit the most satisfactory adjustment?; what effects will development of the regional infrastructure have on the shaping of the region's own development?

As has been noted in the chapter on Strategies for Regional Development long term strategic planning has increasingly become a feature of the regional policies of most countries. What is said here is not new or original. It serves however to reinforce the view that a strategic planning approach is necessary, because of the important role that infrastructure policies must play in the framework of overall regional development policies.

Sixth, a further principle that is perhaps worth putting forward is that piecemeal and short term changes in infrastructure policies have little long term effect on the major regional problems. This follows from most of what has been said about the role of infrastructure but it is useful to make the point since it is not an uncommon practice in many countries to use public expenditure on infrastructure as a means of coping with short term economic problems. A typical example is the special and temporary public works programme, designed to relieve seasonally or exceptionally high unemployment in regions already suffering from comparitively high rates, as a result of general backwardness or structural change. Though individual programmes may be short term and temporary they are often repeated year after year and so become a more or less permanent feature of current economic management of an economy. In the terminology used above such programmes may indeed be part of the "normal code" which determines the regional distribution of public expenditure on certain forms of infrastructure. The relief programmes are usually in some form of maintenance and/or new construction, public building, roads, land clearance and amenities for all of which readily available plans exist and most of which can be regarded as producing a direct benefit commensurate with the costs. They may mean that needed improvements are provided earlier than they would otherwise be, or at a time when the employment they produce is more necessary than at other times. Sometimes they may entail the use of substantial funds and a substantial proportion of the total funds currently expended on public works throughout a country as a whole.

Though they produce immediate benefits the regular recurrence of such programmes, usually at the same time of each year, itself suggests that they do little to alter the underlying structural problems of a region with which regional policies seek to deal. The reasons for this are inherent in their nature. They relieve unemployment during the construction period but not when this is completed. The improvements they bring about may be helpful to the economy and hence to employment in the longer term, but if the improvements or developments would have found a place in expenditure programmes anyway then inclusion in a seasonal relief programme constitutes only a change in timing rather than a total increase in the scale of infrastructure development. The use of labour on maintenance of existing infrastructures provides for no net expansion in them. Insofar as the selection of programmes is not related to the long term plans for regional development they do not contribute to their objectives. They may even cause a diversion from longer term objectives by diminishing the resources available for them in order to meet the more pressing needs of the short term unemployment situation.

Clearly it is not possible to generalize and assert that such schemes cannot play a part in regional infrastructure policies. They are not, however, for the most part, designed to do so. Their usefulness for long term regional infrastructure policies could perhaps be enhanced if it is recognized that they are a recurring feature of some regional situations and that there is some scope therefore for fitting them into the scheme of infrastructure development to change the regional situation.

Seventh, the need for infrastructure development policies and the contribution they can make to regional development generally cannot be assessed by "rule of thumb" statistical techniques. By "rule of thumb" techniques is meant the use of formulae, such as the regional distribution of particular types of infrastructure and investment therein per head of population or per square kilometre, to measure interregional disparities and to serve as a guide to the policies that should be followed. It is not suggested that Governments themselves, who perforce are aware of their unrealism and inapplicability, employ such techniques. Nonetheless they are not unfrequently used to exert pressures upon them to modify their regional policies, whether to remedy "disparities" or to increase the share of resources devoted to infrastructures in particular regions. It is a matter of common observation, that much of the public debate on policy issues is conducted in a somewhat make-believe manner in which statistical techniques are often used as much to confuse issues as to clarify them. This is particularly true in the regional policy field since the core of the regional problem is the differential standards, and the differential rates of growth, which find their quantitative expression in statistical and often over-simplified terms. A few examples may be given to show, in the light of the previous analysis, the lack of validity of the techniques referred to.

a) The mileage of roads needed in a region is indicated by comparisons with other regions on a population or area basis

This is clearly nonsensical. Not only would the two comparisons yield different results since population densities vary but needs can also be measured by the capacity of existing roads to carry the existing and prospective traffic which may bear no direct relation to either area or population. A given mileage in roads, costing the same amount but in different areas can generate quite different amounts of traffic and produce different benefits in terms of economic growth. The need for roads can therefore only be assessed after appraisal of the effects and a comparison of the rates of return or benefit they would bring in relation to prescribed standards. The technique used in the United Kingdom of judging the need for road construction by reference to TAL (Traffic and Accident Loss), though not of itself requiring a uniform standard for all parts of the country, is a recognition of the inadequacy of simple statistical criteria. Even such sophisticated techniques may not provide a sufficient measure of economic benefit and regional growth that may be brought about by road construction: but only when the fullest assessment of benefit is made can relative need be judged. It is still open to Governments, on political or other grounds, to give preference to areas where presumed benefit is less but the judgement requires more than the simple comparison in the example.

b) Public expenditure on new construction and works shoud be proportional to regional populations and areas.

This is a generalized version of the proposition in (a) and is equally invalid. The need for new construction also turns on the adequacy or otherwise of the existing structure and the contribution it would make to specific regional problem. Discontinuity is also a feature of some public works, e.g. in energy and water supplies, since they are planned to meet future as well as present needs and, once constructed, reduce the need for further development for some years ahead and alter the priorities between regions, irrespective of areas or populations. The amount of new construction that can be financed is also a function of the fiscal structure of a country, the part that local authority and private sector resources play in the financing of new constructions and the rate of return that is required to justify an investment. It is to be doubted if any known system of finance could ensure a proportionate distribution of total expenditure on infrastructure; or if it could, the results in terms of regional growth and development would not bear any relation to the desired pattern.

c) The need for "social" infrastructure can be measures by indices of disparities in provision per head.

This is another version of the general proposition that needs are greatest where standards of living are lowest; including the standards in the social services of housing, health, education and amenity. It may be true in a philosophical or moral sense but as a guide to a regional infrastructure policy has no more validity or practical use than the previous propositions. There is a wide range of indices of social needs, from the number of dwellings or units of accomodation (housing), to the "quality" of the units (provision of living rooms, separate bed rooms, toilets, piped water or bath rooms) and the staff/pupil or doctor/patient ratios in the education and health sectors. Such indices, interesting though they may be as an indication of regional disparities, afford no guide to the infrastructure policies that should be adopted. The effective demand for houses or bathrooms is not governed by absolute standards but by income levels and rent or price policies. These have their own dynamic conditioning factors; the supply by costs and the degree to which they are matched by effective demand. The provision of a housing infrastructure of a region, and all that goes with it, such as water supplies, drainage and sewerage, roads, gas and electricity can only be based on appraisal of both demand and supply factors. Government policies can influence these factors, e. g. by rent support and building subsidies and may use indices of disparities in framing such policies. It remains true, however, that the level of housing infrastructure which is needed in practice is the one which equilibrates supply and demand after taking account of Government policies. Moreover, the need for housing, measured by effective demand, will tend to be higher. If "real" housing needs in poorer areas are to be satisfied the answer may lie, not in the direct provision of housing for which effective demand does not exist, but the development of those infrastructures which are necessary for the economic growth from which higher incomes can result.

Similar considerations apply in the education and health sectors. Staff ratios are, by themselves, no indication of the adequacy or otherwise of the level and quality of educational and health services which are needed or can be afforded by a regional economy. Regions in which there is better provision may still be inadequately staffed, but have more scope for expansion of services.

It is not necessary to multiply the examples. The conclusion can be drawn that infrastructure deficiencies in regions, as measured by the kind of statistical indices mentioned, are only symptoms of a problem. As with medicine, cure lies in treating causes rather than symptoms and the infrastructure policies needed are those that result from a full appraisal of the underlying relationships, of infrastructure and economic development, regionally and interregionally.

CONCLUSIONS

A number of points can be made as conclusions to this discussion.

The first is, that in its various forms, the infrastructure of a country is, in total, one of the large claimants on the national income. It is complementary to, or a partner with, the industrial and economic structure with which it jointly generates the incomes and social products out of which consumption, savings and investments, and standards of living are assured. Management of the national economy is management of all these things, in relation and not in isolation from each other. The management of the economy to secure regional objectives implies the shaping of regional infrastructure policies in keeping with those objectives. The economic objective involved is the same as in other directions: to see that resources are applied to the best advantage to secure the maximum economic and social benefit possible. Infrastructure policies whether national, regional or local, which depart from this criterion are not made the less wasteful of national resources simply because certain objectives are deemed desirable. There is no valid reason therefore, simply because regional objectives may be in view, to exempt regional infrastructure policies from the tests of costs and benefits to which all resource use should, in a world in which resources are limited compared with the needs of society, be subjected. The development of suitable costs and benefit techniques, as opposed to the use of simple criteria of regional differences is a necessary part of well founded infrastructure policies.

Second, it would seem, in some countries at least, regional infrastructure policies are seen as diversionary or corrective, involving some switch of resources away from where they would be used under normal cost benefit criteria to regions where, under the same criteria, they would not be used. Such policies may be complementary or alternative to the policies for influencing the location of economic growth or distribution of economic growth different from the one which would be brought about by normal economic forces. It cannot be argued that such policies are wrong or of no effect though they may have the disadvantage of promoting infrastructure as an end in itself and with less than adequate regard for costs and benefits. What has been argued however is that marginal shifts in resources devoted to infrastructure can have little effect on the regional structure of a country as a whole, when by far the greater part of the country's infrastructure is developed according to criteria in which regional objectives play little part. The problem of changing the regional structure of a country to bring about fundamental changes, whether for social or economic purposes, is one of great magnitude. It would seem that not until regional and national policies are more closely integrated, and national policy criteria are adjusted to feasible and well based objectives of regional policy can regional infrastructure policies play more than a limited role. As has been said elsewhere the true regional policies that a country follows are denoted by the regional effect of all its policies rather than those which are specifically designated to be "regional".

Third, it has been suggested that regional infrastructure policies, whether marginal or global in concept, are closely linked with strategic planning. There are two problems involved here. The need for proper survey and diagnosis of regional infrastructure requirements and the relation of the infrastructure of various kinds to economic development is one. This requires also the making of considered judgements both on the order of priorities of the different types of infrastructure, which must vary from region to region, and on the relative priorities of economic and other objectives which infrastructure policy can influence. The second problem of strategic planning is that of organisation, coordination and institutional competence. If this problem is not adequately tackled many of the resources devoted to improvements in regional infrastructures can be misapplied and fail to achieve their purposes.

Finally, there would seem to be a need to establish some limits to the departures from the normal criteria by which investment in infrastructure has to be justified. One means by which this is sometimes done, and which has much to commend it, is to fix, and adhere to differential required rates of returns or benefits in those regions which require special consideration. Subjecting investment projects to cost benefit criteria is one means of using scarce capital wisely and the use of differential favourable rates would not only place the regions concerned at an advantage but place a brake on investment which cannot yield a definite return. It is suggested that some such overt limitations are necessary if regional infrastructure policies are to be properly attuned to needs without leading to a misapplication and possibly wasteful use of resources; a consideration which may become all the more important as international co-operation in regional policies progresses.

IX

PUBLIC FINANCE ASPECTS OF REGIONAL POLICIES

Some information on financial resources devoted to regional policies was given by the Working Party in their report RFED pp. 61-66. The Working Party observed that in a number of countries various expenditures in respect of regional development were grouped in a central fund, although these generally were supplemented by additional resources which could not be readily quantified from regular budgetary appropriations. Of the countries discussed in that report only Denmark, Finland and the United Kingdom did not have central funds. A further generalization made was that in most cases regional expenditure varied between one per cent to three per cent of total expenditure of central Governments.

The precise form and amounts of central Government expenditure devoted to regional policy purposes is subject to constant review and change and an up to date examination of the current situation would no doubt show many differences in detail from the picture presented in RFED. The financial and budgetary situations of Governments are susceptible to rapid changes from year to year as are the policy aims expressed in terms of financial resources. The same applies to particular aspects of financial policies, whether for regional or any other of the multifarious purposes to which public resources are applied. The frequent, if inevitable, changes make it difficult and almost impossible to obtain, at any one point of time, a meaningful picture of the financial resources currently devoted to regional policies and their importance. Moreover absolute global figures mean little of they are not broken down into their components, and variations in percentages can equally mean little if it is not clear to what they are due, e. g. to a change in total Government expenditure or to the part from which the percentage is calculated. Changes in the value of money, due to inflation, also distort the picture.

Such difficulties are often brushed aside by commentators on regional policies who wish either to assert that not enough is spent on regional policies to secure their objectives or, conversely, that too much is spent out of the limited resources available for all purposes. Since concepts of "too little" or "too much" are themselves question begging, a debate conducted in the absence of agreed methods of assessing the available data lends itself more to political controversy and subjective argument rather than to objective answer. Nonetheless, since public finance provides one of the principal ways in which resources can be deployed for regional policy purposes, an understanding of its role and methodology is a necessary part of any discussion of the "issues" of regional policy.

Among the questions which are thrown up by the sort of information contained in RFED the following might be listed as worthy of consideration:

1. Should all funds for regional development be concentrated in a separate budget? If so how should the size and role of the budget be determined?

2. In cases in which there is no single budget should there be a national budget, comprised of the regional elements of each separate (Departmental) budget?

3. How should the scale of public finance required for regional purposes be determined?

4. What contributory expenditure, from non central Government sources, should be deemed expenditure for regional purposes?

5. What, if any, limitations, should be imposed on the growth of public expenditures for regional purposes, or what criteria should be used to judge adequacy or otherwise in relation to policy objectives?

6. How should the impact, or effectiveness, of public expenditure for regional purposes be assessed?

7. What relationship should regional expenditure bear to expenditure for other purposes, or to the total budget?

8. Should regional expenditure be the responsability of autonomous Agencies distinct from Government Departments?

These and similar questions are interrelated and overlapping and there can be no single "right" answer to any of them which would fit all circumstances. In all countries public finance is an instrument for the carrying out of policies and its organisation reflects the constitutional, political and administrative structure. The place which regional policies find in the total activities of Government and their relative role and importance also differ so widely that what would be appropriate in one country could be quite unsuited to the circumstances of another. Discussion of these questions is most likely to be helpful therefore if confined to the advantages and disadvantages of alternative principles in given circumstances, rather than directed to a search for "ideal" solutions.

The advantage of a single central fund or budget incorporating all expenditures on regional policies is three fold. It permits centralized and uniform direction of the use of available funds, in accordance with a single set of policy aims and priorities; it enables a distinction to be made, and clearly drawn, between "ordinary" expenditure which takes place in all regions, and that "additional" expenditure which is required to modify, correct or enhance the regional effect of normal expenditure; and it enables the scale of the effort involved to change the regional situations to be more readily assessed, and therefore to be expanded or contracted if the assessment shows this to be necessary in relation to defined objectives. Derivative from these advantages are an enhanced ability of the legislative authority to ascertain and control the direction of policy and the expenditure of funds associated with it, and to weigh the expenditure against other claims on the nation's resources, which find a place in State expenditure programmes. In addition, it eases the problem of interdepartmental co-ordination, since each Department can pursue its own objectives in accordance with its national criteria, leaving to those in charge of the central regional budget to supplement their efforts where necessary for regional policy purposes.

Thus, under such a system, Departments concerned with, say, housing, roads, water supplies, economic or social development would pursue their policies without regional differentiation, so avoiding conflict between them on the nature and scale of such differentiation. The role of the central regional budget would be to provide the means to effect regional differentiation within the framework of a single self-consistent set of criteria. The size or scale of the regional budget would thus provide an indication of the extent to which the Government as a whole saw the necessity for regional differentiation in its policies and was prepared to devote resources to it. The system would therefore also lend itself more easily than one in which regional expenditure is dispersed among Departments to public control and accountability. The regional policy budget would be subject to the same scrutiny as others.

The various advantages can also be expressed in a more positive and less "defensive" way. It is sometimes said that, in some countries at least, regional policy is only a statement of aspirations and does not "bite" because it has no "teeth". If it is true that a "bite" is only as strong as the teeth, the bite of regional policy can only be as strong as the financial "teeth" available to it. The regional budget, on this basis, can be seen as the teeth by which it can obtain its share of the "national cake". Instead of being dependant on the readiness of individual Ministers or Departments to modify their own policies to take account of regional needs, which they may see as having less priority than other aims, regional policy can be implemented by the application of funds directly assigned for the purpose.

A central regional budget is not, however, free from disadvantages. Unless sufficient funds were allocated to it, it could not achieve its aims, while it would relieve, or offer an excuse to other budgets to ignore the claims of regional policy. Such a situation could well arise, especially in the initial stages, since new budgets, or new fields of expenditure inevitably diminish resources available for other purposes. Secondly, it could provide a temptation to "unload" normal expenditure on the regional budget and enable other Departments with their own budgets to disregard the regional implications of their policies, on the ground that they were now catered for by the regional budget. If the latter were insufficient the achievement of regional policy aims would be diminished rather than enhanced by the creation of a regional budget. Thirdly, the problem of drawing a distinction between "normal" expenditure and expenditure required for regional differential purposes is a difficult one and likely to offer scope for interdepartmental "squabbling" about the Vote on which given expenditure should fall. There could also be genuine conflicts of view over the desirability of incurring expenditure on regional policy grounds which is rejected on grounds of "normal" criteria. (Thus the Department responsible for planning road expenditure according to standard national criteria may consider that expenditure to promote regional development could better be applied to remedying deficiencies in accordance with specific criteria). The creation of a budget also involves an administrative problem, of deciding for example on the need for a separate Ministry devoted to regional development, or for special co-ordinating machinery to manage the central regional fund.

We do not pretend to know how far the considerations mentioned above, in favour and against central funds, have determined the practices of Member countries. It will be noted from RFED that the majority of Member countries appear to have opted for systems of central funds, including the creation of the Department of Regional Economic Expansion in Canada, the setting up of fund endowed Agencies in the United States, and various forms of regional development funds in other countries, some of which represent only a part of the total resources applied. The fact that certain countries with vigorous regional policies adopt different policies, as shown by the contrast between Italy and the United Kingdom, serves to emphasize that there is no obvious balance of advantage between one method and the other.

Even it is decided that a single budget is undesirable or impracticable question (2) still arises, whether the pursuit of regional policies requires at least a notional budget. The advantage of a notional budget is that it would bring out one statement of all the forms, and quantities, of public expenditure devoted to regional policy objectives. This would no doubt be a complex task, requiring a distinction to be made, within each spening Department, between the regional policy elements of its programmes and those which fall within the "normal" category. It would enable attention to be focussed on the total scale of the regional effort, and the diverse elements from which it is composed, thereby serving both public accountability and the formulation of judgements on the adequacy or otherwise of the regional policy effort. The fragmentation of information on public expenditure can well be an obstacle to understanding the policies and to assessing their effectiveness. The Working Party has not considered this issue and we do no more than suggest that it is one deserving some thought.

Our question (3), of how to determine the scale of public finance required for regional policy purposes is an important one. Though it would be posed more acutely if central or notional budgets are adopted it arises also in any attempt to relate public expenditure rationally to the achievement of policy objectives. In an earlier chapter a distinction has been drawn between ultimate, intermediate and specific objectives. Insofar as these call for public finance the test of their realism is in the scale of public finance that is allocated to them. Alternative methods for determining the scale are, basically, to adjust the scale of public finance to the objectives, or to adjust the objectives to the scale of public finance that can be made available. In practice both procedures tend to be adopted, the former as pressures are felt to make greater progress towards the objectives and the latter as aspirations give way to the reality that there are insufficient resources to go round.

The adoption of certain statistical criteria, such that public expenditure on regional policies should not fall below a fixed percentage of the national budget, or that public investment should bear some prescribed proportion to the size of regional areas or their populations has the attraction that they provide some sort of measurable target to which to aspire. Such concepts are often based on the notion that if "disadvantaged" regions are to move closer towards the national average they should receive a more than proportionate "share" of national expenditure. This would certainly seem to be implied in the concept of narrowing the "gap" or regional "disparities"? The provision in the Italian national programme for the allocation of not less than 40 per cent of the total volume of gross fixed investment to the Mezzogiorno (RFED p. 67) is an illustration of the use of this technique. While this is roughly proportionate to the area and population it represents a raising of the area's proportion of national investment which tended to be lower than in the more developed regions of the country. It affords a measurable target, providing both a stimulus to Government Departments to find means of increasing investment in the Mezzogiorno, and a standard by which to judge, and to examine, and possibly remedy, the reasons for any short fall in achievement. The contrast between such a figure and the 1 per cent to three per cent which central regional funds represent in a number of countries (see above) is not necessarily as real as it might seem. The central funds referred to are no measure of the total public expenditure in the regions and the operation of both "normal" and regional policies can be such as to produce an interregional distribution bearing much closer to the distribution of population where relative needs and potentialities may not be so markedly different as in Italy. It may be noted that in the United Kingdom, one of the countries which did not have a central regional policy fund, the proportion of public expenditure on new construction in 1969 was roughly proportionate to the population in the S. E. region and exceeded it in Scotland. (Source: Abstract of Regional Statistics 1970. HMSO Tables 5 and 34).

The use of predetermined targets, whether in terms of absolute figures or percentages to settle the scale of public finance for regional development carries with it certain dangers. It is, for example, easy to assert that 1 per cent of total public expenditure is only a "small" proportion and that raising it by half, or doubling it, ought to be well within the bounds of possibility. This is of course a logical fallacy but one which can produce absurd consequences. Every 1 per cent of a total is a "small" proportion, but raising each 1 per cent by half or more would mean raising the national total by the same proportion, a very different proposition. What matters is the possibility of raising one particular segment of public expenditure by more than others and this depends on the relative importance of the segments and their capability for expansion. In countries with a growth rate of say, 5 per cent, most of the growth arises from, and is needed for, the expansion of existing activities and is not necessarily transferable to a new purpose. The "disposable" new growth may only be a fraction of the total and not all of that can be earmarked for a specific purpose. The important question is how marginal movements of growth can be allocated between the many competing claims on it, of which regional objectives are only a part.

While these considerations do not rule out the use of "target" figures, they do mean that such figures can only be realistic if they follow from a careful analysis of the existing pattern of expenditure and the directions in which marginal change can be secured for regional policy purposes.

No picture of public finance available for regional policy purposes would be complete which made mention only of funds derived from central sources. These themselves take several forms, from the direct expenditure of central Government departments on specific objectives in regions, to the allocation of central funds to regional or local authorities whether for general revenue support or particular projects, and the provision of central finance to State supported agencies with defined regional functions. The real, as distinct from the theoretical, regional policy that is being followed by central Government is in part indicated by the way central funds are in fact distributed between regions. Locally generated finance may however play a complementary part, varying between countries according to their financial system, which provide different roles and different scope for local financial systems. Regions themselves tend to vary a great deal in financial capacity according to their economic base and the systems of local revenue raising. One function of central finance may be to encourage, by the use of "matching" arrangements, the greater mobilisation of local resources to secure greater local participation or initiative in regional development. The "matching" contribution put up by local or regional authorities towards a regional development programme, if falling outside the normal range of local public finance, can be regarded as a contribution to expenditure for regional purposes.

The importance of the role that may be played by locally generated public finance in a region depends not only on the financial capacity of the region itself but on the nature of the public finance system, and the range of functions assigned to local or regional authorities. In highly centralized countries in which very limited functions are carried out by small and financially weak local authorities the great bulk of public expenditure is in the hands of the central authorities and the ability of local authorities or institutions to make an effective contribution to regional policies is correspondingly limited. In contrast, strong regional institutions, whether States of Federal countries or large local authorities in centralized states, command a larger proportion of the public financial resources required for all purposes, including those of regional development. In assessing the need for changing the interregional distribution of central public expenditure, or the capacity of regions to increase their contribution towards regional objectives, regard has to be paid to the structure of the public finance system as a whole. This entails consideration not only of the expenditure side of the account but also the revenue side, i.e. the way in which central and local tax systems provide the revenue to be spent by the various authorities.

In highly centralized countries in which local authorities play a small part and in which revenue systems are more or less uniform throughout the country the revenue contributed by each region will tend to be a function of population and economic product. The expenditure in each region may bear no special relation to this. Not only will a certain proportion be devoted to the central "overheads" of the State in the shape of central administration (mainly in the capital region), defence, and other central purposes, but the remainder may be distributed in relation to potentiality as well as "need". The proportions in which central expenditure is divided between regions can be quite different from the proportions in which revenue is obtained from the same regions. In a sense the real contribution which is made by the centre to the regions is measured by the excess of the revenue derived from the region over expenditure in the region, in both cases after deduction of appropriate contributions towards central "overheads". In such countries regional disparities may be a reflection not only of differences in the economic structure or capacity of each region but also of the workings of the public finance system which may enhance or diminish the disparities, according to the way it works. The ability of a region to contribute to its own development is correspondingly limited by the fact that the greater part of its revenue capacity is at the disposal of the central authorities. This is not, of course, to say that centralized public finance systems may not be effective in dealing with regional problems. They may be much more effective than alternative decentralized systems if these are unable to provide the manpower and skills required for administration and development.

In less centralized systems, in which local or regional authorities are effective and efficient and which retain a higher proportion of the locally generated revenues their contribution to regional policies and development may be much higher than in the centralized countries and the need for redistributive action between regions by central authorities much less.

The answer to question (4) is therefore not a simple one. In a sense all public expenditure in a region from non central funds can be deemed expenditure for regional purposes, since it is spent in and for the region, whether for the maintenance of services or for their development. However, a distinction can be drawn between "normal" or running expenditure and expenditure designed to enhance the region's development through expansion of services, new construction and new infrastructure. If by the term regional policies is meant those policies or activities designed to enhance the capacity of the region within the framework of national policies it is only that part of the expenditure which is "extra" or over and above the normal, that can be regarded as expenditure for regional policy purposes. Its contribution is then in the extra effort it makes to mobilize financial resources for regional development.

In most writing on regional issues comparatively little attention is given to the question of mobilisation of regional financial resources or to "self-help" since regional policy tends to be seen largely as a question of transfer of resources from the centre to the disadvantaged regions which often have insufficient resources even, for the maintenance of necessary services on a satisfactory level. This is not universally true since disadvantaged regions may, by virtue of the system of public finance, still command important resources capable of expansion. Another reason for ignoring the potential regional contribution is that many regions have no administrative or financial organisation or autonomy and the financial resources available for regional development are entirely made up by central funds. This is not the case however in Federal systems or in those countries which have created new forms of regional organisations with powers to raise revenues.

It is, perhaps, a question meriting consideration whether it would not be worth attempting making a closer assessment of the financial contribution that a region makes, or would be capable of making, to the objectives of regional policy as applied to the region. An advantage is that it would permit a better evaluation of the need for central contributions. It could also reveal, by comparisons between regions, whether there was scope for a greater regional effort. Assessments of the net contribution made by regions to central revenues could be of some help in formulating or revising the principles on which central assistance is distributed between regions. It has to be recognized that such assessments can lead to highly charged arguments as to what constitutes "fair shares" of central expenditure as between regions and to such arguments as that each region should receive a share corresponding to its population. Such arguments cannot be justified in economic terms, since the needs and scope for expenditure in each region will vary with its economic and social situation. Nonetheless the lack in most countries, of any attempt to ascertain the total inward and outward flows of public finance makes it difficult to determine in what ways, and to what degree, public expenditure patterns should be modified to secure defined regional policy objectives. Where there are central regional funds to support regional programmes they could also be used more rationally if the total funds available from regional resources could be assessed, through an actual or notional regional budget.

This can also be illustrated by reference to the concept of "matching" contributions, by which the central authority provides a proportion of the total expenditure on a project on condition that the regional or local authority provides the remainder. This is designed to act both as a stimulus and a safeguard against irresponsible use by the local or regional authorities of central funds. The rate of central contribution, or the matching contribution required from the local authority may be varied from region to region, usually by requiring a lower contribution from the poorer regions than from the others. (Thus, in the United Kingdom the central Government makes grants for the clearance of derelict land varying from 50 per cent to 80 per cent of the cost according to region). The actual value of such grants however depends both on the scale of the problem they are meant to tackle and also on the total resources available and the competing claims in them. In some circumstances a 50 per cent grant may achieve more results in one region than an 80 per cent in another. For the former the ability and willingness to raise the matching 50 per cent may be greater than the ability and willingness to raise the matching 20 per cent in the latter. The effectiveness of the system can therefore only be gauged by relating the matching contribution required to the totality of claims on the regional financial resources.

One further general point about local finance can be conveniently made at this stage. As has been indicated some of the problems of regional backwardness or disparities are due to the comparative paucity of necessary services which act as a deterrent to growth and development. To secure the right remedy it is necessary to establish the reasons why local or regional authorities are unable to provide the services at an equivalent level to those obtainable elsewhere. The reasons may be in the poverty of the region, but they may, in some cases, also lie in the lack of a suitable system of local administration and local finance which enables local resources to be fully mobilized. The solution to some types of regional disparities may be found therefore not in the greater provision of central funds but in the better organisation of local administration so that it can utilize local resources to greater effect. The movement in many countries towards local Government and regional Government may be seen perhaps as recognition of the principle that regions have a greater part to play, and can make a greater financial contribution to the solution of regional problems.

Questions (5) (6) and (7) are so closely related to each other that it is useful to discuss them together. The issues they raise are central to any consideration of regional policies as a whole and are linked with the problem, discussed elsewhere, of the conflicts between different objectives of Government. As has been noted, it is easy to infer from such data as are given in RFED that the resources devoted by Governments to the regional problems, however defined, are quite insufficient and the answers must be found in a steady increase of the proportion of resources allocated to it. This attitude is indeed often adopted by Governments, either when explaining the insufficient progress hitherto or in expressing intentions to make greater progress in future by increasing financial resources for regional policy purposes. Such attitudes are more easily adopted when dealing with regional policies in isolation and it usually falls to the financial authorities to adopt the less popular attitude that regional problems are only one aspect of the total problems for which available resources are never adequate.

Though it may be true that many countries devote insufficient financial resources to tackling regional problems and that the fixing of expenditure "targets" may be a useful device for securing greater results we see no reason for exempting regional policies from the normal principles which govern public expenditure, viz that expenditure must be justified by its expected results, that the expected results should, in some definable sense, be as good as would be obtained by using the same resources in alternative ways, and that the expenditure should be applied effectively for its purpose. Such principles preclude not only the adoption of "the sky is the limit" as a basis for determining the expenditure on regional policies but also the adoption of arbitrary limits which bear no relation to what results from their application. When the working out of the principles reveals that the regional policy objectives cannot be achieved the choice - ultimately a political one - then lies between the revision of the objectives or the abandonment of the principles. The dilemma is often resolved in practice by relegating the objectives to the category of "ultimate" and pursuing those "specific objectives which can be justified by application of normal financial principles.

It is not, however, necessary to be pessimistic about the possibility of achieving a continually higher rate of public expenditure on regional objectives. Public financial resources, though not unlimited, are capable of continual expansion as the economy grows and a higher proportion of available resources can be devoted to objectives which are deemed to be feasible and can be justified by comparison with alternative fields of expenditure. There is an interplay between resource use and objectives and neither is fixed at any point of time. The path to higher justifiable-expenditure on regional objectives is through the continual appraisal of the possibilities of feasible projects which conform with the objectives. The limits to further expenditure, within the "normal" financial principles, need only be set by realities, the actual scope for worth-while development and the feasibility of calculating costs and benefits and carrying out projects. The impact, or effectiveness of public expenditure for regional purposes, as in other spheres, cannot be judged by the amount of the expenditure but by the results it can be expected to produce.

The observance of such principles implies also a flexible approach to the question of the relationship regional expenditure should bear to the total budget. If regional expenditure is subjected to the same criteria as expenditure on other purposes the proportion is a resultant rather than a determinant of the criteria. The adoption of an arbitrarily fixed proportion could either result in too much, or too little being devoted to regional purposes, too much implying a wasteful use of resources, and too little implying insufficient exploitation of the real possibilities that exist for regional development.

In short, public finance is neither the controller of public policies nor a passive instrument for giving effect to them. What matters is the criteria adopted to ensure that public expenditure is most usefully and effectively applied to competing objectives. Rules of thumb for determining the volume or proportion of expenditure on selected objectives, whether regional or otherwise, are no substitute for careful appraisal of needs and scope for regional development. If public expenditure on this has been too little in the past the answer must lie, not in arbitrary increases in the amount of public expenditure but in increased effort to determine the scope for justifiable expenditure.

The final question (8) in our list is in part an administrative one but the question of the advantages or disadvantages of separate Agencies from an administrative point of view is best dealt with in the section on administrative problems. The public finance aspect of the question is whether autonomous agencies provide a better means of applying public financie to regional purposes than the ordinary machinery of Government.

As has been stated there can be no simple answer to this which applied equally to all the divergent circumstances of different countries. General discussion can serve only to indicate some of the considerations which may be relevant in particular cases.

One of the considerations is whether sufficient, justifiable, expenditure can be generated for regional purposes if regional policies are dependent in the decisions of individual Government departments. A second consideration is whether, if each individual Department is responsible for its own priorities the resultant pattern of regional expenditure will provide the right "balance" between expenditure programmes. A further question is whether an autonomous agency is more able than a number of separate Departments to secure a co-ordinated approach both towards and within the local or regional authorities whose programmes may be complementary to those promoted at the centre. These questions are also relevant when considering the case for a central Government Department responsible for regional policy as opposed to separate Departments with co-ordinatory machinery between them.

The case for an Agency as such may itself rest on the answer to the first question and on the belief that, in the circumstances of a particular country, even a single Government Department may not have the flexibility or initiative of an Agency which is not subject to the same public control as a Government Department. In many countries such Agencies exist, in the regional and in other fields, and the contrast between, say, the Economic Development Administration in the United States and the Department for Regional Economic Expansion in Canada shows that the same considerations may lead to different conclusions by the Government concerned.

A decision in favour of an autonomous Agency turns, essentially, on a comparison with the alternative. If the need is to apply considerably greater resources to regional development would existing Departments be prepared to meet this need? To do so can require a diversion of resources from other purposes, already well established or the adoption of new criteria. New directions are often more difficult to follow than well trodden pathe. If the belief is that existing Departments will not, or cannot readily switch the resources they control to the objectives of regional policy the case for an Agency to which the necessary resources are granted will seem stronger, though its effectiveness will still depend on whether it is in fact granted adequate resources.

The second consideration turns on the fact that central Government Departments have a range of functions in relation to the country as a whole, and that each Department may have different priorities in respect of individual regions. The result may be collections of programmes which, looked at from the point of view of individual regions, may give greater or less emphasis to particular programmes than would be the case if regional programming was an integrated whole. Thus roads might take a lower priority if weighted against water supplies in a region, whereas if separate Departments were responsible for roads and water supplies the former might receive more attention.

The third consideration may turn on the practicability of co-ordinating the Government's contribution to a regional programme as a whole, if each Department is able to negotiate separately. Since negotiation involves a certain amount of "give" and "take", a single central Agency may be able to reach compromises with the regional organisation better than if each Department can decide for itself.

None of these considerations are conclusive but a possible generalization is that the case for an Agency is stronger where regional policy constitutes a real departure from existing policies and where relatively considerable resources need to be diverted from existing uses. We see little point in Agencies however where the resources allocated to than are negligible in relation to the problems with which they are supposed to deal.

CONCLUSION

A number of conclusions would seem to emerge from this discussion. Public finance is a means both of implementing policies and of expressing them in measurable quantitative terms. Though the way in which public finance is applied reflects the administrative organisation for determining policies and carrying them out, the way in which public finance

resources are deployed afford a specific indication of the real public
sector policies that are being pursued, as distinct from policies which
are no more than statements of aspirations. An evaluation of the total
financial resources that are deployed for specific objectives, and of
their predicted effects, is necessary in reaching any conclusion about
the likelihood of attaining the objectives.

Regional policies differ in one important respect from most other
policies, in that their application is geographical or spatial, embracing
the greater part or the whole range of functional or sectoral policies.
Their purpose is to bring about changes in the regional distribution or
pattern of activities in a country, different from what would occur as a
result of "normal" functional or sectoral policies which are not regionally differentiated. Insofar as public sector policies play an important
part in determining the spatial distribution of a country's economic and
social life changes in the regional distribution of public finance as a
whole are both a determinant and consequence of the regional policies
pursued.

The use of central regional budgets, which bring together all the
public funds designed to make an impact on regional problems is an
administrative question, and has advantages and disadvantages which
preclude any single recommendation regarding their adoption. Whether
such a system is adopted or not no central budget is likely to comprehend
all the forms of public expenditure which have a bearing on regional
policies. The concept of a notional budget which does this could prove
helpful in making a rational assessment of the prospects of achieving
the desired results of specific regional policies. The case for such
notional budgets is stregthened by the fact that very few if any countries
have attempted to survey their regional policies as a whole or to match
their objectives against the public expenditure that would be involved.
A prerequisite for assessing whether the scale of effort is sufficient or
should be increased is an appraisal, preferably a continuing one, of the
public sector resources that are deployed. We would recommend that
in countries in which a sustained long term effort is required to modify
the regional distribution of activity, thought should be given to the establishment of comprehensive notional budgets as a tool for the assessment of the scale of the problems to be tackled. The Working Party
might with advantage seek to revise its picture of the financial resources
used for regional purposes and develop a model form to provide some
degree of comparability.

An examination of such information as is available would suggest
that few countries devote more than minimal marginal finance resources
to the objectives of regional policy. This impression can be misleading, since special funds may represent only a small fraction of the
total resources which are applied, or diverted, to bringing about shifts

210

in regional distribution of activities. It is difficult to see how any conclusion can be drawn as to the impact effect or adequacy of public expenditure in the absence of a comprehensive survey of the total resources deployed. Nonetheless there are some reasons (developed in the chapter on "Rectifying Imbalances") to suppose that the scale of public resources devoted to regional policy purposes is not adequate in relation to stated or presumed objectives. Survey of the total scale is therefore all the more necessary if rational decisions are to be made, either to modify the scale, or, if this is not practicable, to modify the objectives themselves. Moreover, the real effect of public expenditure policies can only be gauged against the net balance of expenditure and revenues.

Since public expenditure for regional purposes is not confined to central Government the complementary role of regional or local authorities has to be taken into account. Some regional problems result from the deficiencies of the local Government system rather than from inherent lack of resources. In such cases the remedy may not lie in increasing transfer of central resources to support those of local authorities but to improve local Government so that it can play its proper part in mobilizing local resources. In any case comparisons of the proportions of central resources used for regional policies would not be valid without regard to the differing organisation and role of local and regional financial systems.

The use of percentages of total expenditure to provide "Targets" can produce a stimulus towards greater effort to resolve regional problems but it is suggested that the true key towards progress lies in the careful appraisal of regional development possibilities rather than in the adoption of predetermined targets. Despite the importance and urgency of many regional problems there are no good reasons, in economic terms, for exempting public expenditure on regional problems from proper cost/benefit criteria on the principles of alternative costs and of effective administration. Such exemption could only lead to wasteful expenditure without achieving the desired results. Public expenditure can only be fruitful if it is used intelligently. The basic aims of regional policies are long term and can only be achieved by a sustained effort to apply resources where they can produce the greatest benefit.

Finally, the question of separate Agencies denotes an assessment of the comparative merits of normal administration in particular circumstances. Some of the arguments for and against have been indicated and can be summed up by saying that their advantages are most definite when substantial resources need to be diverted from ordinary purposes to give new impetus to the tackling of regional problems.

X

THE PROBLEM OF ORGANISATION

Since each country has its own constitutional and political structure, its own systems of administration and its own peculiar set of problems it is not to be expected that there would be any kind of uniformity in the forms of organisation which exist to deal with any of the major problems. This is as true in the field of regional policies as of any other. Moreover, in each country organisation is anything but static. Organisation is constantly modified as the tasks to be accomplished change, as more or less weight has to be given to particular tasks and as existing organisation is found wanting. It is hardly necessary to describe the many changes which have occurred in recent years alone to establish that as new policies are adopted, or as existing policies are changed, the organisation that is required for their implementation also changes.

It is also true that some forms of organisation are better than others as a means of carrying out particular tasks. The tasks with which Governments are faced are not, however, single tasks, each of which can be tackled separately, with its own specific organisation. They are multiple, virtually infinite in number. The problem of organisation is therefore not only that of finding the best way to deal with individual tasks but also that of grouping tasks together in such a way that inter-related problems can be tackled as a whole in the most convenient and effective way. The manner in which the totality of tasks is divided or grouped is itself a major problem of organisation, to which no one permanent solution has been found in any country, let alone a common solution among different countries.

Though some tasks of Governments are of a continuing and permanent character, the permutations and combinations in their relative importance and in the success or otherwise to deal with them are many. Constant change and adaptation of organisation is required therefore even to deal with those problems which are of a permanent character. Since new problems also arise and present additional organisation

213

problems it is a fair presumption that the maintenance, for any very long period of time, of the same organisational structure is more likely to be an indication of inadequate response to needs than of its suitability to its tasks.

Even the most central tasks of Government do not lead to any single pattern of organisation which could be described as the most efficient or reflect any norm. Political considerations themselves play an important part. They involve such questions as the relation of the head of Government to other Ministers, the size, in terms of numbers of the central executive body (Cabinet, Council of Ministers) in which political as well as technical factors are relevant. Seniority, experience and "quality" of Ministers and their political standing can determine the groupings of Departmental responsibilities and the Departmental structure of the work of the Government as a whole.

All these factors help to account for the varied ways in which the same set of problems are dealt with in different countries, or, at different times in the same country. The wide range of economic problems can be divided or grouped among Ministries and Departments - Treasuries, Finance Ministries, Ministries of Economic Affairs, Industry, Trade, Development, Employment and Economic Planning. The economic infrastructure, ports, harbours, energy, can be the responsbility of separate Departments or grouped together in various ways under one or more Department. Similarly, in the social field, housing, health, welfare and social services generally can be split or grouped in a variety of ways, none of which are necessarily better than the others.

In all these fields the two general desiderata - coordination and effectiveness - do not dictate any one solution. Coordination may be hampered if there are too many separate Departments with overlapping responsibilities and the solution may be to reduce the number of Departments with consequential increase in size. It is not the only solution, since coordination can also be effected by various forms of inter-departmental coordinating machinery at various Departmental and Ministerial levels. Effectiveness of a Department is a function not only of its size but of its internal organisation, the knowledge and expertise it can bring to bear and the complexity of the problems with which it has to deal. The nature of Government policies, the degree of intervention, for example, may determine whether large or small Departments are necessary and the kind of coordination machinery that is appropriate.

The problem of organisation is not only one of the structure of central Government. In unitary States there are various ways in which local and regional administration can be organised and in these, as in Federal States, the division of power and responsibilities between the central and local bodies must influence the organisation of both. In highly "centralized" unitary States in which the central authority not only lays down general policy but has a large degree of executive power in the local sphere local authorities have a corresponding small role. Policies of decentralization, which may be necessary if central Departments are too large or unresponsive to local needs, can take different forms, from delegation to, or extension of the powers of, local authorities, to the creation of regional bodies. In less centralized unitary States the existence of large local authorities with a wide range of executive powers reduces the size and functions of central Departments. Decentralization policies may present a choice between further development of local authority systems or the introduction of regional authorities the scope for which will depend on the nature of the problems and the capability of the local authorities to deal with them. In Federal States the way in which organisation can be adjusted to meet various problems is governed by the arrangements in the Constitution but there is still an interaction between the central, regional, State and local bodies which influences the organisation of all three.

The degree to which reliance is placed on non Governmental agencies to carry out particular functions also has implications for the appropriate organisation of Government at all levels. Agencies are of many kinds and can be centrally owned or sponsored or be the responsibility of local authorities, individually or collectively. They include Development Agencies of various types, public utilities and State enterprises to manage nationalized industries to mention only some. The number and role of such bodies is itself an indication of the type of response to organisational problems and inter-acts with that of Government, and so conditions the way in which Government needs to organise its own Departments.

Since there can obviously be no single answer to the question of what is the best organisation for all the customary tasks of Governments it is otiose to pose the question of what is the right organisation to cope with regional policy problems. It is still possible, and useful however to consider whether the pursuit of regional policies poses special problems of organisation, of which account should be taken in the ordinary processes of adapting and changing organisational systems in response to needs.

Organisation is not an end in itself but a means to an end. What is it for? is the question that has to be asked in devising an appropriate organisation. As has been suggested in an earlier chapter, regional policies have many objectives, "ultimate ", "intermediate" and "specific", but a listing of such objectives does not describe the organisational problems which are entailed. The regional objective of raising living standards, of increasing employment, improving the infrastructure can, as has been noted, be sought by a variety of policies and methods.

Different organisational problems arise, if, for example, the method by which employment is to be raised is by incentives to manufacturing industry or, alternatively, the overcoming of deficiencies in physical infrastructures (or by both). If the regional problem is lack of skills and education quite different organisational problems arise in providing a remedy. Examples need not be multiplied. It is necessary, in considering the organisational problems posed by regional policies, to go beyond objectives and methods and break them down into the tasks which they involve. Organisation in the broad sense is the allotting of tasks, of knowing what has to be done (what tasks must be carried out) and who is to do what.

The tasks which are implied in the objectives and methods of regional policies which have been discussed elsewhere in this work are innumerable and must be classified into broad categories for convenience of discussion. The following is only one of a number of possible classifications which would serve to illustrate the organisational problems inherent in regional policies:

1. Intelligence, forecasting, research and diagnosis;

2. Definition of aims and objectives;

3. Devising of policies and methods;

4. Implementation and operation of projects;

5. Coordination;

6. Supervision and control;

7. Monitoring, review and revision of policies.

No particular importance need to be attached to the order in which these broad tasks are placed. Such a list only designates some main, basic and distinct, tasks which are involved in the formulation, implementation and modification of regional policies. As is to be expected, in substance they are the same tasks as fall to any organisation which has to cope with a variety of complex problems. This does not invalidate the list. As has been remarked in other contexts, there is nothing so "special" about regional policies that they should be exempted from the application of the normal criteria by which the wisdom or feasibility of any policies must be judged. They do however present special problems and therefore organisational tasks under each head and these are considered below.

1. INTELLIGENCE, FORECASTING, RESEARCH AND DIAGNOSIS

The importance of establishing and appraising the relevant facts has been brought out in several of the preceding chapters. All regional policies rest on certain assumptions and judgements about the way economic and social forces at work have affected, and will in future affect the different parts of a country. The adoption of regional policies is based upon beliefs that they are necessary to modify the regional patterns that result from these forces. Even in countries in which regional policies play only a small part there is an implied judgement that the forces at work will not create such regional problems that special policies will be needed. Regional policies themselves involve the application and diversion of resources, in some cases substantial. Judgements of the scale on which resources should be applied rest on the same foundations of fact or interpretation of fact, as judgements of the need for the policies themselves. Inadequate knowledge of facts, or their incorrect or unobjective use can lead to wrong diagnosis, inappropriate or ineffective policies and misuse of resources.

"Intelligence" is of course necessary in all other fields but one of the distinguishing features of the regional policy field is that it is concerned with a wide, if not the widest, range of facts. Knowledge and appraisal is required of population, composition and trends, industrial structure, occupational skills, social conditions, environmental and infrastructural needs, people and preferences, and interregional differences to mention only some. The way in which external factors operate on a regional situation not only requires knowledge of those factors themselves but the way in which they act on a region add to the complexity of the task inherent in providing an adequate factual base for policy.

Whatever organisation is adopted to meet these needs several distinct tasks are involved: deciding what information is required; organising and gathering it and filling gaps; ensuring its availability to different branches of the administration or administrations concerned with its use; developing proper techniques of interpretation, forecasting, diagnosis of the reasons behind the problems; recruiting and deploying the necessary technical and professional experts (scarce in most countries) in the most effective manner; and, finally, disseminating the results of inquiry and research to the bodies and organisations, planning or executive, which need them or can make use of them.

These tasks are, theoretically, distinct from those in (2) - (7) of the main headings given above, but organisation is a practical problem. It cannot therefore be argued that they must all be carried out by the same organisation or that there is a preferred way, in all circumstances, to distribute such tasks among the organisations concerned with the other tasks. There are a number of reasons why, in most countries, these tasks tend to be split up between different Government Departments or other bodies and organisations.

First, much of the statistical and other information about regions originates from the work of the Government Departments, local authorities and agencies which need it for the formulation of their own policies. The use and interpretation of the data often calls for an expertise which is available only in the originating Department and cannot easily be duplicated or dispersed. Second, such information as is available is required for a multiplicity of purposes, for purposes of national as well as regional policies. Departments concerned with regional problems are not the only claimants on the data, and their claims may carry much less weight than those of others. Third, particular types of regional intelligence work will be more important in some directions than others. Thus much information about a particular region may be of little relevance outside the region except for the purpose of interregional comparison.

These reasons do not dispose entirely of the case for a greater unification of the handling of the regional intelligence task. Not only is it a comprehensive one requiring a balanced appraisal of many different kinds of information but the purpose is to provide a basis for what is, essentially, a collection of regionally differentiated policies. Each Department, or indeed each regional or local authority may have its own view of the significance for policy of the data and information it has at its disposal. That view could well be different from the one that would be based on a collation of all necessary information, without any element of bias such as an interested Department or regional organisation might well have. This is, perhaps, particularly important in diagnosis or investigation of all the factors which contribute to a situation. A Department which is concerned only with some aspects, for which it has policy responsibilities, is unlikely to be the best equipped to make an objective diagnosis of a regional situation as a whole.

The Working Party has, on more than one occasion, drawn attention to the importance of improving the factual information required for regional purposes, by research and development of suitable techniques for interpretation of data. There is however, still, in many countries, a considerable lack, at least in published form, of regular and comprehensive surveys of regional information, while the undoubted progress in research and statistical techniques which has taken place has not noticeably led to any significant change in the manner in which regional problems are appraised and policies justified. These deficiencies, insofar as they exist, may in some cases be due to the absence of any machinery to ensure that the various tasks described above are adequately tackled. The Working Party might well therefore find it useful to consider some of the alternative forms of organisation which might

enable these tasks to be better performed. Since all the main tasks in
(1) - (7) are interrelated, discussion of possible alternatives is better
left to a later stage.

2.   DEFINITION OF AIMS AND OBJECTIVES

The definition of aims and objectives of regional policies is a
distinct task in itself and poses its own organisational problems.   It
involves not only assessing the desirability of attempting to modify the
regional consequences of the many forces at work but also the degree
to which it is necessary to do so, the feasibility of the objectives, the
resources with can justifiably be diverted from other objectives and the
acceptability of the methods which would have to be employed to achieve
the aims.   Obviously, those regional policies which aim to change the
"balance" between regions pose national issues and the definition of
aims and objectives is an essential task of Central Government.   How
far Central Government has the task of defining aims and objectives of
an internal regional character, or the regional objectives of non Governmental bodies, depends on the constitutional division of responsibility
though the nature of the task is basically the same.

The need to define aims more closely and to take account of feasibility, cost/benefit and acceptability of methods has been stressed
in earlier chapters.   What should be noted here is that the task is a
complex one, in the sense that it divides into several sub-tasks, and
the way in which the sub-tasks should be approached constitutes the
organisational problem.   To define objectives means to refine and narrow them down as a preliminary to devising the policies and methods
by which they are to be achieved.   The process of refinement involves,
as has been suggested, making a distinction between ultimate, intermediate and specific objectives.   A test of the adequacy of any organisation is whether it is conducive to making such distinctions.

It is inherent in the many aims of regional policies that the task
of definition falls on individual branches of Government as well as on
the Government as a whole.   The peculiar feature of regional policies
is that they out across Departmental boundaries so that Departmental
regional objectives must not only be reconciled inter - se but with those
general objectives of regional policy which call for concerted action
by all Departments.   Thus a Department concerned with the promotion
of industry and its modernization in each region according to its potential must reconcile its policy, or its objectives, with those of a Department whose concern is with physically planning or environmental improvement.   Such a Department may have contrary regional objectives,

to prevent the growth of industry where it may be environmentally damaging, even though conducive to economic expansion. Both Departments must reconcile their separate, and possibly conflicting objectives, with whatever objectives are implied in the concept of "balanced" regional development.

There is thus a central task in the definition of objectives which belongs to the Government as a whole rather than any individual Department. To define these objectives it is necessary not only to digest the results of the work carried out in the broad task under the first heading, but to identify those special features of regional problems which justify departures from the "normal" criteria on which Departmental policies would otherwise be based.

These are clearly some very difficult questions of the "central" kind which have to be answered before aims and objective can be defined. For example, what differences in employment or standards of living constitute a case for special measures? Where should the line be drawn in deciding upon the areas to which the measures should apply? To what extent should national growth be sacrificed in the interests of "better balance"? Should objectives be limited by the application of criteria such as minimum rates of return, or by insistence on the same standards in all regions irrespective of what can be afforded from local resources, or, indeed, of local effort? What balance should be struck between economic and social objectives in regions, or how should priorities between economic and social development in assisted regions be determined? Should the strategic objectives be set to enable a region to be self supporting within a given time scale, or an indefinite continuance of support programmes be envisaged? How far should such principles as competitive efficiency be subordinated to the needs for employment at almost any cost?

As with (1) it is unlikely that all these questions can be adequately considered within the walls of any one Department, and this too is an instance of the way in which regional policies present a special problem.

3.   DEVISING OF POLICIES AND METHODS

If tasks (1) and (2) have been successfully accomplished the next task, logically speaking, is to devise the particular policies and work out the methods which are called for by the prescribed aims and objectives with their defined limits. This, too, is not a sequence peculiar to the regional policy field. The special problem in this field is that two types of tasks are involved.

220

The policies and methods suited to a given objective can only - or, at least, best - be devised by whichever body or institution is competent in that field. If the specific objective is to overcome deficiencies in certain kinds of infrastructure, such as housing or roads, it is to be presumed that the task of devising the ways in which this should be done is best carried out by the body which is expert in this domain and is able to assess the financial, technical and practical problems involved and make a proper choice between various alternative possibilities. The body in question may be a Government Department, a local Government or regional authority, a public utility cooperation, a public Agency or even a private sector entreprise.

There is also, again logically speaking, a prior task. It has been made clear, in the chapter on strategies for development, that both intermediate and specific objectives can be achieved by a variety of policies and methods, e.g. that raising the relative levels of employment may present a choice of industrial policies or between industrial and infrastructure development. The task that is prior to the working out of policies by competent agencies is to weigh the advantages of attempting to secure the objectives by one line of policy rather than another. In other words, to devise suitable policies and methods which would achieve defined objectives, a process of comparison between totally different lines of approach is necessary. When this is done, individual tasks - the development of housing or water supplies in particular regions - can be allotted to whichever is the appropriate body. A problem of organisation in the regional policy field is to ensure that the choice between alternative methods is made in this way rather than through the "ad hoc" decisions of individual bodies interested only in one line of development.

In practice the two tasks would not necessarily be tackled in their "logical" sequence. The weighing of the pros and cons of alternative lines of approach is not an abstract exercise. A "dialogue" between those who perform the central task of choosing between alternatives, and those who know the possibilities and limitations of particular policies and methods is itself required before the range of real alternatives from which a choice can be made is established. The performance of the equally necessary tasks requires a continuing and two-way process of consultation in which initiative may lie as much with those responsible for one kind of policy as with those whose role is to compare and make choices between alternatives. It can be added that the task of devising suitable regional policies and methods cannot be performed adequately unless the former are fully informed of the aims and objectives of regional policies and are infused, if not enthused, with the need to devise, in their own sphere, the policies and methods by which the objectives can be achieved.

It is in this light that the need can be particularly seen for the creation of machinery within regions, and within specialized Departments
or agencies, which encourages such initiatives in devising policies and
methods from which choices can be made. The forms of such machinery
are diverse, from advisory councils to executive bodies and from bodies
with specialized functions or broad regional scope.

4. TO 6. IMPLEMENTATION, COORDINATION AND CONTROL

These three are grouped together since, though each presents its
own problems for organisation, most of what has been said in the preceding sections can be applied, mutatis mutandis, to them. Implementation and operation is clearly a matter for the expert bodies, coordination
is necessary to secure adequate attention to priority, timing and phasing
of inter-related projects, and supervision and control may be needed to
ensure that implementary bodies do not lose sight of the purposes for
which resources have been allocated to them by those responsible for
central policy decisions - a possibility that is not at all remote when
the greater part of the funds involved do not have to be raised by the
implementary bodies. The point deserves to be stressed since it is a
particular characteristic of regional policies that they are normally
implemented by various kinds of assistance or support in which there
are two separate parties, those who provide the resources and those
who use them. When each are answerable to different electorates or
constituencies, as is the case with central and local Governments, or
when autonomous public and private agencies operate on commercial
principles judgements and motives are differently conditioned.

Outside supervision and control is necessary for another reason
which especially reflects the characteristics of regional policies. Many
projects are on a large scale from dams and irrigation schemes, to
steel works, roads and development of new urban centres. Experience
suggests that calculations and assumptions made at an early stage often
prove to be wrong, as costs escalate as completion dates recede, and
as rates of return are proved to be unattainable or over-estimated. The
longer the construction period or period before full operation is
reached the greater the possibility that initial estimates of costs
and results must be revised, and that new decisions must be taken,
whether to continue, abandon or modify the project. The motto of "once
started, must finish" or "let's get things done, regardless ..." are
spurs to vigorous action but hardly sound principles of public finance.
Regional policies, in greater or less degree, require the use of public
finance in those very adverse conditions in which boldness may result
in failure rather than success, and caution in well-founded progress.

7. MONITORING, REVIEW AND REVISION OF POLICIES

These too are normal functions for which an organisational framework must be provided and be suited to its subject matter. Any continuing operation requires constant monitoring of how it is working, of changes in the conditions within which it is working and review and revision in accordance with the findings of the monitoring system. This is true of regional policies insofar as they have become a continuing and permanent feature of Government policies as a whole. Their limited scope, impact and success hitherto, their experimental nature and the frequent changes which have been made in many countries suggest that all these tasks constitute a specific problem in the field of organisation for regional policies.

Their inclusion under one general head does not mean that they have to be carried out together or by one body. Decisions to review policies, and changes in policies themselves can only be made by those who have the responsibility and power, the Governments and other bodies. But the purpose of monitoring is to provide the basis on which review should be made and policies revised if necessary.

As has been noted, monitoring can be regarded as part of the "intellignece" tasks under heading (1) since it requires survey of facts, research and prediction. Its purpose is different, however, in that it is geared to ascertaining the need for review and revision of actual regional policies rather than providing a complete conspectus of all the information that is required in order to know whether regional policies, and if so, what kind, are needed at all. The distinction may of course be so marginal that it may be found convenient, in terms of organisation, to put monitoring under the same roof with whatever organisation or organisations perform the tasks under (1).

The subjects which require monitoring would seem to include the following:

a) The specific results of regional policies in terms of their objectives. For example, if a policy aims at creating X thousand jobs in a given region over Y years, how many new jobs have been created and how far are they due to the policies pursued, or other causes?

b) Changes in regional situations which invalidate the assumptions on which existing policies are based. For example, if existing policies are based on an assumption that there is a large pool of labour available for employment this can be invalidated if new developments, possibly unrelated to regional policy measures, have absorbed or appear likely to absorb the labour in question.

c) The actual benefits obtained from regional development projects compared with the benefits which it was assumed would flow from them. Thus if the development of a steel-works, or roads, or the improvement of environment or education were undertaken in order to promote, respectively, secondary industries, general growth, the attraction of outside industry or the filling of gaps in technical or professional skills, have they done so, and, if not, why not?

d) Have the policies or measures produced different results from those intended. For example, if incentive schemes are designed to promote an inward flow of industry from outside has there been such a flow commensurate with the expenditure on the incentives (if not, again, why not?). Alternatively, if the aim has been to encourage expansion of existing labour intensive industry have the measures succeeded? Have restraints in "prosperous" regions succeeded in diverting industry to disadvantaged regions or only in preventing growth or modernisation in the former?

e) What particular new problems may have been created which were not foreseen when the policies were devised? For example, have new bottlenecks arisen, in skilled labour, or traffic congestion which limit the possibility of further development despite the need for it? Have the incentives been "dissipated" in wage increases rather than new employment?

f) Have new factors emerged? Do they nullify the results of measures, e. g. new forms or degrees of international competition which make impracticable or frustrate the development of certain types of industry? Does the growth of world steel supplies invalidate the concept of a regional steel industry as a trigger for secondary industries? Will competing demands for water, basic materials or contraction of markets require revision of previous assumptions? Do some of the new factors work so favourably that some policies or measures may no longer be necessary, such as the discovery of new resources, or adjustment in exchange rates which improve a region's competitive ability? Should regional policies be modified to allow such new factors, rather than artificial support measures, to make their contribution to the solution of regional problems?

g) How has the "balance" between regions shifted over the years? Have "gaps" in incomes between regions widened or been reduced and for what reasons - outward migration or regional growth? Has such national growth as may have occurred been accompanied by an improvement, or worsening of regional "balance" or other symptoms of a regional problem?

h) What are the financial results of regional measures, in terms of viability of projects or revenues to local authorities? Are they commensurate with the resources deployed or do they signify a net loss to the economy as a whole?

Such a wide range of questions, which is by no means exhaustive, is sufficient to establish that monitoring is a major task. It clearly embraces a much wider range of subjects than would normally fall to any one of the specialized bodies concerned with particular aspects of regional policies. To be carried out properly, it also requires a degree of detachment and objectivity in appraising results which is (if the understatement is permitted) not always to be found among executive bodies which plan and implement policies by the results of which they may be judged. (One may, of course, in truth, be the best judge of one's own cause but it is legitimate to believe that objectivity is best secured by other arrangements).

CONCLUSION: IMPLICATIONS FOR ORGANISATION

The multiplicity of tasks which are inherent in regional policy formulation and operation point, as has been made clear, to no one system of organisation. They do, however, help to bring out some of the more important considerations which should influence the framing of the organisation required.

A preliminary consideration is, of course, whether regional policies are so important, either in their aims and objectives or in the resources devoted to them, that special attention needs to be given to organisation as such. It is hardly to be doubted that this is so in the majority of countries, and more particularly in those which are aiming at a far reaching restructuring of the economy in regional terms, or are attempting comprehensive physical planning in relation to economic growth and a broad strategy of national development. Even if such policies are still at a relatively early stage considerable resources have been. and are still being applied (sometimes ineffectively) and if it is accepted that regional and national policies are closely interlinked it seems additionally necessary that organisation should be adapted to the tasks that are implied and are described above.

A first problem is how those "central" tasks, which obviously fall more particularly to Central Government can be most effectively tackled from the point of view of organisation. The answer need not be the same in all cases. The basic requirement for "intelligence" and "monitoring" is comprehensiveness and objectivity, plus professional expertise in assembling, interpreting and utilizing data. The objection that these cannot easily be separated from their sources or the operative Departments is neither insuperable nor universally true. Modern devices for extracting, copying and distribution can be, and are used for making data available to interested bodies from numerous sources. The creation of an autonomous, professionally staffed and statutorily regulated institute to carry out the specific tasks of intelligence and monitoring would permit the comprehensive, objective and competent preparation of the necessary information and would not have to encroach on the policy responsibilities which are the domain of Governments and other authorities.

Such functions could of course be carried out, though perhaps not with the same objectivity, within the Government Department with particular responsibilities for analysis and digestion of the information necessary for policies, as an alternative to the dispersal of these functions between Departments according to their policy interests. The former may have the advantage of avoiding fragmentation in the use of scarce professional personnel or too much diversity and inconsistency in methods of analysis and research. It would also permit integration rather than coordination of study and research, as well as a centralized relation with outside bodies, local authorities and public agencies, whose co-operation in providing a comprehensive coverage of information relating to all regions is likely to be required. If the tasks are allotted to a central Department, in preference to an independent or autonomous institute, it would still seem desirable, in view of the nature of regional problems, to establish a unified organisation within such a Department to deal with regional intelligence (and, possibly, monitoring) separately from the many other subjects with which a central intelligence Department might have to deal.

Though no detailed study has been made by the Working Party of the various ways in which information required for regional policies is gathered and utilized, it would seem that few countries have so far given much attention to these problems. What has been said might suggest, however, that they deserve to be carefully considered wherever regional policies are taken seriously.

The "central" tasks which have been described under headings (2) - (6) as well as the review and revision of policies which follow from monitoring pose similar questions of organisation. It can be taken for granted that machinery is required, at Ministerial and official levels, to secure inter-departmental coordination and consultation in the matters of joint concern. An additional problem is, however, where the "central" tasks themselves should be performed. Can a distinction be made between "strategic" policy matters which provide a common background to the regional policy questions with which each Department deals, or are these so interlinked that regional policy as a whole would best be dealt with in one Department? In any case should the main

226

strategic issues - the broad aims, the amount of resources to be diverted and principles to be observed - be resolved only by inter-departmental discussion with the inevitable compromises, or in a central organisation attached to the office of the Head of Government (as is the case in some countries) or to a major "economic Department", such as the Finance Ministry, Treasury or Industry Department (as in some others)? Can the issues be split in such a way that half can be located in an "economic" Department and the other half in a Department responsible for main forms of infrastructure development? If they are split, which Department "takes the lead" for reconciling economic and land use or planning strategies? (Such questions are posed, e.g. by the form of organisation in the United Kingdom as set out in the White Paper on the Machinery of Government, October 1970, in which the lead "falls" to the new Department of the Environment but economic measures are mainly the responsibility of the new Department of Trade and Industry). Is there a general case for a Ministry of Regional Development of which an example is to be found in Canada? If there were such a Ministry would this be the right "home" for the tasks in (1) - (7).

As a penultimate point, there is also the question of how far any Central Government Department, which has responsibilities for some aspect of regional policies, should decentralize its activities to regions. This is perhaps not as basic a question of organisation as those mentioned which concern the allocation of regional policy functions between Departments themselves. But working closer to the regions may have administrative and other advantages, particularly in better appreciation by a central Department of the problems of a region and in developing relations with its authorities and the private sector. It does not however provide a substitute for the proper organisation of the regional tasks of Central Government as a whole.

Finally, it has been noted that the organisation problems are not limited to the way in which Central Government can best handle regional policy matters. Attention has been drawn to the interrelation between central and local or regional bodies as well as the public and private agencies. The organisation problem as a whole turns on these interrelations which influence the location of initiatives in developing regional policies and the way in which resources are applied to them. It may seem a reasonable inference from what has been said in this chapter that the success and efficacy of regional policies may well depend on the way organisational problems are resolved.

XI

INTERNATIONAL ASPECTS OF REGIONAL POLICIES

It will be clear from the Introduction and from the discussion of incentives that regional policies are a matter of international as well as domestic concern. Their effects can be felt outside the country in which they operate, and they provide a field for co-operation between countries based upon an understanding and degree of acceptance of the special features of the regional problem which may be held to justify measures which might not otherwise be acceptable in the framework of the general rules governing international economic relations. It has also been suggested that there is scope for international co-operation in a variety of ways, whether by mutual assistance to ensure that regional imbalances are not worsened, that competition in incentives and attraction of foreign investment does not get out of hand, or simply in the exchange of information on techniques for regional development and planning. In Europe the important changes that are taking place, with the widening of the membership of the EEC are throwing up questions relating to the role of regional policies.* The way in which they are answered can have repercussions outside the EEC itself. In any serious study of regional policies therefore their international aspects merit attention.

It is convenient to begin by acknowledging that most, if not all, Member countries are at one in agreeing that regional policies, however defined, are a necessary element in the context of general economic policies for growth and progress. There is also more or less support for the view that special measures for the support of declining or stagnating regions are justifiable on economic as well as social and political

---

* It should be borne in mind that all references to the EEC in this report antedate the declaration on regional policy made at the "Summit" conference of October 1972. The text of the declaration is given in the Annex to this Chapter. In the author's view the declaration, as well as the report of the High Level Group of the OECD (vide Prefatory Note) tend to reinforce the conclusions in this Chapter.

grounds. Argument may revolve over the precise nature and extent of the measures which are internationally acceptable but there would be little point in querying, from an international point of view, that regional policies are necessary. The purpose of this Chapter therefore is to examine, in a general way, some of the issues that arise internationally without calling into question the basic principle of the desirability of regional policies as such.

The Working Party have themselves drawn attention to the international aspects of regional policies. In their report, the Regional Factor in Economic Development, p. 96, they pointed out the need to study regional problems in an international context, mentioning particularly the problem of frontier areas, the way in which regional factors can be taken into account in the policies of countries co-operating in the economic sphere and the bearing of regional policies on international competition. It is perhaps fair comment to say that the need for such study has been accentuated by events since the report was produced but also that there is not, as yet, very much in the way of agreed conclusions on any of these matters.

It would be beyond the competence of an individual and outside the time-scale of the present study to examine all these matters in any detail. It would require a study in itself of the particular situation in individual sectors and regions in which regional policies may have an international impact. If such a study were deemed desirable the Working Party is better equipped to consider how it should be undertaken and the specific detailed questions which should be examined. In the present work we shall seek only to offer some general observations which may be of help if further detailed study is decided upon.

The question of border areas of adjacent countries offers perhaps a useful starting point, as prima facie it exemplifies a field of regional policy which provides clear-cut scope for international co-operation, at least between countries sharing common land frontiers. Most of the OECD countries fall within this category - e.g. France/Spain, Spain/Portugal, France/Italy, Switzerland/Austria, Austria/Germany, Belgium/France/Holland/Luxembourg/Germany/Denmark, Sweden/Denmark/Norway, United States/Canada, etc. The United Kingdom, though separated (or linked) by the sea from (or with) the European continent is sufficiently close for its S.E. corner to be regarded as adjacent to N.W. France. With Japan as an exception there is clearly a sufficiently wide context, within the OECD itself, for consideration of the regional policy implications of the "border" problem.

Frontiers are demarcation lines behind which each sovereign nation works out its own destinies. Since they are the outcome of

historical processes and often of conflict between nations they bear no
necessary relationship to any standard criteria. The development of
border regions or areas take place in accordance with the progress of
the nations to which they belong and regions on opposite sides of the
same frontier can, and mostly do, have markedly different characteristics from each other. Different political and social institutions,
different concepts of national aims and progress, different technical
standards and levels of accomplishment, and different national economic
conditions all have their effects which are often most noticeable as
frontiers are crossed.

The degree of co-operation between nations sharing common
frontiers is a matter for the voluntary decision of the countries concerned. A frontier can be a place where co-operation stops, or where
it begins. It is only when countries are pledged to co-operate with one
another to their mutual advantage that frontiers and border regions
can be seen as an obvious place for co-operation.

Presupposing that co-operating countries are anxious to make
the best use of the opportunities which border regions offer for mutually advantageous action, it is worth therefore considering in what ways
border regions present special problems for regional policies.

Firstly, it would seem that the planning of infrastructure and basic
services, such as communications, water and energy supplies will
take a different course if they are planned with regard to the needs of
adjacent regions taken as a whole, rather than for their separate parts.
This in itself would require a considerable degree of co-ordination by
the responsible authorities on both sides of the frontier, but the benefit
could be mutual through the avoidance of duplication of facilities, or
by providing common facilities on a more economic scale than might
otherwise be practicable.

Secondly, insofar as barriers to trade and mobility of persons is
reduced through, for example, the workings of the EEC, factors affecting the location of industry and commercial activities are altered,
some border regions becoming less attractive and others more so.
The consequences for employment and unemployment and the provision
of social services may also call for a co-ordinated "across the border"
effort to mitigate the effects, just as with similar problems within
countries.

Thirdly, efforts by one country to deal with its own imbalance
problems in border regions may be nullified by the action of the neigh-
bouring country, with which it is otherwise co-operating. Thus if the
latter has a more effective incentive policy, or has otherwise more
favourable conditions for the attraction of industry, the lowering of

barriers between the two may cause a further worsening of conditions in one of the border regions. It would seem that the very lowering of barriers, which is a reflection of the degree of willingness of countries to co-operate in economic policies to mutual advantage, will call for a further effort of co-operation in the field of regional planning to avoid such effects.

These points may perhaps be framed more generally. Within a country a "region" for planning purposes is an area which is sufficiently large to be regarded as warranting consideration as a whole. A frontier may in the past have served to split what would otherwise be an area capable of benefiting by a co-ordinated approach to all its problems. As the "barrier" effects of a frontier are progressively diminished, and as the desire for cross frontier co-operation is increased, so the need for treating formerly divided border regions as one whole would seem to increase.

Since the Working Party has not itself as yet made any detailed study of border problems we are unable to judge how significant they may be in current conditions, or where the need for co-operative action is most pressing. It is worth noting however that the reference to the border problem in RFED was based upon the experience of several countries represented on the Working Party.* What has been said above may serve to reinforce the view that this aspect merits study in greater depth.

The border problem is only one aspect of the wider problems to which the Working Party drew attention (see above).

We have commented, in Chapter VI, on the desirability of international agreement on the principles of regional incentives and subsidies and on improving methods for evaluating them in the context of the economic and fiscal system of the country concerned. It is interesting to note that the EEC Commission has drawn attention to the difficulties of evaluation of regional aids and that, in one country (the United Kingdom) the increased emphasis on fiscal aids make calculation of the total amount of aids extremely hazardous.** The problem extends of course not only to relations between countries within particular economic groups, such as the EEC, but to those of all countries participating in international trade. It is related also to the question of improving evaluation of the regional disparities which incentives and other measures are intended to correct. This question has been discussed in the Chapter on "Rectifying Imbalance". It is not therefore

---

* See "Salient Features of Regional Development Policies in the Benelux countries", OECD, October 1969 for an account of regional economic policy in the Benelux frontier areas.
** Report in Guardian, 29th June, 1972.

necessary in this chapter to do more than draw attention to what is said on these subjects, and on distortions of competition, in those chapters.

There are however further important international implications of regional policies, one of which is the effect which regional policies may have on the pattern of development and therefore of international trade and investment. Some appreciation of these implications may help in further evolution of the policies themselves.

In a hypothetical world in which regional policies are not necessary, trade and investment will tend to flow in accordance with the simple criteria of profitability and the pattern of location of industry and other activities will be determined by the comparative advantages of each country and their different parts. The introduction of regional policies is intended, and according to their effectiveness, may succeed in modifying that pattern. An understanding of the way in which that pattern may change is important not only for Governments seeking to devise suitable policies in concert with each other but also to the private sector whose marketing and investment constitute a large proportion of economic activity.

So long as countries regard regional policies as entirely a matter of redistribution of economic activity within their own borders it is unlikely that the full significance of the fact that so many countries pursue regional policies will be appreciated. Nonetheless, events are beginning to create their own pressures to bring about a greater realisation that regional policies in individual countries can have a marked effect internationally. The most striking of these events is perhaps in the prospective widening of the EEC which is already beginning to pose the question of the role of regional policies and the economic pattern within which they will be set. The solutions of the problems which may be thrown up are of course a matter for the EEC itself and we do not presume to offer advice. We quote the example however to illustrate some general points.

When a group of countries decide to remove the barriers or obstacles to trade and investment between them a new dimension is added to the "regional problem" in their individual countries and between them. The progressive elimination of barriers and the harmonization of institutions and regulations for the conduct of economic affairs constitutes, in effect, the creation of a new economic entity, virtually transforming individual countries from separate "independent" units into regions of the new, enlarged wholes. The context in which all decisions are made regarding location of economic activity - the heart of the regional problem - is equally transformed. Firms accustomed to looking first at the "home" markets, and secondarily at export markets are confronted with a new enlarged "home market". The process works in both, or multiple, directions and affects inward as well as outward flows of goods and services and investment. It is not to be reasonably expected that these processes will leave regional patterns unchanged. Left to themselves, the changes in the basic conditions for international activity must result in a reappraisal by firms of the geographical pattern of their activities and give rise to new "centres of gravity" for organisations, plants and establishments. Regions which were previously "central" in their own countries may become more pheripheral in the new context. Some regions which were previously peripheral may, per contra, become more "central". Other peripheral regions, furthest away from the central areas of their own countries in an opposite direction from the border regions of the participating countries will remain peripheral in a larger community.

To illustrate by naming a few examples, N.W. France, Belgium and Holland are on the periphery of the existing EEC. When it is widened their position becomes more central. In the United Kingdom, the Midland regions are centrally placed within that country, but the enlargement of the Community pushes their relative position more towards the periphery, compared with N.W. France. Southern Italy, Scotland and N. England, inevitably peripheral remain so to a much larger economic entity.

It should not of course be supposed that the mere geographical situation of centrality or "peripherality" will of itself determine the economic viability of the regions concerned. In economic terms centrality is not a matter of geographic location alone. London is not geographically speaking at the centre of the United Kingdom though it is the centre of economic life. The extreme peripheral areas of Europe may, in economic terms, come "closer" to the central areas than they are at present, as a result of the progressive removal of obstacles to trade and investment. The capacity of any region to survive or progress depends on many other factors besides physical distance, itself a factor of diminishing importance as improvements in transport and communications of all kinds take place All that can be said that the economic situation of each region within a country will be strongly influenced by the new network of international economic relations conditioned by the removal of traditional barriers. Only if account is taken of the potential effect of the widening of an economic community can regional policies be correctly attuned to realities.

Countries may well be faced with some paradoxical situations necessitating some reviews of policies. The new economic pattern may increase and diminish opportunities for existing regions in many, often unforeseeable ways. The role of incentives and restraints may need to be adjusted to take account of such changes. Competition in incentives pursued without reference to the changing economic pattern may produce

234

different results from those intended. Thus restraints in the United Kingdom designed to steer industry from the South to the North, may result in movement, not to the North, but to other regions of Europe in which restraints are not practised. Incentives for the South of Italy, designed to modify preferences of domestic concerns for the North may become insufficient to offset the new advantages of other locations in the widened Community. Alternatively they may have a greater attractive force to foreign enterprises which can benefit from a location in Europe and are subjected to regional planning restraints in areas they would otherwise prefer.

Whatever the outcome in the shape of changing regional distribution of economic activity the likelihood of such changes poses significant questions of policy for the authorities concerned. Because the outcome is largely unforeseeable the tendency may persist for some years to pursue policies based upon the pre-existing situation rather than the one that will exist in the future. Some warning of the possible dangers in such a course is given in the chapter on the impact of national factors on regional development. At any rate the need will exist, despite all the difficulties inherent in all economic forecasting, for an attempt to assess the way things are likely to go, in terms of regional distribution of economic activity, as a result of the creation of greater European economic unity.

Some of the questions to be asked, and their possible answers will be of concern to outside countries which may participate in European economic development or may be affected by it. The ability of the centralized institutions of the EEC to develop more effective policies for specially disadvantaged regions, whether through trade preferences or concerted investment policies can have both favourable and unfavourable effects ou non-participating countries: Favourable through the opportunities that economic growth may provide for large export markets. Unfavourable if preferential arrangements add to the problem of regions in non-participating countries through the relative weakening of their competitive capacity.

While it would be hazardous to make any predictions of the future regional pattern of economic development in the EEC countries certain inferences are often drawn from the experience in the past of individual countries. By and large, the depressed or declining or disadvantaged regions have tended to be peripheral within their own national situations. The decline or disadvantages have not been solely due to their peripheral location, but to their economic structure as well as to the changing fortunes of their traditional industries. But relative remoteness from the main centres of economic life has also accounted for the difficulty in keeping pace with the progress elsewhere which results from the more favourable locational conditions and economic structures of other regions. Not all peripheral regions have similar problems. In Germany, perhaps due to its greater decentralization and also to its situation within Europe as a whole, some peripheral regions, e. g. in the South and West, have more than participated in the general progress in the German economy.

The question - on which no prediction is made here - is whether in the future those peripheral regions, already at a relative disadvantage in their own countries, will be further disadvantaged. Alternatively the question can be posed the other way round, whether in fact the central regions, already at a relative advantage, will be further advantaged. The question does not permit of a single answer. The central areas in some countries will be difficult to sustain, either through the lack of manpower where conditions of full employment exist, or through additional problems of congestion and inadequate social facilities. The scope for locating additional growth in hitherto disadvantaged regions may therefore well grow and the regional problem take a different shape. Nonetheless not all central regions have the same problems of congestion, etc. and some have more scope for accomodating additional economic growth than others and may, in total, absorb more of the growth than the disadvantaged regions.

Perhaps one conclusion may be drawn, namely, that if each country continues to pursue regional policies without regard to the regional policies of others, then, as with the border problem, they may achieve less than through acting in concert. The need for some co-ordination of regional policies may also be enhanced if central institutions, endowed with substantial investment resources, seek to allocate them without regard to the new regional situation that may emerge.

Much would depend on how far the co-ordination goes. Should central funds be allocated to the same regions as those chosen by country authorities in applying their own funds? If so, how far should account be taken of the national resources available for regional policies? Should, alternatively, central funds be allocated for disadvantaged regions in countries with less adequate resources in relation to the problem? What criteria for the measurement of depression or decline, or disadvantage should be adopted to provide either for equitable treatment between regions or to ensure that resources are applied to the best effect? Should central resources for regional development be applied outside the development regions if by so doing their problems can be alleviated (for example by national communications or infrastructure development serving interregional purposes)? If, as is suggested in the chapter on regional imbalances, the regional problem cannot necessarily be resolved without migration, should central regional funds be allocated to regions affected by inward migration?

Similar problems arise in the case of incentives. Can disparate national systems of regional incentives be made compatible with each other or with the changing regional situation arising from the effects of economic union? The development of multinational enterprises and the possibility of co-operation between State fostered development organisations may also present a need for co-ordinating their activities with the objectives of regional policies, just as they arise within individual countries.

As with individual countries the answer to such questions may turn on whether the attitude to regional problems is whether regional imbalances must be "corrected" at whatever cost or whether some degree of regional imbalance, even a new degree, has to be accepted as the price of economic growth. Since, as has been pointed out in the "Growth of Output" there can be conflict between the two objectives in national contexts, there can also be similar conflict in the international context of the EEC.

How far such questions are really relevant, and what answers should be given to them are a matter for determination by the EEC authorities. The purpose of drawing attention to them here is only to show that a "simpliste" approach to the problems of regional policy is no more possible in an international context than it is in a national one. They also perhaps suggest the need for caution in applying, to an international situation, the same concepts of regional policy as may be appropriate to the internal situation of an individual country. Finally, they may indicate the scope for working out a common approach to dealing with the regional effects of the new situation created by the trend to economic integration.

A further international aspect of regional policies is, as the Working Party has pointed out, that of "competition" in incentives. This had been touched upon in the chapter on incentives. Evidence that countries deliberately modify their incentive schemes to make them more internationally competitive, and thus create a climate in their disadvantaged regions would be hard to come by. The fact that regional policies have traditionally been regarded as primarily an internal matter make it probable that Governments do no more than "cast an eye" as what may be offered elsewhere.* Moreover, the attraction of foreign investment may play a relatively small part in incentive policies designed primarily to influence the direction of internal investment. Nonetheless an increasing awareness that incentives do tend to play a part in attracting foreign investment could lead to the danger of rivalry and overbidding, with consequential escalation of incentives and their "distortion" effects.

* As the OECD High Lelve Group, op. cit. paragraph 210, puts it, "In Government planning the complexity of the problems to be solved often pushes into the background the international repercussions of domestic decisions".

Any attempt to regulate incentives to avoid international competition would require the formulation of rules as to what is and is not permissible. It is interesting to note that regional policies and incentive measures taken by Member countries of the EEC are subject to scrutiny of the Commission and that a beginning has been made in the development of rules such as a 20 per cent limit to incentives in "central" areas and the confining of incentives to well designated areas. As yet there appear to be no firm rules limiting the incentives that may be applied outside the "central" areas. A further principle which has been put forward is that development incentives must be open to easy evaluation, a principle which in the light of the analysis in the chapter on incentives is not without difficulty in practical application.

To decide what is and is not permissible between co-operating countries, whether in the EEC or wider groupings, can clearly be no easy task in the current situation in which regional policies, aims, objectives and methods differ so widely and change from time to time in accordance with situations as they develop. Allowance must also be made for the very different nature of regional problems and the differing institutional arrangements in particular countries, each of which tend to call for quite specific systems for promoting regional development in selected regions. The view of the Working Party which seems to have been borne out by experience, is that particular circumstances vary so much that there "can be no question of a single uniform approach to the regional problems of all countries" (RFED, p. 11).

Though this conclusion may not put paid to the idea that some measure of international agreement is necessary to ensure that regional policies work to mutual benefit rather than the opposite it is a warning against being unduly sanguine that common internationally acceptable rules can be developed. Possibly the most fruitful course is to explore some of the questions that would need to be considered in a slow approach to greater "harmonization" of policies and practices.

Some of these questions can perhaps be listed as follows:

1. Which regional situations justify "special" measures of economic intervention?

2. What tests should be applied to determine whether such situations exist?

3. Over what proportion of the economy can "special" measures be accepted?

4. Which types of "special" measures should be regarded as suspect from an international standpoint?

5. In what ways can "special" measures for regional purposes conflict with other internationally agreed objectives?

6. What, if any, time limits for special measures would be appropriate?

7. How far should account be taken of the impact of regional measures on the interests of other countries?

8. What aspects of regional policy measures should be the subject of agreement, formal or informal, between co-operating countries?

On (1) it would be necessary to consider the many different types of regional situations and to distinguish between those that could be deemed "eligible" for acceptable special measures and those that were not. Since the justification for special measures may lie not only in the nature of the situation but in the way it could be expected to develop in the absence of special measures it would call for looking at the situation in dynamic terms, i.e. to consider future prospects as well as past performances.

Thus a "classical" regional situation is that of areas in which staple industries are declining with high and persistent unemployment. The need for special measures arises from the belief that the play of "normal" economic forces would not be sufficient to remedy the problem. Other "classical" situations include "backward" regions, regions with unacceptably low income levels and social conditions, and regions with high growth potential whose development may be necessary to relieve over-developed regions. Another "regional situation" is one in which problems of backwardness, decline or otherwise unfavourable conditions are scattered throughout a country or whole regions which are generally prosperous. This very diversity of regional situations indicates the difficulty of confining eligible situations to one or two of the classical varieties, but nonetheless, it would be necessary to reach agreement as to which of such situations should be deemed eligible. The danger is that almost all countries could find such situations in many parts, thus opening the door to more or less universal systems of "special" regional support. It has been noted elsewhere that "regional situations" cover in many cases up to 50 per cent or more of a territory. Only if the problem is recognized however can some progress be made towards resolving it, and, perhaps, towards confining special support to more limited areas.

The problem (2) of devising tests to determine whether a regional situation justifies special measures is also not an easy one. Political acceptability of regional disparities - or political sensitivity to them - vary quite considerably from country to country. If unemployment is a criterion, does a deviation from a national average constitute sufficient

239

justification, and, if so, what degree of deviation? If special measures are justifiable in one country where regional unemployment is X per cent higher than the national average are they equally justifiable in another country where the national average is higher, but regional deviations less? Similarly, what disparities in income levels constitutes a justification? Are average incomes per head of the population as a whole a sufficient measure or should more sophisticated calculations be required, differentiating according to age, sex and occupational structures? Should common concepts of "E" values (as discussed in the chapter on rectifying imbalances) be a pre-requisite for tests of the severity of imbalances?

What tests would be appropriate to determine the justification of special support measures in regions with favourable conditions for growth which are to play a positive part in national economic growth in planned areas of development? Should the test be the rate of acceleration of growth needed to relieve the pressures on less favourably placed regions, by encouragement of migration and the provision of new employment in the favourable placed regions? Should there be a test of adaptability, to exclude special support measures in regions having strong recuperative elements in their structure? The mere posing of such questions exposes the difficulty in any attempt to reach internationally agreed rules between countries with greatly varying conditions. They are however implied in such an attempt. If, because of the difficulties no attempt is made, it would carry the implication that "rules" would be so flexible that almost any regional situation could be held to justify special support measures. The dilemma is a real one and it is a matter for judgement whether to regard the difficulties as insuperable or to make an attempt to resolve them.

If some agreement could be reached as to the regional situations justifying special measures the next step would be to consider what types of measures could be deemed appropriate to those situations and also acceptable in an international context. One range of measures widely used would not seem to be open to question, namely the use of public finance to develop public infrastructure and social services in designated regions. This is, after all, a normal function of Governments and public authorities and the fact that some Governments are more able than others to finance necessary infrastructure development, to the benefit of industry and commerce, would hardly lay them open to charges of promoting industrial growth by "unfair", or "distorting" procedures. Nonetheless public finance can be used to provide hidden subsidies, e. g. when State or local authorities undertake to incur expenditures which would normally fall on the private sector. Since public finance systems vary a great deal what may be normal in one country could constitute "special support" in another. The fact however that public finance support may sometimes be administered in conjunction with direct financial incentives and subsidies to industrial enterprises means that any rules for direct assessing, evaluating or determining the acceptability of direct incentives and for comparing them would have to take account of the support given in other ways from public funds. This would be necessary, for example, if a rule were established that State support for a regional enterprise should not exceed a given percentage of the enterprise's own investment.

In the incentive field itself any rules would have to cope with the variety of forms in which incentives are provided, from tax relief grants, soft loans, subsidies, to advance factories on favourable terms and from automatic and general incentive schemes to selective and conditional support schemes. For the reasons discussed in the chapter on incentives regard might also have to be paid to the degree of effectiveness of incentives which, as has been shown, is not necessarily directly related to the scale or form of the incentive. If emphasis is laid on ease of comparison and evaluation some incentive systems could well be disqualified from international acceptance, but if ease of comparison were abandoned, rules which imposed limits on what could be offered would hardly be meaningful. Again, it is a matter for judgement whether an attempt should be made to simplify incentive systems so that they are comparable and capable of evaluation but it would seem that, unless the attempt is made, the problem of limiting competition in incentives and their "distortion" effects cannot be tackled. The view of the writer is that, rather than attempt to reconcile the multifarious systems which are in operation, or to create a basis for comparing them and limiting their scope it would be more fruitful, and more capable of international "monitoring", to devise model incentive schemes. These would not be applied uniformly, but differences in application could be based on specific criteria from which a basis of comparison, and their justification could be established.

The question whether rules should be devised for time limits to support measures is posed by the fact that circumstances do change. Though it has been generally recognized that major regional problems are not capable of solution in the short term and that special measures may have to be constantly applied over a long period of time if they are to be effective, it is still open to question whether this justifies the more or less permanent retention of the measures. It would seem that Governments find it very difficult to withdraw support schemes even when the original circumstances have altered. The consequence is that "flexibility" in regional policies is more often a matter of widening the areas to which they apply and extending the armoury of measures, rather than pruning in some directions before advancing in others. The reductio ad absurdum of such a process would be if the area of regional supports eventually goes beyond the 40-50 per cent current in some countries to 100 per cent. Agreeing on time limits for internationally acceptable regional support measures could conceivably be of assistance to Governments wishing to resist this process, though, no doubt, the case will often be made out, after review, for continuance beyond the time limit. At any rate, the question of whether time limits were desirable would be one for consideration in a context of international agreement on regional policies.

The impact effect of regional measures in one country on the interests of another has almost certainly grown in recent years, as increased resources have been devoted to regional policies and as techniques have become more sophisticated. Though acceptance of regional policies implies that some degree of distortion of competition may also have to be accepted as an inevitable concomitant the measures to promote new industries, by grants, subsidies, etc. in selected regions can place competing industries in non supported regions at a disadvantage. While this may be acceptable within one political system it is not necessarily acceptable outside. The avoidance of conflict over an issue of this kind is, prima facie, a suitable subject for international agreement.

All OECD Member countries could be affected by the regional policies of others, including those with important regional problems. Since regional policy often involves attempts to establish highly capitalised, modern and efficient industries in disadvantaged regions the impact effect on industries in the same field can be considerable. It is also important to bear in mind that though a region, as such, may be "disadvantaged" in one way or another this is not the same thing as saying that a particular industry in that region would be at a disadvantage. In fact it could be at an advantage, even without regional incentives, for example, if there are good labour supplies (because of the decline of traditional industries) or if locational factors are well attuned to the needs of a new industry. In such circumstances a new industry, needed for the region as a whole, but capable of competing without special support can be placed by support measures in an exceptionally favourable position compared with the same industry elsewhere.

Many regional support measures apply not only to incoming firms but also to existing, well established and efficient firms able to compete effectively nationally and internationally. Regional incentives or other measures may be beneficial to the region in which they are located since the firms may be encouraged to expand, and create more needed employment. Provided they do not lose sight of their commercial viability such firms may equally be placed in a position of advantage compared with their competitors. This too is a distortion of competition but it would seem difficult to devise rules which would distinguish between new or incoming and already established enterprises. The trend in some countries, e. g. in the United Kingdom is indeed to place more emphasis on the possibilities of generating regional growth through assistance to existing industries rather than to rely mainly on incoming firms and enterprises.

To the extent that Governments seek to prevent support schemes leading to "unfair" advantage being obtained by firms in disadvantaged regions any rules might therefore have to apply equally to existing as to incoming firms. The problem would be to devise rules which do not render regional policies and measures ineffective while at the same time ensuring a greater degree of equity in the treatment of firms wherever they may be situated.

Support measures, such incentives, can perhaps be regarded as having two distinct aims. First to make it attractive to a firm to locate itself, or to expand its operations in a region in which it would not otherwise choose in the absence of the incentive. This purpose is compensatory in nature, i. e. the aim is to offset those factors which would have led to a decision to locate or expand in a non-supported region. So long as incentives are geared to this purpose the regional policy aim would not be in conflict with the aim of equity of treatment between competing enterprises. A rule that "compensatory" incentives are legitimate might therefore be acceptable internationally.

"Compensatory" incentives would include payments for costs of interregional transfer or expansion, training and retraining of workers, remedying deficiencies in infrastructure, the environment or amenities which mitigate against the regional location preferred by Government, or additional costs due to unfavourable communications and the like. Such compensating payments would, in theory, do no more than put a firm in a position to compete on equal terms with firms in other regions, or countries, which may not suffer from the same disabilities.

The form in which such incentives could be provided would not necessarily need to be uniform, since administrative convenience could indicate different forms in the varying circumstances of different countries. However the test to be applied would be whether the incentives were genuinely compensatory for specific disadvantages. The administrative problem would be to ensure that compensatory payments did not constitute additional hidden subsidies constituting a distortion of competition.

Any such rule would probably be more easily applicable to systems of "selective" support than to automatic systems in which incentives operate to benefit all firms in a region irrespective of whether they expand or contribute at all to the aims of regional policy. "Automatic" systems however have the advantage that they do not call for administrative judgement in individual cases, and that they contribute a general stimulus to enterprises in the region capable of improving the economic climate of the region as a whole. Their disadvantage is that they can distort competition by helping firms already capable of sustaining it. Special rules would therefore be required to deal with "automatic" systems of regional support.

Where it could be shown that the total of "automatic" incentives do not more than compensate for the disadvantages of operating in a region that are suffered more or less generally these could of course be brought within the rules relating to compensatory incentives. This would not be entirely unfeasible in regions in which it is clear that certain factors, objectively determinable, exist, e. g. remoteness from main economic centres, areas suffering from exceptionally poor environment, areas with inadequate supplies of skilled labour, areas of high cost services (e. g. water, electricity). If such disadvantages were objectively surveyed, and the consequences for enterprises assessed in terms of comparative additional cost, automatic schemes might be devised to compensate for these assessed disadvantages. When applied, they would not constitute a distorting remedy but one which puts firms in the area or region in a position to compete on fair terms with those in more favourable placed regions.

Not all regions which are at present beneficiaries of support measures can, by any stretch of the imagination, be brought into the category of regions with measurable disadvantages, justifying automatic support for all firms, irrespective of their individual competitive capacity. The very fact that assisted areas in some countries extend to some 40-50 per cent of the whole country suggests that automatic support schemes must create distortions of competition which could hardly be acceptable in any agreed international context.

Some countries do of course seek to adopt criteria which limit the provision of incentives to particular areas within regions, to enable aid to be concentrated where it is most needed and justifiable. The policy in the United States of "worst first" areas or the selective area policy of Germany, in which aid is confined to municipalities with conditions falling below specified standards, are examples of the possibility of applying general systems of aid to selected areas. The gradation, in the United Kingdom, of support areas, from "special" development areas, through development areas, to intermediate areas may be seen as a move in the same direction. The point here is that recognition that areas within regions can be differentiated could render feasible the adoption of rules which limit, or permit, the granting of automatic incentives on a basis of selectivity, not of firms, but of areas.

It would seem necessary that rules would have to take account not only of the classical "disadvantaged" region concept but also of the designated growth region or zone. As has been noted elsewhere, regional policy in some countries is not so much a remedial or corrective policy aimed at backward, declining or disadvantaged regions, but is the alternative one of promoting growth in regions, favourably placed or constituted, to bring about a higher rate of national growth, Spain, Japan, France and Sweden are possibly examples of this category. In such cases compensatory payments may be justified by the necessity to encourage movement to the selected areas. Both selective and automatic incentive schemes, applicable to the designated areas, could be justified in terms of the regional policy pursued, as they could be justified in the cases of support for declining or backward regions.

The adoption of rules which would constrict the freedom of countries to do as they think fit, irrespective of the effect on other countries' interests would be no easy matter. A specially difficult problem would be to ascertain the facts which would justify compensatory schemes or schemes applicable to particular regions or areas. This might not be insuperable, since the incentive for international agreement lies in both, in the recognition that regional policies are necessary and that they can do harm, as well as good, to international economic relations. Nonetheless the situation could arise in which derogations would have to be permitted and the rules would need to cover the circumstance for permitted derogations. Here, of course, the possibility of a fixed time term for such derogations would arise.

Another device that could be helpful in a context of seeking mutually acceptable rules would be the adoption of "once for all" techniques in the grading of incentives. Genuine compensatory incentives would fall within this category, and schemes of selective support to individual firms would also lend themselves to such techniques. One of the striking features of the way in which regional policy has developed in recent years is the attention given in some countries to "rescue" operations. Firms of importance to a region, and inheriting obsolete and inefficient equipment or in difficulties through exceptional external circumstances may have to be "put back on their feet" by substantial "ad hoc" schemes of Government support. Often this presents a much better, and more effective means of regional regeneration than schemes affecting the generality of firms or designed to encourage new forms with no "natural" roots in a region. The question that could arise in any attempt at international agreement is for how long, and how often, special support measures would be justified. The test remains that of "distortion" and it could be argued that rescue operations present no danger of "distortion" so long as, once an industry is made viable, it does not continue to receive support.

CONCLUSION

We conclude from where we began, that regional policies and their accompanying support measures are a matter of international and not only of domestic concern; that room exists for co-operation in such matters as border regions, the systems of incentives; and that distortion effects can only be mitigated by an attempt to agree upon rules. The attempt that is being made within particular groups of nations, such as the EEC, to devise rules points also to the need for an attempt to cover wider groupings such as the OECD. We have tried to bring out some of the considerations which would need to be allowed for in drawing up any rules for ensuring that "distortion" of competition in incentives is minimised, without detriment to securing the diverse aims of regional policies. It is suggested that, rather than attempt to reconcile conflicting systems and to judge them, an effort should be made to develop model rules, with appropriate safeguards for necessary derogations. It is considered that the view of the Working Party that further study should be made of the international aspects of regional policy should be endorsed, and steps taken to pursue the questions referred to in this chapter in greater detail and depth.

Annex

DECLARATION ON REGIONAL POLICY
made at the October 1972 Conference
of the EEC Heads of State or Government

"The Heads of State or of Government agreed that a high priority should be given to the aim of correcting, in the Community, the structural and regional imbalances which might affect the realization of Economic and Monetary Union.

"The Heads of State or of Government invite the Commission to prepare without delay a report analysing the regional problems which arise in the enlarged Community and to put forward appropriate proposals.

"From now on they undertake to co-ordinate their regional policies. Desirous of directing that effort towards finding a Community solution to regional problems, they invite the Community Institutions to create a Regional Development Fund. This will be set up before December 31 1973, and will be financed, from the beginning of the second phase of Economic and Monetary Union, from the Community's own resources. Intervention by the fund in coordination with national aids should permit, progressively with the realization of Economic and Monetary Union, the correction of the main regional imbalances in the enlarged Community and particularly those resulting from the preponderance of agriculture and from industrial change and structural underemployment."

XII

CONCLUSIONS

This report has been about the "Issues" of regional policies.
It is not therefore a descriptive account either of the regional problems
as they present themselves in individual countries or of the methods
and policies which they pursue. For these the reader has been deemed
to be familiar with the factual information published by the OECD in
such reports as The Regional Factor in Economic Development, or
available in the OECD country studies entitled "Salient Features" as
well as in the official documentation of the Member countries. This
material has been drawn on to illustrate some of the themes that have
been discussed but the report has been primarily an exercise in the
"problematics" of regional policies.

The basic justification for such an exercise is twofold. First,
that the range, variety, and complexity of problems and policies call
for some systematic appraisal of the lessons of experience which might
be applied with benefit in countries at different stages in the development of their regional policies, or which, for reasons of their own,
need to review and modify existing policies. Second, that countries
are affected by what other countries do in this field. Some understanding of each other's problems is a necessary step towards the framing
of mutually acceptable policies and effective collaboration.

To regard the study of regional policies as an exercise in
"problematics" is, perhaps, itself a general conclusion of this report.
Whether the subject is strategies for development, the problem of imbalances, the effectiveness of incentives or restraints, the objectives
of regional policies, the role of infrastructure and public finance or the
organisation needed, or any of the others which have been discussed,
the characteristic feature of regional problems is the multiplicity of
ways in which they present themselves combined with the variety of
considerations which influence the selection of policies to deal with them.

This characteristic deserves particular emphasis, since it distinguishes them from most other major but more self-contained problems such as agriculture, communications, housing, education, etc. Regional problems cut across these traditional demarcation lines for quite specific reasons. Regions are, by definition, such substantial areas of a country that they contain within themselves virtually the same range of problems as the country as a whole, differing mainly by degree in economic structure or those features which present special problems. The situation in each region is conditioned not only by the features which are particular to the region but by national and international factors which play upon all the regions. Inter-relations between different influences and different types of development - industrial, infrastructure, social - are such that it is only through the balance that is struck between them that overall regional policy can be defined and its potential effects gauged. While regional policies may have complementary aims to those of other national policies, their more distinctive feature lies in conflict rather than complementarity, their aim being to bring about a different regional situation from that which would result from those policies which have only "functional" rather than regional or geographical aims in view.

Conflicts arise when growth policies exacerbate regional imbalances, when criteria for efficiency, higher productivity, or return on capital, favour some regions and place others at a disadvantage, or, more generally, when policies, framed on the opportunity cost principles which underlie the economic use of scarce resources, produce socially or politically unacceptable regional situations. In such cases the primary issue for Governments is how to resolve such conflicts, whether by sacrificing desired regional objectives or the perhaps equally desirable objectives of economic policy as such.

If these are the distinctive features of regional problems it leads to the question whether sufficient recognition is given is most countries to the need to place regional policies in proper perspective. This is a question of fact which could merit the attention of the Working Party. Without trying to answer this question the analysis in this report does tend to lead to the conclusion that the need for a perspective view has grown in recent years as the scope of regional policies has widened. The same consideration points also to a further conclusion, namely, to place regional policies within that framework a systematic approach is needed to the questions which have been the subject matter of the previous chapters. The reasons for this conclusion are to be found in a number of points which constitute common ground to most parts of this report.

The suggestion or initial conclusion, that a perspective view and a systematic approach are needed is not intended as a criticism even in respect of those countries where they may be lacking. It is recognized that regional policies have been in continual evolution and in their initial stages at least have presented but an ad hoc response to particular localized problems to which relatively small resources have been applied. It is only insofar as it becomes evident that such methods do no more than scratch the surface do aims become more comprehensive, and larger resources deployed, to a degree in which something more than an ad hoc approach is called for. The evidence that this stage has been reached in many countries is to be found in RFED and the later studies of the Working Party. At the risk of some repetition of what has been said earlier in this report the main reasons for the conclusion referred to can be briefly summarized as follows:

a)   Regional policies have moved in many countries far away from their historical beginnings of dealing with local problems. They now extend beyond single to several regions, comprising a substantial proportion of a whole country and even, in some respects, the whole country itself.

b)   The scope of regional policies has also widened. They no longer comprehend only single problems, such as unemployment or low living standards but a whole range of inter-related problems which, it is increasingly recognized, cannot be dealt with in isolation from each other - economic, spatial or land use planning, social and environmental needs and the rational and planned development of infrastructure.

c)   Regional policies are concerned not only with the correction of imbalances due to the operation of the forces of the past, but with a forward looking long term adaptation to the needs of the future, arising from population growth, the need for modernizing, re-equiping or modifying the industrial structure in primary industries, manufacturing and services to meet needs in terms of higher standards of living and social welfare.

d)   The widening of the scope and scale of regional policies poses new and more extensive problems in public finance and resource management and utilization, and organisation. As the objectives of regional policy multiply so do the claims on available resources. Not only the manner in which they should be deployed, but the scale on which they should be diverted from other purposes becomes a problem of regional policy itself. An insufficient scale means the problems cannot be effectively tackled; an excessive scale involves the sacrifice of equally important objectives.

e)   The distinction between regional and non-regional objectives fades in significance as the scope of the former widens and as their achievement calls for the increasing adaptation of national policies to take account of regional diversities. National and regional policies which conflict need to be reconciled if they are not mutually to frustrate each other.

f)   Given objectives of regional policy can be achieved by a variety of alternative methods and be approached according to different time scales and orders of priorities. The choice of methods, if resources are not to be wastefullly or ineffectively applied, calls for the use of increasingly sophisticated techniques in forecasting, appraisal or diagnosis and of cost/benefit and planning policies.

g)   The results of the policies pursued hitherto have not been such as to obviate the need for continued effort to secure a better regional balance in the regional economic and social structure of most countries. In some respects regional problems are as acute as they have ever been and measures in force appear insufficient, either to prevent a continuance of such problems for decades ahead, or to secure a regionally satisfactory adaptation to new trends and dynamic forces which can clearly be discerned.

h)   Many of the policies and measures which are applied to internal regional problems have an impact on other countries such that it is becoming increasingly necessary to reach a modicum of international agreement on what is or is not acceptable within an agreed framework of rules governing trade and investment.

It is not asserted that all these reasons for the suggested conclusion have equal application in all countries, an assertion which would contradict what has frequently been said about their diversity. Nonetheless it is suggested that they do apply in most countries in which regional policies are of real significance and constitute a justification for the conclusion that these need to be tackled in a systematic and comprehensive manner.

THE ELEMENTS OF A "SYSTEMATIC" APPROACH

If it is accepted that a "systematic approach" to regional problems and policies is required it becomes necessary to consider what this entails. The task might well seem to be a formidable one since, in any country, which sought to adopt it, it would comprehend an examination, in relation to its own circumstances, of most of the issues which have been discussed in a general way in the foregoing chapters. The task would be difficult enough if the scope of regional policies is the relatively limited one of promoting a differential rate of growth in selected "disadvantaged" regions. A fortiori it would be even more difficult in countries in which regional policies amount to little less than an attempt to shape, in the complex conditions of modern life, the whole regional pattern or structure of a country in terms of its economy, the spatial distribution of its population, the location and size of its urban communities, the development of the infrastructure of communications, ports, airfields, its health and education services etc. in accordance with some all-embracing concept of what is regionally desirable. The cause of the difficulty lies, however, in the scope of the policies themselves rather than the method.

It is also possible to exaggerate the difficulties which are inherent in a systematic approach to regional problems. It is true that they range over a wide field and that there are alternative answers, or combinations of answers to many of the problems. Perhaps it is as well to recognize, as a conclusion, that the achievement of aims which are as far-reaching as those that have been mentioned above and are also considered in the body of this report constitutes, a task of the first magnitude. It is not the only such task, however, nor is it one which is so peculiarly difficult that it does not lend itself to the normal techniques which are employed wherever choice must be made between a multiplicity of purposes and judgement exercised in selecting the methods best suited to their achievement. In some countries considerable advances have been made in placing regional policies within a general framework of national planning. France and Italy come particularly to mind. If, systematic approaches to regional problems and policies are, in the majority of countries that have been studied, conspicuous by their absence, this is not so much due to the inherent difficulties or inability of Governments to approach regional problems systematically as to the way they have evolved, pragmatically, by continuous accretion of new problems, and by the methods of trial and error by which new policies must often be tested. Moreover, hindsight is easier than foresight, and the lack of anything that can be regarded as an accepted body of principles puts a premium on the ad hoc piecemeal, and spasmodic approach which would still be regarded as second-best if a more systematic alternative were available.

This report has not aspired to produce a systematic approach to the regional problems of individual countries. Such a task can only be performed by those in possession of the relevant facts and who can assess, in a given political climate, the relative importance of different objectives and the feasibility of alternative methods which can be employed. It has only sought to identify some of the questions which would need to be considered in a systematic approach to regional problems.

The questions, which in detail have been considered in the context of the particular subjects or themes of the preceding chapters, can be grouped. In a broad sense regional policies are a "management" problem for Government and, as with all management problems, the grouping of the matters to be dealt with, in some logical framework, is the first step in the process of decision making, the primary function of management in any enterprise. There is obviously no one optimum grouping even within a single enterprise and the suggestions made below should be regarded only as a tentative indication of a possible framework. The Working Party itself could perhaps usefully devote some effort to producing a more definitive framework which could be recommended to Governments for their consideration.

The tentative grouping suggested is as follows:

a) Recognition and survey of regional problems;

b) Diagnosis of origin, causes and consequences;

c) Classification of "acceptable" and "unacceptable" situations;

d) Range of policies and measures which come into consideration;

e) Criteria for selection of policies and measures;

f) Factors limiting choice of policies and measures;

g) Appraisal of impact of policies and measures;

h) Definition of objectives and methods;

i) Organisation and operational problems.

It will be noted that "definition of objectives and methods" comes at a late stage. The reason for this will perhaps be apparent from the argument in the chapter on strategies for regional development. If, as so often is said, politics is the art of the practicable, the selection of policies and methods must be governed by what is realistic, i.e. not only desirable but also feasible. It is not until the necessary preliminary work has been done, of the nature of (a) - (g), that it would seem possible to determine those objectives and methods which are capable of successful application. It is perhaps a legitimate criticism of the ad hoc methods which have been tried in the past, mostly with unsatisfactory results, that they are "problem orientated" rather than "solution orientated". In other words the choice of policies and methods is mainly geared to the type of problem involved instead of to feasible solutions. For example, the simple answer to the problem of regional unemployment is to create more jobs. If the initial measures appear to be insufficient the "problem orientated" policy would be to reinforce them, coûte que coûte. The "solution orientated" policy would, in contrast, not only be based on an examination of the causes of the unemployment situation but on investigation of the alternative feasible solutions, e.g. not only the creation of more jobs in a region in which this would evolve excessive costs but in assisting workers to move to other regions where jobs might be available, or created at less costs. It is not the definition of the type of problem alone, that permits solutions to be determined but a comparison of alternative solutions in terms of feasibility, effectiveness, resource cost and avoidance of new problems.

Some observations may be made on each group in the above list:

a) Recognition and Survey

A conclusion that can be drawn, inter alia, from the chapter on the regional impact of national factors, is that every country has a regional problem, or series of problems, whether recognized or not. It might indeed be said, and not as a witticism, that if one can not see a regional problem one ought to look for it. The reasons for this are in the numerous forces at work, described in the chapter referred to, which affect the regional structure of a country. Their effects can be both beneficial and harmful. As has been noted, the past cannot be changed but the future can be influenced. Only by anticipating and appraising the regional effects of the forces at work can it be determined whether regional policies are necessary at all. A possible lesson from the experience of most OECD countries is that current regional problems are the result of failure to anticipate the consequences of the forces at work and to take, in good time, those steps which are necessary to enhance their beneficial and minimise their harmful or undesirable effects. It is a matter for argument whether experience also suggests that the anticipated situations call for specific regional policies or the modification of national policies to influence them in a desired direction. What, on the basis of experience, is less open to argument is that assessment of the regional effects of change is a necessary part of the process of formulating policies for promoting the general progress of society.

It is not, of course, asserted that a survey of the regional effect of change must inevitably result in the conclusion that special policies are necessary. It has been noted that in some countries, e. g. the United States, change including regional change, is accepted as the mainspring of progress and the forces bringing about change should be allowed to work themselves out, so that policies are concerned with the palliation of the social distress that may result in localized areas. In other countries a different conclusion has been reached, that the forces of change must be resisted, or guided towards a regional structure deemed, for various reasons, to be more satisfactory. All that can be reasonably asserted, however, is that such conclusions should stem from considered judgements about the regional effects of the forces at work. The Working Party might consider it a suitable recommendation that all Governments should undertake and maintain, as a permanent feature of their activities, a regular survey of the regional structure of a country from which to determine (as a separate operation) whether regional policies are in fact necessary.

It is not necessary to elaborate in detail what such surveys should cover. Industrial structure, employment, living standards, urban development, communications and infrastructure and the scientific appraisal of regional differentials (vide the Chapter on Rectifying Imbalances) are only the basic ingredients to which static analysis and dynamic forecasting techniques have to be applied. The task is an extensive and costly one and a judgement has to be made whether it is necessary and worth while. It would, however, hardly be consistent with the undertaking of a report of the present kind to conclude this section without expressing the belief that such surveys are necessary and that their absence, in a majority of countries, partly explains some of the adverse regional situations that exist and the inadequacy of the policies which seek to cope with them.

b)   Diagnosis of Origins, Causes and Consequences

This is logically distinguishable from (a) even if in practice it is a task that could be combined with it. The need for proper diagnosis arises, as in medicine, from the fact that cure is not normally effected by treatment of symptoms. To take the classical case of high unemployment associated with declining industries, it is not unless the causes of decline are established that appropriate remedies can be found. The causes may be quite varied, from external competition from low cost producers, to obsolescence of plant and equipment, lack of capital resources for renewal and modernization, inefficiency of management, low worker productivity through lack of skill, absenteeism, development of cheaper substitute products and so on. Each cause may call for quite different treatment, ranging from abandonment of the industry and substitution of others, the provision of capital, temporary or long-term subsidization, education, training and retraining of workers in modern skills, installation of better equipment, reorganising management, enforced mergers, improvement of infrastructure, even the provision of day nurseries to overcome female absenteeism.

Proper diagnosis is also necessary to establish whether "blanket" or "selective" policies of incentives are preferable, and whether reliance must be placed on the introduction of new industries from outside or the regeneration and rehabilitation of existing industries.

The same diagnostic approach is required for other problems, such as backwardness, low standards of living or inadequate social conditions. Are they due to the age and sex composition of the people, their low standard of education and vocational training which reduce the scope for occupations producing a high average income? Could the deficiencies in housing be due to the financial system or the lack of enterprise in the construction industry? Do poor communications inhibit the full exploitation of local resources and so reduce the income earning possibilities? Does the land ownership system, over large or too small farms, account for rural poverty? Is the absence of an enterprising managerial class the primary restraining factor on locally generated growth, or the fact that much better opportunities can be found for their talents elsewhere?

The diversity of answers which can be given to such questions, not only in different countries but in different regions of the same country, suggests that proper diagnosis is a <u>sine qua non</u> for appropriate policies. It also reinforces the case for seeking "<u>solution orientated</u>" rather than "problem orientated" policies since what appears to be the same apparent problem may be due to quite different causes for which different solutions will be required.

<u>The Working Party might therefore also consider recommending that Governments pursuing regional policies should give adequate attention to diagnosis of the causes of situations for which remedial action is deemed necessary.</u>

c) Classification of "Acceptable" and "Unacceptable" Situations

Most regional policies are directed towards correcting or remedying what are deemed to be unacceptable situations. The term "unacceptable" is necessarily a subjective one and reflects political considerations as well as objective criteria; and what is unacceptable in one country (e. g. a given rate of unemployment) may be deemed acceptable in another. Similarly, what is unacceptable at one time may be acceptable at another, e. g. a relatively higher rate of unemployment may become acceptable if it is deemed to be temporary, if everyone is in the same boat, or social security measures are improved to reduce the distress and hardship which accompany it. Moreover, acceptability may depend on beliefs as to the causes or whether there are alternatives. Acceptance may often be gained when the causes appear beyond control but not when it is believed that they can be remedied if only the will were there.

Such considerations make it difficult to say that X per cent unemployment is acceptable, but Y per cent is not, or that certain differential rates in unemployment or standards of living are or are not tolerable. Nonetheless, if regional policies are to be something different from an exercise in the unattainable, some rationale in the definition of what is acceptable or not is a necessary part of the process of arriving at feasible objectives. In the last resort "realism" means that some undesirable states have to be accepted, <u>faute de mieux</u>, while some states which in themselves are tolerable are not acceptable because the possibility exists of an even better state. Most people accept old age or temporary sickness as inevitable accompaniments of life itself. But they are less prone to recognize that in some circumstances unemployment, hardships and poor social conditions are also, to some extent inevitable and beyond the power of the Government to remedy, unless they also play their part in adjusting to the situation according to its causes.

This somewhat old-fashioned view is perhaps particularly relevant to those regional policies which are concerned with "imbalances" between regions. The implications of attempts to "rectify" imbalances have been discussed in the chapter on the subject. A conclusion that emerges from that discussion is that some differences in living standards and employment are inevitable, that some movement of population from less to more favoured regions is a necessary result of change, and that evenness of development in all regions is an unattainable and almost meaningless objective if only because of the differences in resources and capabilities and the unacceptable shift or transfer of resources that it would entail. (It may be noted, en passant, that it is easier to perceive the unacceptability of certain present conditions than the shift of resources required to remedy tham, since the consequences can only be felt later. There is thus an inbuilt predisposition to base remedial policies on shifts of resources to disadvantaged regions, without bothering too much about consequences for other regions, or the economy as a whole which are not immediately perceived and felt).

Some classifications of acceptable and unacceptable situations could therefore be helpful in narrowing down objectives of policy (h). They may also contribute to the survey in (a) by identifying the areas or regions which are below or above the line between acceptable and unacceptable conditions.

It is a problem in itself to decide where "the line" should be drawn and in what fields. The distinction between persistent and short term is a helpful one. High unemployment or low living conditions may be more acceptable over a short period than if continuing and unchanging. The line can however hardly be drawn realistically without reference to the resources available for dealing with what is unacceptable. The practice in some countries of dealing with "worst first" cases, or of allotting aid resources to areas in which a combination of circumstances (unemployment, incomes, travel to work distances - as in Germany) exists is a rational device which permits the line to be drawn at different levels as available resources fluctuate.

The drawing of such lines is, in principle, desirable in respect of all those matters which might call for special regional policies. These include not only incomes and employment rates but the physical and social conditions, housing, congestion, amenities and environment. The classifications adopted may lead to a conclusion, that in some respects regional problems are differently distributed than in others e. g. that environmental conditions or housing may be worse in regions of high employment that suffer from congestion and overloading of social facilities, while in regions of low employment and activity rates outward flows of workers may have resulted in greater availability of housing. The suggestion in the chapter on imbalances that, it is desirable to find some generalized concept (which has been termed "E") to give proper weighting to the general factors which may indicate a need for special policies, implies a system of classification which enables measures to be directed, not only to where problems are most acute, but to be differentiated regionally according to their particular nature and scale.

Finally, it is suggested that some reasonably objective system of classification is desirable in order to enable comparisons to be made internationally. This is not because countries should govern their internal regional policies by the same criteria, but to enable the basis of measures which may affect other countries interests (vide the chapter on international aspects) to be fully understood.

As has been suggested, the Working Party might wish to promote further study of the possibility of classifying regional situations according to objective criteria.

d) Range of Policies and Measures which come into Consideration

A distinction between the "ad hoc" and "systematic" approaches is that the former relies on devising suitable policies to situations as they arise, while the latter not only anticipates the situations which are likely to arise but has already appraised the different types of policies and measures which could be adopted as and when the situation arises. Both have their advantages and disadvantages. No two situations are exactly alike, and foresight is limited, so some degree of "ad hoc-ism" is inevitable. On the other hand prevention is better than cure, and previous periods of experimentation, trial and error and experience can reveal the strengths and weaknesses or applicability of certain policies to given situations. "Ad hoc" responses tend to be short term and palliative in effect and deal with symptoms: "systematic" responses, if well devised, are more likely to cope with underlying causes and provide better long term solutions. The case for a systematic approach in the regional policy field is that regional problems are a normal, continuing and permanent feature and that significant changes in regional structure can only be effected over a long period of sustained effort. There is therefore scope for using time for reflection as well as action and for building up an "armoury" of policies and methods in the light of both practical experience and theory.

What has been said in the chapter on strategies for development shows that there is in fact a considerable range of policies and measures which constitute alternative methods for dealing with particular problems. To adopt the "right" policy involves not only asking the question whether it will work, but also whether it will work as well or better than other possible alternatives. This cannot be done unless the latter are available for consideration at the same time.

Each country has its own specific problems and range of relevant alternative policies. By arranging them in categories a bird's eye view can be obtained of the alternative choices and their applicability to particular situations considered. The following list covers the range discussed in this report:

1. Industrial;
2. Land use and environmental;
3. Infrastructure;
4. Social;
5. Public finance;
6. Administrative;
7. National.

1. Industrial

There are several types of regional industrial policies: rehabilitation, reorganisation and improvement of existing industries; diversifying the industrial base by introducing new, locally or externally based industries; developing industry for local or external markets; concentrating on labour intensive rather than capital intensive industries (or vice versa); industrial development based on local or alternatively imported resources and materials; service industry development for local or nationwide purposes; altering the balance between primary, secondary and tertiary industries; fostering large or small-scale enterprise.

None of these policies are an end in themselves. They can only be judged by their efficiency in overcoming the problems which occasion the need for such policies and by the ratio of the benefits to the costs that they entail. Each policy also calls for its own specific kind of measures so that it is only by the study of the requirements of each that rational decisions can be made about incentives or other encouragements.

2. Land use and environmental

Regional policy involves, as has been indicated in the body of this report, the formulation of a land use strategy, or a strategy for the geographical distribution of population in a way which best serves its economic and social needs. The size and location of urban centres, their relation to each other, the serviceability of existing towns and capability of adjustment to new conditions, or the need for new towns and the pace at which they should be developed, denote the types of policies which can be followed in planning the use of a country's land and its environmental character. The role of the countryside, for agriculture and amenity use mutually interacts with the policies for urban development. Advantages and disadvantages of large and small towns, concepts of "optimum" urban size, play a part in determining the choices from which policy decisions have to be made. So do the changing patterns of external trade, which modify the locational advantages of particular ports and harbours and the urban, manufacturing centres with which they are linked. A "systematic" approach means the listing of the variety of land use policies and an evaluation of each in terms of capability of response to the foreseeable economic and social needs of the future.

3. Infrastructure

The different types of infrastructure have been discussed in the chapter on the subject. Infrastructure policies can be both an alternative to, and a necessary accompaniment of other regional policies. Their effects on economic development in general, or regional growth in particular, are indirect and only by a systematic evaluation of the way each type of infrastructure development produces its effects can a choice be made between them, in relation to given regional situations. Among the factors which determine the regional distribution of infrastructure development is the comparative urgency of need. As has been noted, infrastructure investment is a major claiment on national resources. The comparative urgency of need may therefore constitute a limiting factor on the adoption of regional industrial (or social) development policies which in part depend on improvement of the infrastructure. Assessment of the nature and scale of the needs for infrastructure in the country as a whole, and of the effects it may have in promoting development is a necessary part of a systematic approach to the formulation of regional policies in their interregional, as well as internal regional, aspect.

4. Social

Policies in education, health and welfare are equally part of the "armoury". What has been said on infrastructure applies equally to them and each presents a variety of alternative policies requiring assessment. In education they include the role and effects of primary, secondary and higher education, of vocational and professional training and the location of institutions of learning and research in science and technology; in health the provision of general medical services, hospitals and medical teaching institutions, and the determination of scales of provision and size of institutions such as hospitals in relation to "catchment" areas. Policies on such matters interact with economic policies (the expansion of industry can be limited by lack of education and health facilities) and are relevant to the balance between urban and rural development. Since each has its own governing criteria, e.g. the number or possibility of recruitment of teachers, the willingness of doctors or professional staff generally to work or live in regions, the rate at which hospital or university redevelopment can proceed place limits on the regional restructuring that is possible. The systematic formulation of regional policies requires therefore an appraisal of these factors before realistic choices can be made between alternatives.

5. Public finance

It will be clear from the chapter on this subject that public finance policies have a very direct bearing on the regional policies that are possible. The overall limits that must be set by considerations of taxable capacity, control of inflation, and the relative urgency of different claims poses a need for determining what can be made available for such additional needs as may be called for by regional policies. Regional policies that are feasible may depend on the relative roles of central and local finance and the degree to which either can be expanded by measures of public finance policy. The conclusion that can be drawn from the discussion of the subject is, not that the regional tail should wag the national dog, but that assessment must be made of the overall implications, for public finance, of regional policies. Public finance policies are not, however, inflexible and the way these can be varied to accommodate the needs of regional policies deserves systematic examination so that regional adaptation is not unnecessary restricted by public finance considerations. On the other hand some limits must be set, whether in economic, infrastructure or social policies, which condition the choice of feasible regional policies.

It is the role also of public finance policies to prescribe the terms on which it can be provided for specific purposes. In essence this means

fixing required rates of return for public investment and the differentials
that can be justified by regional policy. It means also determining the
degree of participation to be required from beneficiaries and the advantages and disadvantages of various methods, grants, loans, guarantees,
price support or subsidies for equipment, buildings, or other purposes,
and ways of means of ensuring that an adequate proportion of the public
finance available is devoted to regions which require special attention
and for which "normal" methods of public finance would not be adequate.
Separate principles of public finance cannot, or should not, be devised
for each separate objective of regional policy and a unified "systematic"
approach is called for in this field as much as in the others.

6. Administrative

Regional problems are not always the result of underlying economic
or social causes but can reflect deficiencies in administrative organisation, the correction of which may be an essential precondition for regional progress. The various organisational tasks which are necessitated by regional policies have been examined in the chapter on organisation.
The range of administrative policy questions which could benefit from
systematic approach includes: how to promote regional initiative in
identifying the problems requiring attention and in formulating plans;
how to ensure co-ordination and integration of plans of different bodies;
what changes in local Government systems are necessary to permit an
integrated approach to interrelated problems extending over wide areas
or regions - to combine cities with their surrounding travel to work
areas and to secure an equitable division of financial responsibility
for regional "central" services. The choice between larger and smaller
units of administration, the advantages and disadvantages of separating
some public utility functions from ordinary local Government administration or setting up of "ad hoc" public agencies all pose questions of policy
and merit appraisal in terms of their suitability for dealing with different types of regional problems. The results of such appraisal would
indicate whether the solution to certain problems can be found in organisational changes, which permit, for example, the better mobilization
of resources and their more efficient application. By so doing the need
for "ad hoc" and palliative measures, with their temporary effects might
be reduced or eliminated.

7. National

Some regional problems arise out of, or are exacerbated by national policies, i.e. those that are applied globally to a country as a
whole and are not regionally differentiated. The control of inflation,

by "credit squeezes" or budgetary policies, the pursuit of infrastructure policies according to common national criteria, sectoral support policies, for agriculture and basic national industries, to mention only some of the subjects which have been discussed in earlier chapters, all have unequal bearing on the regions. As has been noted they may sometimes work more adversely in the "problem" regions than in others. It has been suggested, as a conclusion to the chapter on regional strategies, that the true regional policies of a country are as much denoted by the way national policies work regionally, as by those, more limited, policies which are designated as "regional".

It is not always open to a Government, however, to modify national policies to take account or regional considerations at the precise moment when the need for those national policies is most acute. This is true not only in "crisis" situations, but in more normal times. Individual problems come up for consideration at different times, and the case for regional differentiation may not always seem strong when only one subject, such as agricultural support programmes or health or education policies, are under consideration. If a long-term view is taken, it is the joint working of national or "functional" policies as a whole that condition the relative progress of the regions. It would seem to follow that an appraisal of the way various national policies jointly affect the regions would be a step towards devising the modifications of national policies necessary for establishing the range of policy alternatives from which the ultimate choice of objectives must be made.

e) Criteria for Selection of Policies and Measures

In a systematic approach, once the range of alternative policies has been established and adequate attention given to diagnosis and definition of what is "acceptable" or not, the process of selection of appropriate policies to deal with the problems which have been identified can be approached. The criteria for selection then become important and the more they are made explicit the more likely that objectives will be realistically attuned to what is feasible.

The criterion of political acceptability has to be mentioned for politics and policies are inseparable but in a non-political work no comment can be made on them (except, perhaps, that the only explanation that can be found for some policies is their political acceptability).

The more "objective" criteria can be sub-sumed within the term "comparative cost/effectiveness". The point that has been emphasized on several occasions in this report and which can be high-lighted as a conclusion, is that no good reason has been seen for exempting regional policies from the test of comparative cost/effectiveness. Good management, in the regional as in other fields, means that when there are two equally effective courses of action possible, the lower cost one is to be preferred: or that when they are equally costly, the more effective one is to be preferred. The difficulty lies, not in the principle itself, but in its application. Studies made by the Working Party have shown that techniques for appraising costs and benefits are not free from difficulty. Costs can only be properly assessed on a discounted basis but the rate of discount over time has an element of arbitrariness in it. Effectiveness is particularly difficult to judge when a multiplicity of purposes is involved and the results can only be perceived as through a glass darkly. Nonetheless, Governments do reject some policies because they are too costly, or because, their apparent benefits are not commensurate with the costs. In so doing they are adopting the criterion of cost/effectiveness. Explicit recognition that regional policies must have some regard to it means that a whole range of otherwise desirable objectives can be excluded.

The criterion of feasibility is of course related to cost/effectiveness. A policy or project is not, in practical terms, feasible if it exceeds prescribed cost limits or does not meet prescribed standards of benefit in relation to cost or, more correctly, it falls outside the range of what is financially feasible. There are other ways in which a policy or project may not be feasible, even if it were desirable and would satisfy cost/benefit criteria. A land reclamation policy might not be too costly and could be effective in terms of the acres of land that could be reclaimed but is not feasible if there is no market for the particular crops for which the soil is suitable. The construction of a new town for a hundred thousand people might entail no exceptional construction costs, in housing, roads and water supplies and be a cheaper solution than rebuilding an existing town; but it will not be feasible if people will not move to it or it lacks the necessary conditions for competitive industry. As has been noted, an incentive policy may be financially feasible, in the sense that a country can afford it, but not of much use if available labour does not have the necessary skills to enable industry to benefit from the incentives.

Other criteria are derivative from cost/effectiveness, in the sense that they give more precision to principles to ensure that policies are worth the effort or costs involved and do not produce undesirable effects. One such criterion is that encouragement of industry should not create, or perpetuate inefficiency, low productivity or uncompetitiveness. Another is that support policies should lead, within some reasonable time, to self sustaining conditions, so that "propping up" measures can be dispensed with, or do not become a permanent feature. A third criterion is that regard should be paid to certain standards, e.g. in environmental conditions, housing standards and social needs.

All such criteria effect the selection of policies. The first may dictate that, even in "problem" areas only those industries should be supported which have a reasonable chance of attaining competitive levels of productivity and efficiency and that measures should be devised to avoid encouragement of low productivity and inefficiency. The application of such criteria can also affect the choice between policies for regional growth or for encouragement of migration to areas where the criteria can be better satisfied. The second criterion might favour policies or support measures for initial stages of development rather than over the life time of enterprises. The third might also pose a problem of selection of areas for support measures according to their ability to satisfy requirements for environment and social needs, and the criterion might mitigate against attempts to locate industry and population among the detritus of previous ages in which such considerations played little part.

A possible conclusion that emerges from this study is that though such criteria do, in fact, influence the policies and methods which Governments use to cope with regional problems they need to be explicitly stated both in the process of selecting policies and in explaining them. The Working Party might therefore consider it useful to formulate the criteria which should underlie the selection of policies, in relation to economic and other objectives.

f) Factors Limiting Choice of Policies and Measures

The factors which limit the choice of policies and measures are implied in the previous sections though the weight to be given to them cannot be placed in any precise or uniform ranking order. The overall needs of the national economy, for growth, modernization and competitiveness may have over-riding priority over the needs of particular regions and may predispose towards policies favouring migration rather than local growth. The financial and budgetary resources that can be deployed for "low return" policies may, in the light of other claims on them, be insufficient to permit major reconstruction of backward regions, or require that they be deployed in ways which produce an earlier rather than later return. The use of high rates of discount for assessing future benefits itself means that policies must be directed to the near rather than to the distant future - a point which is not always appreciated when regional policy objectives are stated to be concerned with the year 2000. The scope for certain types of policies may be limited by the rate at which complementary factors can be provided, e.g. the development of new skills in the work force by retraining schemes, the length of time required for developing resources of energy or water supplies, the rate at which, e.g. in new towns, community and social services can be provided. The criteria of cost/effectiveness, feasibility and others mentioned in the preceding sections equally impose limitations on the choice of policies and measures.

The review and identification of such limiting factors is clearly a task for individual Governments. The Working Party might, however, consider recommending that Governments should, in defining and explaining their regional policies state the limiting factors which they feel obliged to take into consideration.

g) Appraisal of Impact of Policies and Measures

In a "systematic" approach appraisal of the impact of policies and measures is, logically speaking, the penultimate stage before objectives and methods can be realistically defined. It is a possible point of criticism of the way in which Government policies are sometimes announced that emphasis is given primarily to the kind of effect it is hoped the policies will have rather than to the actual impact they can be expected to produce on the problem. This is perhaps particularly true in the case of incentive policies. These are of course designed to encourage industry to locate in particular regions but, as the analysis in the relevant chapter may have demonstrated, they do not always produce the desired effect, or, if they do, within the time-scale envisaged. Judgement of their efficacy has, therefore, often enough, to be postponed until only the passage of time shows that the incentives have not worked as intended and that new and "stronger" measures must be devised. These too may be "in the right direction" but, in turn, still prove to be ineffective. It is a conclusion from this report that policies are more likely to succeed if, at the outset, attention is given not only to the intention behind chosen methods but to their likely impact on the problem it is desired to solve. Thus incentive policies designed to influence a situation in which, say, there are X thousand jobs required should be accompanied by an appraisal of the number of jobs they are likely, in the known circumstances, to produce. If it then appears that there is likely to be a shortfall there is then a further choice: either to strengthen the policies (incentives) still further, or, if this means abandoning firmly adopted criteria, or is not practicable because of the other limiting factors, devising alternative and feasible policies for dealing with the problems created by the shortfall. As has been suggested elsewhere in this report, regional policies should be designed to deal with the problems of all regions. These may include the problems of those regions into which labour may migrate when there are insufficient job opportunities in assisted regions. Appraisal of the likely effects of given policies are therefore necessary to determine the residual problems that will remain, in both assisted and other regions.

The same reasoning can be applied to other policies. A land use or infrastructure policy may be designed to go in the right direction, e.g. of reducing pressures on conurbations, bringing about growth in medium size towns or establishing new towns in the right "nodal" points from a communications point of view. But their prospective rate of growth and development needs to be assessed to judge how far the desired objective will in fact be attained. If the answer is that it will not be fully attained, or attained within the time-scale necessary, the conurbations it is desired to relieve will still grow, and policies may have to be devised (such as permitting planned expansion into surrounding areas, or improving their capacity to accomodate people or cope with traffic congestion) to cope with their residual problems.

A "concluding reflection" to which this report as a whole leads is that one of the principle reasons for the limited results of many of the policies pursued and that have involved the use of quite substantial resources is that insufficient attention has been given to their possible impact. The Working Party might wish therefore to make a recommendation on this subject accordingly.

h)   Definition of Objectives and Methods

It should by now have become clear that definition of objectives and methods is the end-product of a systematic approach to regional problems and policies, rather than a starting point. It is not until the various tasks discussed in the preceding sections have been adequately accomplished that it is possible to assert, other than as "ultimate" objectives, those objectives to which policy is in fact directed. It has been suggested, in the chapter on strategies for development, that most "ultimate objectives" are no more than pious aspirations and the real task that faces Governments is to define the intermediate and specific objectives and the methods that go with them. It is not necessary to recapitulate the wide range of objectives with which regional policies are concerned, in the economic, physical planning and social fields in order to demonstrate the validity of this conclusion or the complex character of the choices and decisions which are involved. What might be emphasized, as a concluding reflection, is that most of the objectives to which Governments aspire, whether "better regional balance" enhancing regional contribution to national growth, relief of congestion in crowded cities, or the creation of adequate opportunities for the people of all regions will remain pious aspirations unless defined, quantified and appraised in terms of the resources required and the impact effect of specific methods is properly calculated.

i)   Organisational and Operational Problems

This point is placed last in the "systematic" approach in accordance with the principle that organisation follows from or has to be framed in accordance with the tasks to be accomplished. Without repeating the arguments in the chapter on the subject the conclusion that would seem to follow from the descriptions that have been given of regional problems and policies in the report as a whole, in particular the way they cut across traditional "departmental" or "functional" lines, is that they do pose special organisational problems. These are not only in the central Government field but also in the regions themselves and in the relations between central and regional authorities. The problem boils down to how best to ensure a concerted and consistent approach to all the questions which are entailed in regional policies, and which touch upon most aspects of Government policies. The many differences in the organisations adopted and the changes which are made from time to time, do not point to any one solution. The conclusion remains that success or failure of regional policies, and, wider than this, the extent to which regional problems will remain acute, must depend, in large measure, on the organization which is adopted to identify the problems, to survey and appraise the wide range of alternative policies and measures and to implement them effectively. The Working Party might therefore consider that the attention of Governments should be drawn to the special problems of organization for regional policies, having regard to the tasks which have been described in the chapter on the subject.

FINAL OBSERVATIONS

In this concluding chapter an attempt has been made to bring together the main themes which have been discussed in greater detail in the individual chapters, and some of the principal conclusions which seem to deserve particular emphasis. Looking back on the work as a whole certain broad strands of thought may have become discernible which are suited to special mention by way of general conclusions. The principal purpose of the report has been to provide some "food for thought" which, it must be hoped, has not proved too indigestible. The attempt has also been made to discuss the problems in terms of themes rather than individual countries, in the hope that those with expert knowledge of their own countries may find, "mutatis mutandis", some principles and conclusions which are applicable to them. A task which the Working Party might feel it would be worth while to undertake is to examine, in relation to individual countries, the applicability of the principles to them and whether their observance would in fact be helpful in terms of national needs and international co-operation.

An underlying theme of the report is that regional policies are here to stay, that they are growing in importance and that they need to be improved, strengthened and made more effective. Broad though such a generalization may be, it rests on the equally broad one that

regional problems themselves will never disappear and that recognition
of this fact is essential to the formulation of all kinds of policies, whether
they be termed national, regional or local. They stem from the one
constant in all the flux of human affairs, which is change itself. It is
inherent in change that regions should prosper and decline, that change
should bear differently on different regions of a country. Some of the
"problem" regions of today are those that were in the vanguard of
economic progress in the past; some of those that flourish today may
be the problem regions of the future. Since the past is for ever gone
the role of policy is to anticipate and prepare for the future and to apply
those methods which are best designed to help a country, in all its parts
or regions to adapt to the forces of change which are at work. The process of adaptation cannot be in one way only, to resist change and seek
to preserve whatever regional pattern of a country's life happens to exist
at a given moment in time. It also requires recognizing the beneficial
effects that change can bring, and enabling society to take advantage of
them. Since all change can bring social hardship and distress palliative
measures will be necessary, whatever policy is adopted. The problem
is to ensure that palliative measures are not such as to harden the ar-
teries of society and prevent it from ever responding adequately to the
"challenge of change".

For these reasons this report has not been founded on the assumption that the "regional problem" is that of the "problem region" alone.
It is also that of the interrelations of regions, the part they play in support of each other and in the general progress of the country as a whole
as it faces up to the conditions of modern life, the new techniques and
technologies, the new demands of consumer taste and social welfare and
the need to "keep abreast" with other nations in a competitive world.
Nor can regional policies be, on this view, confined to the particular
problem of the problem regions. No region is free of problems for
which apposite policies are required. There is only one source from
which they can all be tackled, the resources of the nation as a whole.
It follows that each set of regional problems has to be given its proper
weight, and priority in the allocation of those resources. If this is not
done it can only mean that some regional problems are solved at the
expense of others. The progress of a country as a whole will not be
advanced if there is an imbalance in resource allocation, if less urgent
problems are dealt with at the expense of the more, or if priority is
given to those that produce the less beneficial results.

Dealing with the regional problem or problems has been seen as a
function of national policies as well as those more narrowly defined
policies which tend to be designated as regional. It is the combination
of those policies which apply to a country as a whole, and those specifically directed towards particular regions, which shape its regional pattern. On this view the dichotomy is not a useful one and serves more

270

to enhance apparent conflicts between them than to bring all the aims of policy into a harmonious framework. That there are such conflicts (as, into example, between national economic growth and the diversion of resources from regions of higher to regions of lower economic potential) has been recognized; but it is in the way they are reconciled that denote the "true" regional policy which is being followed. The proper use of terms can be considered only a semantic question but there would seem to be practical advantage in describing regional policies in terms of what they really are, rather than of what they are not. If policies are in fact designed, and can be shown, to permit the more rapid growth of the regions which have a potential for it (as of course is the case in a number of countries) only confusion, or the wrong conclusions can be drawn from claiming that the same policies are intended for the opposite purpose, such as reducing the disparities between regions or promoting relatively faster growth in the regions with less potential for it.

This leads on to an observation about "closing the gap" or "rectifying imbalances", a subject which has been discussed at length in this report. "Gap closing" can be brought about by raising the lower level to that of the higher, or by lowering the higher to that of the lower, or bringing each towards the other. Conversely, "gap widening" can occur either with falling or rising levels, if the relative rates of decline or growth favour the higher level. For this reason there is no direct correlation between national growth and the narrowing or widening of regional disparities, even if there is progress in all regions. The gap between prosperous and backward regions widens when growth takes place more rapidly in the former, or even when both decline but at a higher rate in the latter; and it can narrow when growth takes place more rapidly in the latter, even if both are growing.

Policies which are designed to enhance the growth rates of backward or declining regions may successfully do this, if sufficient resources are effectively applied and the results may be beneficial. They are not the less beneficial because more rapid rates of growth may have occurred elsewhere. The view underlying this report is that the importance of "closing the gap" can be and often is exaggerated as an objective of policy and that more importance should be attached to the absolute progress that can be achieved than to relative rates.

This view is strengthened by the consideration that regions are interdependent and that in some cases the development of backward regions requires a higher rate of growth in other regions in order that the necessary resources can be generated. As has been noted, the scale of diversion of resources required (particularly when as much as 40-50 per cent of a country may be involved) or the needs of national growth may preclude a transfer of resources sufficient to eliminate regional disparities and the alternative of migration to more prosperous regions which may be unavoidable may still enhance the disparities. It seems difficult to escape the conclusion that narrowing gaps is a more difficult enterprise than bringing about progress as such, and that the latter is more likely to be the realistic objective.

The range and complexity of the many issues considered in this report suggest that some doubts can be felt about defining regional problems in dualistic terms, viz the North/South or East/West contrast, the central and "peripheral areas", "advanced" and "backward" regions, developing and developed regions, "prosperous" and "less prosperous" and the like. There are some countries where this dualism is a convenient way both of describing regional disparities and of narrowing the need for special regional policies. It does not however always fit the facts. Regional problems are not always quite so conveniently distributed, as is shown by the development, in recent years, of shades of distinction such as between "special", intermediate, or grey areas in the United Kingdom. Moreover, regional policies are not only concerned with distinctions between regions in economic terms (employment, standards of living etc.) but with spatial policies (aménagement du territoire) which require special efforts to steer development to those regions and areas within them which have the required physical characteristics, from land availability to location and even climate which render them particularly or more suited to development than others and more capable of contributing to national economic growth. Such regions or areas do not always fall into a simple dualistic pattern.

There are general disadvantages in using the dualistic pattern. "Policy by averages" does not make a great deal of sense. By their nature averages, and differences from averages, do not identify the real problems or the need for and possibilities of dealing with them. Just as the average man cannot be found nor can the average region; and if it could it would provide no indication that, in some respects, it did not require "special" attention. Regional policies need to be directed to the regional problem that exists, and in the regions in which they exist, even if they do not conveniently arrange themselves in a tidy dualism pattern. A further disadvantage is that since resources are in fact limited it is a necessity of economic policy to reduce, as far as possible, the extent of their use in "special" ways, i.e. ways in which normal criteria of economic management may tend to be disregarded. From this point of view the tendency in several countries to adopt a selective approach to regional problems is to be welcomed. The logical extension of this argument is, however, that selection of the regions in which special policies should be applied should be based on something more "selective" than whole regions or groups of regions defined mainly in terms of their departures from average levels in one respect or another.

All this is consistent with what has been said earlier about the importance of proper survey and diagnosis. Difficult though this may be,

272

the need for them lies in the importance of using scarce resources
effectively. The more this can be done the more possible it would be
to concentrate resources on where, throughout a country, the real problems happen to be.

The penultimate reflection that might be made is that, necessary
though it is, to keep regional objectives in mind in framing policies -
and it is part of the philosophy of this report that regional objectives
in the widest sense should find an increasingly significant place in the
general policies of Governments - some dangers must be guarded
against. In particular support policies to industrial development, which
are necessary and which, as has been argued, involve an acceptance
of "distortions" of competition, need to be carefully framed so that,
while achieving their purpose of promoting industrial development
where it is most needed, they do not also store up new problems for
the future. In mind is the possibility, by no means remote, that industries receiving support are so well cushioned that they do not take the
steps that are open to them to remedy the weaknesses which have led to
their decline; that new industries, which have come into being as a
result of subsidisation and support fail even to reach a position in which
they are capable of independent existance; and that those industries are
encouraged which have least chance of providing the base for further,
self-sustaining growth of a modern economy. It has been argued that
incentive schemes do not always bring about the results intended and it
is, perhaps, nowhere more than in this field that the methods of regional
policy need careful scrutiny. This might be considered an additional
reason for the preparation of the "model" system recommended in the
report.

The same must be said in relation to infrastructure development.
Beliefs that infrastructure developments automatically produce economic
development are not well founded and it is only in the careful appraisal
of the relation of infrastructure development to the complementary factors
which determine growth in general that wasteful use of resources can
be avoided.

The danger that regional policies can be pursued to a point that
they may hamper the general progress of a nation, and weaken its
capacity to compete or to adapt to change is an ever present one.

In short, in regional policies as in others, the ends do not necessarily justify the means and most certainly not when the means are not
well designed to achieve the ends.

To end this report on a more positive note, the belief in the need
and potential benefits of regional policies is firmly asserted. Given
their proper and permanent place in the national scheme of things they